DESIGNING
VICTORY

DESIGNING VICTORY

ROBERT P. MADISON, FAIA

WITH

CARLO WOLFF

Designing Victory
By Robert P. Madison, FAIA
with Carlo Wolff

ISBN 978-0-578-43745-3

www.designingvictory.com

March 2019

For more information or inquiries, contact:
Act 3 LLC | 12200 Fairhill Road, Cleveland, OH 44120
+1 216 325 7777

Published by

www.Act3Creative.com

1st Printing

Dedicated to my father,

Robert J. Madison

TABLE OF CONTENTS

INTRODUCTION
SIR DAVID ADJAYE, OBE

Robert P. Madison is more than just a pioneering architect and educator—he is a living example of the American dream. As the first African-American architect in the state of Ohio, Bob persevered and overcame in the face of adversity and racism. Setting up the tenth African-American architectural practice in America, Bob dared to become visible in a world that had historically kept him invisible.

During the past half-century, he has insisted not only on visibility but also on things being better. I think architecture is constantly required to remake the world. It is this constant dialogue that is reflected in Bob's architecture. His designs have not only shaped his hometown of Cleveland, but also impressively the coastal city of Dakar with his US Embassy building.

▲

The Smithsonian National Museum of African American History and Culture, 2016 | Adjaye Associates

Sir David Adjaye and Robert Madison in May 2018.

When I was an architectural student in London, I moved outside of the taught narratives. I found inspiration in faraway examples of architecture from India to Mexico because what I was tutored didn't reflect my imagination or background. But I know that students today can relate to architecture more personally—in part, because of Bob's contribution.

A leading architect of his generation, ***Sir David Adjaye OBE*** *set up his first office in 1994, establishing himself as an architect with an artist's sensibility and vision. He reformed his studio as Adjaye Associates in 2000 and won several prestigious commissions including the Smithsonian Institute National Museum of African American History and Culture in Washington. Born in Tanzania to Ghanaian parents, Adjaye has taught at the Royal College of Art, where he had previously studied, and the Architectural Association School in London. He also has held distinguished professorships at Harvard, Princeton and Yale universities.*

FOREWORD
MALCOLM HOLZMAN

Bob Madison never personally revealed that making Cleveland a better place than he found it was an ambition. His actions could not be mistaken for anything else. He was a strong moral resource. We first met during the competition to expand and renovate the Cleveland Public Library. The URS Corporation formed a team with both of our firms to compete for the project.

My architectural firm led the overall design effort. At the competition presentation I introduced and illustrated the concept for the project. Bob spoke eloquently about the contribution the enhanced library would make to Cleveland. After our team was awarded the commission by the library committee, Bob's firm prepared the documentation for the upgrading of the existing 1925 neoclassical library building. URS managed the project and produced construction documents. Although our project roles were understood, Bob also acted as the community conscience for the team. He was fond of strategizing, presenting, politicking, being an arbiter of good taste and more.

▲

Louis Stokes Wing, Cleveland Public Library, 1998 | Hardy Holzman Pfeiffer Associates, prime architect; Robert P. Madison International, associate architect

Robert Madison and Malcolm Holzman at a presentation to the Cleveland Public Library board, 1993.

After a year of agency and committee reviews, wrangling and approvals, many people in Cleveland wanted a better understanding of the design progress. This need was driven forward by stories in *The Cleveland Plain Dealer*. A small group of architects including Bob and a reporter, but not the client, came to my New York City office. At that time a presentation for the Stokes Wing was advancing. Drawings, renderings, models, marble and glass samples were in development and assembly. A large physical model, eight feet tall, demonstrated the roundness and reverse bay windows of the elliptical Stokes Wing tower. Our unveiling of the specially developed frit glass to limit heat gain and glare was of great interest to the visitors. Portions of the glass were opaque to cover the building's structure and a unique graduated pattern was depicted. The Georgia marble details corresponded with the original library embellishments but did not replicate them, another item of interest to the group.

Following multiple Cleveland visits I decided white, gray, and beige were not appropriate colors for the Stokes frit glass. On too many days the Cleveland phenomenon known as the lake effect produces an overall grayness, not something to be reinforced in the building's colors. After careful design consideration and testing, yellow was the best design choice. The Stokes Wing would emit a warm glow even on an overcast day. We knew it was an uncommon selection, but Bob's instant response was overwhelming. He made it known that yellow was not a Cleveland color. For the remainder of our two days together he could only talk about this color rarely used in architecture. As a team we weathered many public and political storms, but this topic was different.

Two weeks after the office visit, the design materials were trucked to Cleveland for the presentation. Before I could publicly present the project, the library director approached with a directive: The Stokes Wing could not be yellow. Bob upon his return home made sure that the outcome of the presentation would preclude the use of yellow as an exterior building color. A chill was placed on the design in more ways than one and my relationship with Bob was annealed. Two years later, the library construction was complete, the public enjoyed the addition to their skyline, and almost everyone had forgotten the yellow frit glass. The off-white color of the Stokes Wing was publicly described as fitting into the formal masonry tradition of other downtown buildings.

After the completion of the project Bob and I stayed in touch. We served as professional references and met when time permitted. About 15 years ago during his NYC visit to the Metropolitan Opera, we had lunch. For two hours, we discussed the intervening years and many other topics. At the end of lunch, Bob wanted to convey important news. I sat back and wasn't totally prepared for his commentary. The news was that yellow was the correct color for the Stokes Wing frit glass. Even though nothing could be done now about the color, he felt compelled to tell me about his new perception surrounding his original judgment. He physically lived with his color choice but admitted the originally proposed color would have been better.

Bob always speaks his mind about topics and making Cleveland a better city is at the top of that list. His desire to not degrade the color, style, height and uniform appearance of the six buildings of the 1903 Group Plan was initially more important to him than a color choice. Architects seldom revisit previous design decisions, especially with their peers.

Bob's ability to be self-critical is part of what makes him an outstanding professional leader. Speaking the truth as he sees it is an exceptional characteristic, no matter how difficult it might be for those around him. I admire Bob's passions, forthrightness and his unique ability to be magnanimous.

Malcolm Holzman, FAIA, *is an award-winning architect whose career includes more than 150 building projects in 32 states. His diversity of design solutions reflects a wide range of building types and application of materials tailored to projects' regions. A recipient of a Bachelor of Architecture degree from the Pratt Institute in New York, Holzman is globally acclaimed for his insightful use of stone material, earning numerous prestigious awards. He has received the Gold Medal from Tau Sigma Delta, the honor society of architecture and allied arts, and was elected a Fellow of the American Institute of Architects. A native and current New Yorker, Holzman is a founding partner of Holzman Moss Bottino.*

PROLOGUE

The night I began writing this introduction to *Designing Victory*, the temperature in Cleveland dropped to several degrees below zero, the coldest temperature around here in the last 25 years. Summer and the publication of this book seemed impossibly far off. In fact, my publisher told me I would be preparing to celebrate my 96th birthday when the first print run hits distribution centers and the ebook is released. Turns out he was right about the timing. In turn, I confide that now that this process is complete, I am so pleased that my story has finally been properly told.

In one way or another, for more than 40 years, I've wrestled with countless memories, notes, letters, essays, photos and memorabilia, trying to make sense of them and get them in order. At least once a week—sometimes several times a day—over that period, doubt entered my head: "Are you sure it's worth it? Is this story worth telling? What can I say that others need to hear? Will anybody want to read this?"

▲

4B Pencil

There is comfort as the lines of the 4B pencil record my initial design thoughts on paper and before they ultimately are transferred to the final design.

I heard those whispers of doubt in my head over and over; everybody who attempts to create or achieve something new hears them, don't they? Still, after listening to those whispers for far too long, I knew I was ready to raise my voice.

This business of recalling what I saw, what I felt, what I did, and writing down family history from before I was even born, has been remarkable. It's also been unexpectedly gratifying, especially when previously unknown details or long-forgotten memories surface to provide me with new context. But it's hard work and surprisingly fatiguing, both physically and mentally, to patch together conversations, news clippings, photos, and other accounts of all the days of my life. For those of you good at math, you might have already done the calculation—that's nearly 35,000 days (detail-oriented folks out there shouldn't forget to figure 24 leap year days into their calculation).

That's a lot of sunrises and sunsets—much observing, learning, working, enduring, and enjoying life. I've done all that.

I personally connect to a huge swath of American history. Between my life and the lives of relatives I have known, we cover a range of more than 160 years. That's about two-thirds the history of the United States. So far, during my life, 16 different men have held the office of president of the United States, representing quite a diversity of philosophy, leadership, and character.

Unfortunately, many of my life experiences are measured not just by days, years, or even the number of U.S. presidencies. The organized violence of wars also `provides sad milestones for me and my family. You'll learn about Grandma Land, my great-grandmother, who was born before the Civil War. I was born not quite five years after the end of the Great War, as it was called then. I fought in the war that followed that one, World War II, the greatest and worst the world has ever seen. I almost died, several times, in that war.

But not all violence and hatred happen within the boundaries of war. Those close to me—family, friends, colleagues—have experienced plenty of examples of those. I have also known the sweetest, most personal love. Without that, what life is worth living?

Along the way, I received a first-class education and graduated from the best schools before opening my own business, the first black-owned architectural firm in Ohio and just the tenth in the United States. I learned early on, however, that the halls of academe and the corner offices of the workplace are not the only way stations where one learns about life.

Family—wonderful, warm, messy family—is a school unto itself. For most of us, family provides the most meaningful education.

My family goes way back, and I recall many times that I benefited from older members who looked out for us. So it's appropriate for my story to begin not with my physical birth, but with the kind of birth many of us go through in adolescence. This is a birth of greater awareness, I guess. It's about awareness of the world—where you come from, how you fit in, where you want to go. My adolescent sensibilities included all of that. While family members were looking out for me, I carefully observed them to learn how life works, how success is achieved, how victories are celebrated, and, unfortunately, what happens when circumstances conspire to doom some to failure and sadness.

The summer of 1936 provided the setting for my youthful awakening. Little did I realize that, at the very same time, my parents were going through an awakening all their own.

CHAPTER ONE
COUNTRY COMFORT

Not long after my 13th birthday, my parents, Robert and Nettie Madison, revealed a plan for us. They explained that our grandmother was on her way to pick up the two oldest Madison brothers—me and my brother Julian. We would travel the nearly 1,000 miles from Washington, D.C., to stay for a while in Alabama.

Our relatives lived in Mobile, in the far southwest corner of the state, not far from the Mississippi line. That part of the country was familiar to us, as my parents were born in Alabama and I had spent much of my early childhood in the region. Our stay would allow us to get a taste of the South and become better acquainted with family there. At least that was the reason we were given.

▲

Downtown Mobile, Alabama, circa 1936

Mobile wasn't a large city when we visited—it had about 70,000 residents then and peaked at just over 200,000 in the year 2000. The indigenous population and French and Spanish cultures blended into language, food and the buildings of downtown and residential neighborhoods. We became very comfortable there, maybe too comfortable. Even a friendly, sleepy, small city could become dangerous and inhospitable to young black men who didn't account for lingering Jim Crow attitudes.

It's only when you become a parent, however, that you learn the insider's secret. Parents often speak one form of truth to protect their children from harsher realities.

We would figure out, much later, that the main purpose of that "vacation" was to provide a breather for our parents. In more ways than one, they desperately needed a break. The country was mired in the Great Depression, the worst economic crisis in our history. While the stock-market crash of 1929 provides the most dramatic symbol of the Depression, it was crushing unemployment that caused the most profound and longest-lasting effects. At the Depression's depths, the general population unemployment rate was over 25 percent.

For African-Americans, matters were much worse; the rate was essentially double—nearly 50 percent of colored people who wanted to work could not find a job during most of the 1930s, and those blacks who were lucky enough to have jobs usually were paid 30 percent less than white workers for comparable jobs.

While the Depression's staggering impact was felt by virtually everyone, it was felt most deeply by African-Americans.

One of the few surviving early photos of Bob, about one year old, in the summer of 1924. Most early family photos were lost in the shuffle of forced moves and evictions.

Throughout most of that decade, my parents were battered; they struggled mightily to maintain their footing. So, even if Julian and I were out of their care for only a couple of months, to our parents our absence meant two fewer mouths to feed and more flexibility to pursue work. A break like that could make all the difference for a family living on the edge. My parents couldn't have pulled this off, though, without some help: Our grandmother traveled alone from Alabama, then packed the two oldest Madison boys and a few of our belongings into her car for the return trip to Mobile. Our trip would take three days.

Rushed, often random moves, with new places to live and new schools to attend, were routine for us, so the trip with our grandma seemed more like a pleasant adventure than a desperate move. We were seasoned, although often reluctant, nomads.

We would miss our parents, but we knew circumstances back home meant Mobile was where we had to be. Still, a strange city could be frightening, even though we would be shepherded by my grandmother, Mother Julia, who was quite a woman of influence in that city.

As it turns out, that summer in Mobile was largely uneventful, except for one awful incident. Only the quick thinking of Mother Julia spared me from the most dire consequences. It was in downtown Mobile that I first felt the most dangerous taste of racism. As a result, I learned a lesson no young man should have to learn.

Mother Julia had rounded up Julian and me after a long weekend in the country. She had to get back home that Monday to meet with church elders, but she also wanted to get Julian a new pair of shoes and knew just the store. The journey from the country back to the city was quite calm. The children's shoes section in that department store, however, turned out to be anything but.

While Julian tried on a pair of dress shoes, I explored the store in the way curious boys do. All of a sudden, Mother Julia started screaming at me, "Bobby, don't. Please don't. Stop!" I remember the event clearly—it felt like a crowd was running toward me. Mother Julia, store clerks, the manager, the security guard, and even Julian, with one shoe on and the other foot in only a sock, were waving their arms, falling all over each other.

"Can't you read the sign?" they screamed. It wasn't a question—instead, it was an expression of utter disbelief. Stunned, I asked, "What have I done? I'm only getting a drink of water."

My crime: I had picked the wrong drinking fountain.

There were two fountains side by side. One was clearly marked colored, one marked white. Even though I was a good student and one of the most literate in any school I ever attended, no, I hadn't read the signs. Why would I read a sign in order to get a drink? But even if I had, neither I nor any other non-native could have known what they meant.

Segregation was the rule in the South in those days, governing behavior in classrooms, bathrooms, swimming pools, trains and buses. Segregation was also the law of the land governing the proper use of water fountains. That was the only time I ever saw the confident Mother Julia fearful. Seeing her shaken, I knew this was big. We left the store immediately, without Julian's shoes; they would not sell us any that day.

Later, Mother Julia explained the rules to me. We rode in the back of the bus. We did not eat downtown, and we could drink only from appointed water fountains. I certainly didn't understand all this, but I learned the rules fast; it was explained to me that my very life depended upon doing so.

Even though that incident left a scar, our trip to a community about 60 miles north of Mobile was a highlight of our time in Alabama. The small town of Millry will always remain vivid in my memory. It was there that Julian and I truly connected with our past. It also was the first and only time I bonded with my great-grandmother, the remarkable Louise Land.

Going to Millry

How we got to her place was a revelation unto itself. As we came to learn, getting there was just as significant as the arrival. The journey to Louise Land's property was a voyage back in time. City distractions, noise, and congestion peeled away to reveal country spareness, quiet, and openness.

In Millry, we would connect to a shared past: We were all children of the South. But because circumstances led my parents to pursue better

Robert J. Madison and Mother Julia, circa 1920.

educational opportunities for their children, it's almost as if we were two families. To this day, that separation remains hard to fully appreciate or assimilate. While there were times conversations in Millry seemed to veer into another language, there was never any doubt about a shared sensibility and a central person and a central historical fact that bound all of us.

That person was Louise Land, our great-grandmother. The key historical fact was that she was a black woman, born in the South before the Civil War.

My great-grandmother, a woman I quickly learned to respect, was born a slave.

My memories of her speak to a past that would help shape my own path. Remembering all this now, I think it's funny how looking in the rearview mirror can help navigate the way forward.

By the time I met our great-grandma, she had been running her own place for years, and keeping a tight ship. Our trip to her property that August made me realize where I came from—and led me to understand the rewards that determination like my great-grandmother's could bring. But before I could learn all this, we first had to make a long journey.

Getting there

After we left Mother Julia's place on the outskirts of Mobile, we were on the main highway, probably U.S. Route 45, for about 20 minutes, and then turned onto a two-lane country road, likely Alabama Route 17, for about an hour. Along the way, we passed agricultural land and cotton fields, but we rarely saw people. We eventually turned onto a deeply rutted dirt road; travel was slow and bumpy. Welcome to the red clay of Alabama.

We drove on like this for about two hours, mostly through thick forests. The very few people we did see were colored, all walking toward a clearing. We passed several shacks propped up on large stones or concrete blocks. Once in a while we'd see a two-room house with a porch, and people sitting outside would wave as we drove by. Common sights in rural Alabama: half-naked children, a few dogs, a chicken house, a couple of pigs, an occasional goat, and plots of land hard-put to yield any crop. The sun was blistering and the car kicked up clouds of dust. Mother Julia—that's what two generations of Madisons called my grandmother on my father's side—told us we were driving past sharecroppers. We didn't know the exact origin or meaning of "sharecropper," but based on what we saw along the way, we knew for sure we didn't want to be one. I secretly hoped we wouldn't be disappointed to learn that our great-grandmother was a sharecropper, either.

I remember miles and miles of cotton fields, forests, occasional clearings for a shack, and a few people, along with out-of-service automobiles propped up on bricks in front yards, rusting and fouling the landscape. I remember the red clay and the heat and the dust—and the absence of people. To a city boy, used to the volatile and sometimes chaotic nature of life in central Washington, D.C., that last observation may have been the most striking. Our adventure carried us into the interior, our country's southern heartland, full of unknowns.

At about 2:30 p.m. that Thursday, we arrived at the home of my paternal great-grandmother, whom everyone called Grandma Land. Mother

Julia stopped the car in a clearing in the forest, a clearing with a difference. There was a white picket fence with a gate. There was cultivated land in the front yard and all around. The house was small, as were the others we had seen, but hers stood out. It was more like a well-constructed log cabin, neat, clean and well-maintained. Unlike most of the buildings we had seen on our trip through rural Alabama, Grandma Land's house had a solid foundation. There were no cars in the front yard, no dogs, no visual mayhem. There was a sense of order and definition. There was evidence of hard work, caring, and opportunity. We were relieved: Louise Land clearly was not a sharecropper.

This was her land, her home, her pride, her place.

CHAPTER TWO
LAND OF MY ANCESTORS

That summer in the deepest South, we would meet family we didn't know we had and do things city kids like us couldn't begin to imagine. Living simply could mean living well, we would discover, and the phrase "living off the land" would no longer be a cliché, thanks to what we would learn first hand from, appropriately, our Grandma Land.

When the dust settled and we got out of the car, we saw a little old lady approaching the gate to greet us. Grandma Land looked to be about 75 years old, but in the way she carried herself she seemed younger. Besides, if we had sought proof of her age, that would have been difficult then. You see, so many records were not kept, or perhaps the family Bible had been destroyed in the war—the Civil War. Louise Land lived on this land all

▲

Mother Julia's home, Mobile, Alabama, 1936

The home base for me and my brother Julian's summer sabbatical in 1936—my grandmother's property in Mobile. Hers was a broader version of the traditional "shotgun" house. Some say that name comes from the house's narrow configuration; so simple in construction that a bullet fired through the front door would pass straight out the back door without hitting a wall. I prefer to see the house's architecture as reflecting Caribbean, American, and West African roots, including the word "shogun," which in West African culture means "God's House."

her life, inheriting it after her parents died. According to the 1930 census, Louise's age was listed as 71, placing her birth year at 1859. On that same census, the birthplace of Louise's mother—our great-great-grandmother—is listed as North Carolina, while her father's birthplace is listed only as "U.S." Such are the ambiguities African-Americans encounter when they attempt to trace their lineage back through the dehumanizing fog of slavery. Her exact age remains one of those family mysteries. My father insisted that she lived to be 90 years old.

A warm welcome

The first thing Grandma Land did when we arrived was kiss Mother Julia, and, as we were introduced, she hugged and kissed us, her grandson Robert's oldest sons. She was ecstatic and so were we: We finally met the legendary Louise Land. Next we met one of our many cousins, Cousin Etta, who lived with Grandma Land. Etta was a large woman, very dark-skinned, and about 40 years old at the time. Soon thereafter, five other cousins, all women, crowded around to meet us. At this time of day, all the menfolk were working in the fields, on the railroad or at the sawmills.

Much joy, merriment and laughter marked the occasion. Not only had Mother Julia come from the big city, driving her late-model car, but Cousin Robert's sons had come to pay a visit. Cousin Robert—our father—had left Alabama a long time ago to go to a real university up north. Cousin Robert was the first of the Land clan to graduate from a university, and he was now an engineer. Of course, none of them knew what an engineer did, but they knew it was something very, very important.

Julian and I didn't know what to make of all of this fuss, but it was fun meeting all our relatives—and to be treated like celebrities.

The true celebrity, though, was Grandma Land.

Perhaps that's because she did far more than persevere; Louise Land thrived. She kept an immaculate home, grew and harvested most of her food in her own fields, and raised her own chickens, cows and pigs. Standing about 4 feet 10 inches, at a bit over 100 pounds, she was petite and elegant. Louise Land was a handsome woman, too. Her skin was a very light brown, her complexion ruddy and sunburned. She grew her hair long, to her waist, but she'd usually wear it in a bun at the base of her neck. She wore a very simple shirtwaist dress with a half-apron in the front. No jewelry, no make-up, no stockings, and sandal-style shoes. Stylish, but no-nonsense—that was my great-grandmother.

But her looks didn't tell her whole story; on the inside, she was tough. In the field, she stood erect as could be, and she picked cotton well into her 70s. She had been doing that all her life, so she was great at it. My great-grandmother was an independent woman with 40 acres and a mule all her own, and in no way was she a slave. She was a person of powerful bearing and pride.

After a flurry of introductory hugs and kisses, we went into the house for cake and milk. We entered a large room. At one end was a stove, with pots and pans hung on the wall. There was a storage cabinet where food was kept, and next to that was a metal pan that contained wood logs. At the other end was a table with six chairs around it. Near the center was a rocking chair with a footstool and an end table. A large oval hooked rug spread out on the wooden floor. There were plantation scenes on pictures on the wall, and there were neat, white tie-back curtains at the two windows. Behind the stove was a storage space containing more firewood, a large tub, buckets, and shelves of jars, some filled with preserves and canned foods. The room was spotless and, in a way, very business-like. This was where very organized living happened.

Off of this room were four small sleeping rooms. Each contained a double bed, a chest of drawers, and hooks on the wall for hanging clothes. Each had a window to the back field. The rooms were Spartan in their appointments and clean as a whistle, and there were piles of handmade quilts, pillows, lots of needlepoint and crocheting. There was a four-poster brass bed in Grandma Land's room, with a down mattress and fluffy, feather-stuffed pillows. On the outside of the house, just to the right of the porch, was a pump for well water. And back about 20 yards was an outdoor appliance that wasn't familiar to us city boys—the outhouse.

Settling in

Mother Julia, Grandma Land and the cousins talked about things ladies talk about when they get a chance to visit—babies, men, illnesses.

Occasionally, Julian and I were brought into the discussion, but mostly we were smart enough to only sit and listen. Even just listening to our Alabama kin was hard work. Their pronunciation, unfamiliar colloquial expressions, and heavy southern drawl forced us to concentrate in order to process the conversation. While we spoke the same language, our dialects were different. As the evening wound down and some of the cousins left for home, each made us promise to visit their houses before we left, and all promised to see us in church on Sunday. That's when the preacher would be coming.

After dinner, Mother Julia left to drive herself back to Mobile. Then the rest of us went back out on the porch and did something simple but wonderful. We talked. Grandma Land's people wanted to know everything about our parents, Robert and Nettie, and our brothers who hadn't made the trip. They also wanted to know what life was like up north, which was just as foreign to them as the South was to us. Cousin Lucy had been to Mobile for short stays on about a dozen occasions, but Grandma Land had been away from Millry no more than five times in her life—three times on the train and twice in Mother Julia's car. She could not write, and she could read only certain passages in the Bible that she basically knew by rote. She could also scribble a reasonable facsimile of her name to serve as her signature. That was the extent of Grandma Land's literacy skills.

Cousin Lucy, however, had some formal education. She attended a one-room schoolhouse and completed the eighth grade. Although she learned basic reading and writing, those skills were slowly fading because she had few opportunities to use them. No books, magazines, or newspapers in the house, no radio or phonograph. For our Alabama relatives, Millry was the whole world.

Julian and I were totally unprepared for this encounter, and we could not believe the isolation. And so it began to dawn on me why Cousin Robert, our dad, was such a hero to them and why their questions were so elementary. We answered them as best we could, with as much detail as we could, and our use of words had to be defined and explained over and over because our language and expressions were as foreign to them as theirs were to us.

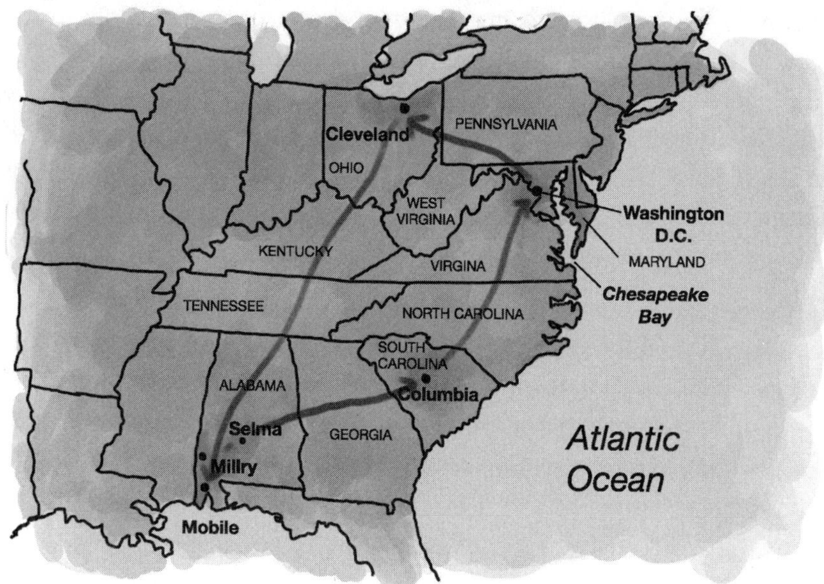

The Madison family migrated several times between the northern and southern states, beginning in Cleveland, Ohio, where Bob was born in 1923. Other Madison brothers were born in Alabama, South Carolina and Washington, D.C. before the family circled back to Cleveland in 1937.

As the evening wore on, though, communication became easier and we began to really warm up to these human beings, our relatives, our ancestors. We developed love and genuine respect for whom they were in their world. I thought to myself, tonight is for your questions, but from now on we have questions, too. Like "How did you get this land?" and "What happened at the end of the Civil War?"

We would soon learn that formal education is one thing but survival is quite another. Survival requires a different measure—and a different level—of intellect, perseverance, dedication and skill. My ancestors in the deep South had mastered the art of survival. Just staying alive and healthy in a hostile community where the Ku Klux Klan was the law was quite an accomplishment.

Soon the four of us were enjoying a good time just talking. It was fun, and we lost track of time. But quite suddenly, or so it seemed, the sun dropped low in the west, and Grandma Land announced that we should start getting ready for bed. I was confused, because it was only 8:30 p.m.

Everybody moved fast, closing windows, drawing curtains, doing what had to be done every night at this time, like snuffing out the candles and turning off the kerosene lamps. That's when I realized how in so many ways Julian and I were far from home, in both distance and culture. It struck me that there was no electricity, no light anywhere. The sun was the primary source of light. No street lights, and no streets, really. Total darkness except for when the moon was out—and it wasn't that night.

Cousin Lucy showed us to our room, then showed us how to use the night candle and the kerosene lamp. She also located the night pan for us in case we had to go in the middle of the night. It wasn't something Julian and I looked forward to using, but we also knew that if our country cousins had reasons for not using an outhouse, then those reasons were good enough for us, too.

Once we were in bed, Grandma Land and Cousin Lucy came back, tucked us in, kissed us, said good night and left for their own rooms. How beautiful, warm and tender. How nice. I felt very special. I'm sure Julian did, too.

No matter how special we felt, however, Julian and I did not sleep much that first night. We were lying in strange beds in an unfamiliar house in Millry, Alabama, a town we didn't know. Most unsettling to us was the total blackness; not a light was to be seen anywhere. And then there were the noises of a country night—crickets, dogs barking, horses neighing, coyotes, raccoons, possums and owls. We had never heard such noises before, let alone in such a symphony.

There was another reason for my sleeplessness: the nagging realization that we were sleeping on the very site of an old plantation where my forebears were born. They grew older, worked the land (for nothing but a place to live and subsistence), wore down, then died, leaving barely a trace. How many generations? Who were all those people? Did their spirits still roam this land? We could never know.

It was downright spooky. It was a night in the deep South.

CHAPTER THREE
DAWN OF A NEW DAY

After that long and startlingly dark night, a truly new day began for us. It was 5:30 a.m., and the country world was already alive. The sun peeked in, chickens clucked, dogs barked, and Grandma Land and Cousin Lucy stirred into action. We had never gotten up that early and didn't know what to expect. A couple of things we did know: We didn't want to miss anything, and we knew we were expected to help with the kinds of chores us city boys had never done.

So we fetched water from the well, collected eggs from the chicken coop, hauled wood for the stove, lit the fire, and heated water for the bath Julian and I would take in our room. While Cousin Lucy was preparing breakfast, we made our beds, hung up our night clothes, and then completed the worst chore of all: taking the night pans to the outhouse.

▲

Classic field plow, circa 1930

Julian and I discovered firsthand what a magnificent and powerful tool the plow can be when the horse responds as the handler dictates. Grandma Land was a master at this—she did it all her life, and her way.

Breakfast was delicious—eggs, bacon, grits, biscuits, potatoes, and milk. This was the best cooking I had ever tasted. The eggs were absolutely fresh; we gathered them right after the chickens had laid them. The milk was warm and fresh from a cow nearby.

After breakfast and the dishes and pans were washed, dried and put away, we headed to the fields for the day's work. Grandma Land led the way, and I was impressed by her agility. At her age, she was still doing things I thought only younger people were supposed to do or could do.

When we got to the fields, she hooked up the plow to a workhorse and showed us how to make the furrows straight. After furrowing for a few hours, we put in the seed and covered the ground over—peas, spinach, collards, cauliflower, broccoli and other crops suited for late summer and early fall planting in southern Alabama. Working in the fields was new to us, and the idea that you planted and harvested different crops for over six months a year was hard to grasp. After plowing and planting, we went to a different field to pick cotton.

Imagine: city boys Robert and Julian Madison in the field, picking cotton. Grandma Land and Cousin Lucy did it with such skill and ease it seemed like nothing at all. I'm sure we thought, if they could do it, so could we. And we did it, but it was hard work, and we weren't very good at it either. This was a lesson in how to pick cotton—a lesson in humility, too. Julian and I were more about motion and frantic action, while Grandma Land and Cousin Lucy seemed to work much more slowly. Julian and I quickly learned that these city boys were no match for two country women. No motion of theirs was wasted: bending, picking, shuffling through the rows; placing cotton bolls in burlap sacks; then dragging the sacks forward to look for the next plant to pick. To watch was to look at a kind of dance. Try as hard as we could, though, it was impossible for us to keep up. After a few hours in the field, we went back to the house, fetched water, boiled it, cooked a big lunch, ate, and had a rest period.

Then, much too quickly, it was back to the fields to harvest crops for food on the table and for sale. We picked ripe tomatoes, okra, sweet potatoes, white potatoes, green beans, peas, lettuce, greens and corn. Fruit trees were next and by now it was 5 o'clock. The 10-hour workday was

One of the few photos of the four young Madison brothers: Julian, Bernard, Stanley, and Bob.

almost over, but we still had to feed the chickens, pigs and the horse. Even so, we still had time for a bit of fun, so Grandma Land taught me how to ride the horse bareback. I had never been on a horse and I was scared, but this was an old horse, gentle, slow and patient. I thought he was as old as my grandmother. Not so; I learned that horses typically live only about 30 years.

Then came supper: chicken, sweet potatoes, beans, cornbread and black-eyed peas, most of it straight from the fields. Sumptuous.

After dinner and cleanup, we went to the front porch, which we came to realize was where country folk come together. In a world without air-conditioning or television, it was the natural place to be. From the porch, we waved at cousins passing by and talked some more. This time we asked, "How did you get this land?" The talk went on until bedtime.

All of a sudden it hit me just how long that day had been, packed with work we had never done before. Julian and I were overcome with the warm feelings from time with family and working harder than we had ever worked. It was high time to get ready and rested for a weekend of cooking, feasting and the word of God. We fell asleep exhausted.

Ready for another journey

Saturday came much too soon, but we were up and ready from the moment the animals announced their hunger. It's remarkable how quickly we adapted to country living. We did our morning duties, readying ourselves for another busy day. At breakfast, Cousin Lucy asked me to head into town with her to pick up staples for the Sunday feast, when the circuit rider would come for services. She didn't want to take Julian because he was too young for a long walk through rugged countryside.

Because we would be gone most of the day, Cousin Lucy checked my shoes, pants and hat to make sure I was prepared. I passed inspection, so we were ready to leave. Grandma Land, meanwhile, stuck to her kitchen, getting everything set for the preacher.

I noticed that Cousin Lucy wore a straw hat and carried several burlap sacks, along with a rather substantial stick. It was clear to me that the hat was to ward off bugs and the blazing sun. The bags, of course, were for carrying home groceries and supplies. But I wondered: What was that stick about? I would soon find out.

Not long after we began our trip, I more fully appreciated that rural Alabama wasn't like Washington, D.C., where you got around by bus or car. This was the country—no buses or taxis or private automobiles. The roads were too rutted even for bicycles. If you needed to travel, even five or more miles, most likely you'd need to rely on your own two feet.

So we set out, walking down a dirt road for about a half-hour, then following a trail through the woods for another 40 minutes. We kept switching between woods and dirt roads until we traveled through a thickly forested area with lots of animals: possums, skunks, rabbits, raccoons, squirrels, and beautiful birds I'd never seen before. That was all quite exciting—but it was also scary when we came across snakes, turtles and stray dogs. Cousin Lucy jumped into action when needed, beating them back with her stick. So that was one of the uses for the stick.

Every so often, we'd run into someone, and Cousin Lucy would tell them I was Cousin Robert's oldest child. "You know Cousin Robert?" she would say. "He's the one who went up north to a real college."

"Yes, I heard about him," they would reply. "Sure enough, son. How are you? Welcome, and I'm sure I'll see you at the church meeting tomorrow." These random encounters were wonderful, and we enjoyed quite a few. For someone accustomed to moving around so much, it was a welcome change to experience the stability of a rural community. While my Alabama relatives endured the poverty associated with a lack of creature comforts, they also enjoyed a wealth of personal, long-lasting relationships.

Town and country

After about three hours, we finally arrived in the center of town, a paved intersection with maybe a dozen free-standing buildings. I walked past a post office, saloon, barbershop, sheriff's office, and a lockup. There also was a locksmith, a pharmacy, a grocery store, gun shop and horse trough. Clearly, I was a stranger in a strange land. It felt like I had been dropped into a Hollywood set.

When we entered the grocery store, I saw that all the people behind the counters were white and that all the dirty jobs, like sweeping floors and hauling heavy loads, were done by colored men. As I also recall, all the folks in town were white except for that store's customers.

The storekeeper greeted Cousin Lucy by name, with warmth and great respect; she'd clearly been going there for years. She introduced me to him, too. Everything felt cordial, and like we were players in a cowboy movie.

Cousin Lucy bought sugar, flour, cornmeal and a few other items, putting them in her bags. She tied the bags to her stick, balancing them on her shoulders. After an hour or so in town, we headed for home. While the town had been welcoming, the weather on our way back was not.

When it started raining, Cousin Lucy took off her sandals, leading us to a one-room schoolhouse where we took shelter until the downpour stopped. We took a different route home, crossing a stream where we saw alligators, rattlesnakes and other critters. It was all so wild to watch, but pretty scary, too. We kept our distance, and, as you can imagine, we stepped carefully.

Cousin Lucy had been making this trip for years, so it was like being in the care of a guide. She truly was in touch with the land and culture. Guiding us through chaotic landscapes, fending off wildlife, negotiating rural commerce, and then leading us to a place where she knew we could get some fruit to eat for our journey home—she did it effortlessly.

We finally returned to Grandma Land's in mid-afternoon. After a short rest and substantial food, we arrived at the heart of the day's real work—getting ready for Sunday's "go to meeting time."

I had never had an experience like this. And because we rarely appreciate moments like these, I didn't realize that I'd never live through such wonderful days like these again, either.

CHAPTER FOUR
A FEAST OF FAITH

Those staples and ingredients Cousin Lucy and I brought to Grandma Land's home would be our contribution to an important event the next morning. Because Millry was too small to support an organized church, a traveling preacher would pass through every three weeks. The preacher was called a circuit rider, and he was anxiously awaited by everybody in the area. He was scheduled to preside over services shortly after arriving at about 10 a.m. Plans also called for us to enjoy a picnic dinner with all my relatives—the whole community.

"Picnic dinner," I would learn, was quite an understatement. Grandma Land worked around the stove all day. Frying chicken and baking desserts would take her time and talent, praise be to God that pies and cakes were her specialty. After the cooking and baking were done, we started getting

▲

Worship tent, Millry, Alabama, circa 1935

At Sunday go to meetings, the revival tent marked the spot where the community came together as one body to praise the Lord. The circuit rider arrives on horseback every third Sunday; the tent is raised, and depending on weather conditions, the sides can be left open or closed.

clothes ready, pressing, sewing, whatever it took to look sharp for the circuit rider. Hurry sundown, see what tomorrow brings. Sunday's coming.

Sunday morning arrived sunny, warm and beautiful. We had breakfast, cleaned up and dressed up to get ready for church. This was clearly a big deal, so it was no wonder Mother Julia had packed a special suitcase with church clothes for me and Julian.

All of us—Cousin Lucy and Grandma Land, Julian and I—set out to make the journey. We walked on a morning that grew hot and humid, over uneven terrain, in our Sunday finest clothes and shoes, carrying baskets of food and all the fixings we'd need for the day. We walked for perhaps three miles, in about one hour. Our destination was a clearing in the woods where we'd rendezvous with another 75 people coming from up country, all dressed up and carrying both food and great expectations for a glorious day. To know us Madison folks, you have to appreciate that scene and how special it was.

Cousin Lucy, proud to share Cousin Robert's sons with these country kinfolk, introduced us all around. "You know Cousin Robert, he went up north to college, and he's an engineer?" she said. "These are his boys. They're here for a few days." Everybody came over to give us a hug. I felt very special.

While all this was going on, the men set up the tent, the portable benches and a makeshift pulpit. Then the ladies began to put the food on the tables, along with placemats, dishes and silverware. It was very picnic-like.

At the same time, the children assembled in groups for Sunday school Bible study. It all felt very well-organized and made me humble and proud at the same time.

Feeling the spirit

"He's almost here," someone announced, so we looked up that dirt road to see two men riding beautiful white horses. It was 10 a.m., right on time; the preacher and his assistant had made it. I thought seeing everybody in that big tent, seeing the circuit rider come riding up on his horse, was the greatest scene I would ever witness.

The preacher was a dashing, well-built man about six feet tall, weighing maybe 175 pounds. He was handsome, very light-skinned, and well-spoken—someone I would later identify as a ladies' man. He wore a white cape over a three-piece suit, and boots. His appearance—a man on horseback, wearing a white cape—was similar to men on horseback I saw as a much younger boy in rural South Carolina. While back then I was filled with dread, in Millry I was filled with warmth.

The preacher's assistant was his opposite: portly, very dark, and less flamboyant. But his warm demeanor made him a perfect front man for the preacher, who clearly had white blood in him but nevertheless was colored and so still subject to discrimination.

The two dismounted, and their horses were led away to be tied up and fed. The preacher and his assistant mingled with the crowd for a few minutes, then started the service. Several members of the congregation sang *a cappella* to usher in the preacher, who began with a long prayer, then swung into Bible reading.

Those who had schooling read along with the minister to the accompaniment of Negro spirituals I knew very well. Somehow, these familiar songs had a very different feeling when sung in this environment. Those Madison folks could really sing.

At around the same time, a collection was taken so the traveling minister and his assistant could be paid. The minister then started the actual preaching—all fire and brimstone—and captivated the congregation. Afterward came communion and baptism.

The service, which lasted about three hours, ended after another collection, and then fellowship began. At 2 p.m., dinner was served. The preacher sat at the head of a table, joined by a local deacon representing the Millry area.

It certainly was a feast. Most everybody brought something—chicken, duck, rabbit, chitterlings, corn bread, biscuits, greens and squash—and on and on. The preacher ate well, and led a lively conversation about happenings outside Millry. As I think back, listening to him was like hearing a news report from the outside world. Remember, there was no television, no radio, no newspaper, no telephones, after all—nothing but this microcosm of Washington County, Alabama, in 1936. The people devoured the circuit rider's every word.

After dinner, the children scattered to play games while their elders caught up on the news. Later there was Christian Endeavor for the kids and Vespers for the others. Singing, marching, preaching, all blended together as dusk approached. The women cleared the tables, the men folded them up, and the preacher and his assistant prepared to leave, passing through the crowd one more time to wish everyone health and happiness until the next visit three Sundays out.

All of us watched the circuit rider and his man mount their horses, giving a gallant salute as they trotted into the setting sun. It truly was like a scene from a movie. Then we pressed our kerosene lamps into service so we could see our way home. On our way out, everyone gave Julian and me a hug and told us to give Cousin Robert, our dad, their best.

This was monumental. I have never felt so loved and appreciated by people whom I had never met before, people who were related to me through the centuries and certainly through slavery, people I felt I would never see again.

We walked home by lantern light, ending a go to meeting day with a once-in-a-lifetime memory of the circuit rider and the extended family I didn't know I had.

The events of that Sunday kept buzzing through my head, making for another sleepless night. I kept thinking about all those cousins in the backwoods of Millry, Grandma Land's 40 acres and a mule, her picket fence, her four-room house with no plumbing or electricity, her cows, pigs, horse, cat, dogs, greens, potatoes, cotton fields, the total darkness at night, the total silence.

In Millry, I learned that many worlds exist. Separate from most of the reality I knew, Millry was a self-contained and self-sufficient world with a beauty, language and economy all its own. How wonderful.

For Julian and me, the teachings of Millry—do well by whom you know and with what you've got—would influence us for the rest of our lives. And the next day, when we drove away from Millry to return to

Mobile to spend the rest of the summer at Mother Julia's house, we left a region we would never experience again, along with many relatives we would never see again.

Rounding out comes hard

Despite the many teachings of Millry, I was a square—and I would be one for years to follow. Probably the first time I realized I was a square was later in 1936.

Mother Julia, my dad's mom, had divorced my grandfather and married a man named Craig. Together, they had a son and two daughters, one of whom was also named Julia. One Saturday night, the younger Julia took me to a dance presented by one of Mobile's many all-boy social clubs.

The Diablos was the premier social club, and the Diablos Dance was widely considered to be the best. The club drew the elite—the sons of doctors, lawyers and the like—and Julia was dating a Diablo, so my presence created a hardship for her.

Julia was upset because her mother—my grandmother—had required that Julia look out for me at the dance. She was worried that I, this little drip who didn't know anything, would embarrass her, maybe even spy on her. I ignored her threats and went anyway. To this day, I'm glad I did.

The decorations alone made it a worthwhile event. The Diablos spent three days and nights transforming a ballroom on the second floor of the Elks Hall. When I saw the way that ballroom looked, it put me in another world. It was a masquerade dance and everybody—except me—was looking spiffy. People spent lots of time and money on costumes, and I had never seen anything like it. This was my first dance, and I didn't know the first thing about dancing. I was such a nerd.

It was a beautiful party. Everybody was happy except those who weren't judged winners in the best costume contest. Everybody had a lot of fun except for some sweethearts who found themselves without their one and only, usually because their one and only was with someone else. There was much hugging and kissing and fooling around. Julia was right—I was square. And mostly, I was squarely alone.

On the sidelines, I watched people party and dance, and boy, they could really move. Although everyone was dancing to their own beat in their own way, from my sideline seat as a spectator, it seemed like they were performing as participants in a choreographed show.

The popular notion is that colored people can really move, and I'm here to tell you it's true; I know, because I was the exception who proved the rule. I thought the band, an aggregate of young, local musicians, was fantastic. And even though it was hot as blazes, the partygoers danced until it was nearly dawn. They were fueled by a lot of special food and soft drinks. There must have been a special room where the drinks were extra-special, because I kept seeing people disappear down a corridor. When they returned, most of them acted a little strange. Even though Julia had planted me in one spot and warned me not to move while she did her thing—whatever that was—I had a good time. Even though I was on the outside looking in, I sure did enjoy the view.

These people knew who they were and what the rules were. Even though there were constraints, they understood life was to be lived and enjoyed, and that everybody had a place.

At 4 a.m. Sunday, however, my place was to be home, and Mother Julia was waiting. After looking us over with a very searching eye, she reminded us we would be in church in five hours. I slept well those few hours—and then I slept through Sunday school and the sermon. Perhaps I dreamed about one day being like all those other kids. But dreams don't always turn into reality, at least not on cue.

It would be years before I shed my squareness, which is a bit surprising considering how smooth and "with it" my father was. Robert J. Madison was cool and connected from his very beginnings.

CHAPTER FIVE
BALLAD FOR MY FATHER

Robert James Madison was born in Mobile, Alabama on July 21, 1899. On November 18, 1900, my mother, Nettie Josephine Brown, was born about 150 miles to the north in Selma, a city legendary in the history of civil rights. Both my parents were talented and, even more importantly, that innate talent was sharpened by their own highly educated parents and schooling. For at least the five generations I'm able to track, an unusually strong emphasis on education has flowed through my family.

My father's parents, Robert Madison and Julia Land, had three boys. Tragically, my father was very young when he lost both brothers—Ollie drowned in a swimming pool and Marshall was killed in an auto accident. Their deaths essentially left my father an only child and, later, a solitary man.

▲

Survey Transit, circa 1950

Working with a surveying crew and our transits and other gear was part math and part magic. Not only did the entire process transform a rough piece of land into a plat ready to be built upon, it also transformed my father. Looking back and forth with his unaided eyes and through the scope, my father was transformed, and he was happy. When his sons assisted him on the job, we would move in small increments according to his commands. He was in control, and the world came to order.

Even as a young man, I was aware of and proud that I was at least the third in a family line of Robert Madisons. But not even a strong, proud family lineage can make up for a loss of brotherly camaraderie. His parents divorced when my father was in his pre-teens, the collapse of their marriage perhaps collateral damage from the stress brought on by the loss of two sons.

When my dad turned 15, he was enrolled at Snow Hill Normal and Industrial Institute, a boarding school for boys in southeastern Alabama. Because he attended a boarding school, it might sound like he was privileged, but he was not. In fact, Alabama at that time did not provide public school education for black children beyond eighth grade. Ironically, a private school like Snow Hill was the only quality education option for a black child in the South.

So, although my father was in an advantaged educational environment at Snow Hill, he was isolated and virtually alone at an early age. By fate and circumstance, this solitary condition and the loss of close connection seemed to run through my family. My mother, Nettie, was an only child. Her parents also divorced when she was young, and each remarried. During his last year at Snow Hill, my dad met my mother. Perhaps their similar family circumstances drew them together.

At Snow Hill, he excelled in mathematics and science. For reasons known only to him, my father decided to become a civil engineer. Upon graduation, he enrolled at Howard University in Washington, D.C. At Howard, a historically black university, he was accepted into the school of engineering and architecture. Financially, he benefited from a similar out-of-state aid program that would later assist black students of my generation. My father also was a star on the baseball and football teams. As the team's quarterback, you could say he was the Tom Brady of Howard University.

Like Brady, my father would forcefully call out plays in code to communicate with team members so they would know the play without tipping off the opposing team. But while Brady barks out commands using terms like "Omaha," "three-nineteen," or "jaguar," my father took a more cerebral approach. He signaled the play call and snap count by shouting out in Latin, a language he and his teammates knew. Across the scrimmage line, the other guys had no way of deciphering those Howard plays, as they were not similarly versed.

Robert J. Madison, Bob's father, with a college friend at Howard University.

At Howard, Robert J. Madison cut a sporty figure, both in his athletic uniforms and in the attire he wore for school or social activities; he was a dandy, classy dresser. But mostly he was a hard worker. To pay his way, he worked a night shift in the post office. And he worked hard in the classroom, graduating cum laude in 1922. He was Numero Uno in his class, valedictorian. Had he graduated in 1972 instead of 50 years earlier, he would have worn his stylish clothes and used his education and work ethic to build an executive career at NASA, Ford, General Electric, or Big Blue. Had he graduated in 2002, he would have entertained multiple offers from Apple, Boeing, or Exxon. But like all of us, his time was not of his choosing. And this was the early 1920s.

His Howard graduating class was said to include the first colored engineers in the country. As for my mother, while I know nothing about her secondary school education, I do know that she graduated with a degree in drama from Morris Brown College in Atlanta. That was an extraordinary accomplishment for a black woman—or any woman—born in late 19th-century America.

To this day, it remains difficult for me to comprehend that my black parents, born two generations removed from the Civil War in the very heart of the Jim Crow South, each earned degrees from prestigious universities. What are the odds? If any couple had set themselves up for success through a combination of determination and education, it was Robert and Nettie.

My father married Nettie shortly after his graduation from Howard, confident he had found his intellectual equal in a woman with whom he would share successful careers and a rich family life. In short order, the "family" aspect of their lives began to be fulfilled. On Saturday, July 28, 1923, a year after my father's graduation from Howard, the next Robert Madison—me—came into the world. For reference, Vice President Calvin Coolidge succeeded Warren G. Harding as president five days after I was born. For only $300, you could sit in the driver's seat of a brand new Ford Model T, the country's best-selling automobile. This was the peak of the Roaring Twenties, when booms in economics, technology, and entertainment propelled America's recovery from World War I. Until I was about eight years old, life for me and the Madison family was good. From 1929 to the middle of the 1940s, though, worldwide events would test all of us and eventually bring most of us back to earth.

My life began in Cleveland, Ohio, sometimes called "Alabama North." My parents had moved to Cleveland not long after they got married. Including my grandparents' generation, my family's journey intertwined with what is known as the first "Great Migration." My family members were smack in the middle of more than 1.5 million African-Americans who, between 1916 and 1930, moved from the rural South to the urban North. The Great Migration was not some organized march or guided tour. Instead, it was a physical response to opportunities black people learned were possible in the North. The grapevine of family and friends was the social medium of its day and a powerful tool that helped trace a path for many.

Friends or family who found better job opportunities and weekly pay of $20 a week in an auto factory up north? Interesting. People like you getting a better education, a fairer shake, in Michigan than in Mississippi? Let's check that out. Not much more than two generations after the end of the Civil War, the South remained a virtual captive region for blacks. For us, the South and its repressive laws and culture held us back. Better to take a chance and plunge into the unknown waters of the North, even if those waters held unknown dangers.

I came into the world on Central Avenue at 31st Street in a building called the Maternity Clinic for Colored People. If that name sounds quaint, consider that even in the most forgiving northern environments of that time, colored doctors could not deliver colored children or treat people of color in hospitals. The Maternity Clinic probably presented a better environment than a kitchen table to bring a child into the world, but it was not a modern, well-equipped hospital, either. So, while the Great Migration brought African-Americans many opportunities, it's clear that in Cleveland we had not migrated to some enlightened promised land. No such land existed in the U.S. at that time.

For my first six months, we lived with my grandmother, Julia, and her second husband, my step-grandfather, Prince Watkins, the inspiration for my middle name. While living with them, my father earned his first substantial full-time job: a teaching position. Teaching was no match for engineering work in either earnings or status, but my father had not found any of those opportunities in the North. Employment in education was the next-best professional option, so he was ready to grab it. As is often the case with opportunities, this one came with a catch—the teaching job was at Selma University in Alabama. So, after six months or so, the Madison family was on the move once more, heading back south for what my parents hoped was a better long-term situation in my mother's birthplace.

In Selma in 1923, my father taught physics, chemistry, and mathematics. He also coached the football team. In fact, that last job provided me with one of my fondest memories of Selma, maybe even of my entire early childhood: sitting on the team bench at a football game with my dad when I was four years old. Just imagine the view through my eyes during the game, looking up at these large men engaged in physical battle on the football field. They were heroic figures to me, warriors striving to notch a victory for my father. My father was my hero, too.

My mother was an educator as well, teaching courses in drama. And my parents' professions came with some unexpected benefits—the stu-

Robert J. Madison on the campus of Howard University.

Nettie J. Brown, about age 18.

dents, the co-eds, adored me and clamored to be my babysitters. We were the youngest members of the university elite, and we happily lived that part. And while it's difficult to be objective, then or now, we truly deserved the respect and attention we received.

Our means of transportation? A Hudson touring sedan, a very exclusive motorcar my father's earnings made possible. We also had maids and cooks, all kinds of help in running a professor's household. It was the good life. That's what we lived.

In that environment, the Madison family began to comfortably grow: my brother Julian was born in Selma on February 28, 1927. Even though I was nearly four years older than Julian, I bonded with him quickly.

It was no longer just me. I had a brother, someone to play with. My parents began to drill into me: You and Julian will do great deeds and change the world. Before I could do great deeds, though, I had to first do great in the classroom. At an early age, I began to assert myself as a student. I was diligent and proud to study and achieve. And in first grade, teachers discovered another talent: I could draw. Not long after, my mother told me the path my life must take; study hard, work hard, become an architect. And I said, Yes, Mother, I'll become an architect—even though I really didn't know what an architect did, or how outlandish this dream was for a young black student.

My dad was very good at his job and soon was offered an opportunity to teach and coach at another historically black university, Benedict College. So the Madisons were moving again, over 400 miles to Columbia, South Carolina. By the time I was five years old, I had already lived in three states. But when you're surrounded by the promise of improvement and a loving family marching together to make that promise become reality, moving is not a hardship, it's a mission.

Our time in South Carolina was fine, and at Benedict, my parents did well. My mother was director of the department of theater and drama, and our tight little family would expand again. The third Madison boy, Stanley, came into our world in Columbia on August 10, 1929.

Beneath the placid surface, though, my father was restless and anxious. He had received the finest training and education. He was qualified to design sturdy highways, majestic bridges, and soaring buildings. But even the best teaching position at the finest university wouldn't enable him to put all that knowledge to work. He was a thoroughbred, trained to run a great race and score great victories. No matter how solid the academic opportunity, however, he would be teaching, not doing.

After numerous applications, interviews and background checks, he received his big break: an offer of a prestigious position as a civil engineer for the federal government in Washington, D.C. He would become the first "colored" engineer in the U.S. War Department.

For us, a new life was about to begin. Robert James Madison would practice engineering in a big job in the nation's capital, doing what he was educated for and what he always wanted to do. He was happy, my mother settled into being a housewife raising three happy sons (a fourth was soon to come), and all seemed good.

CHAPTER SIX
ELEGY FOR MY FATHER

Riding a wave of optimism, my father bought a house on Gresham Place in an elegant neighborhood in Washington, D.C., near Howard University. Little did any of us know that this would be the last house we would own as a family. Perhaps fate is kind when it keeps foreboding secrets from us.

So we packed up and said goodbye to faculty, students and staff at Benedict College to head to our new house and new life. Outwardly, my parents expressed hope, excitement and joy, but even though I was only seven years old, I could sense they were anxious about the future. No colored man had done this before, and they were conflicted about the comfortable life they were leaving. But because they viewed themselves as pioneers of our people, somebody had to do this. Those somebodies were us. The year

▲

Hudson Touring Car, Detroit, Michigan, 1928
For one great and memorable year in my life, we were at the top. My father was a college professor, coach of a championship football team… we were a joyful family of five! Why wouldn't we travel in a Hudson touring car?

was 1930, the first full year of the Great Depression. For that and other reasons, the trip north was fraught with both hope and dread.

The car was packed and we left Columbia early, at about 2 a.m. Our parents were up front, sometimes with my mother holding our brother Stanley, who was just a bit over one year old. No child car seats or even seat belts back then. Stanley would sleep on the back seat with Julian, three years old, and me, the seven-year old big brother. Less than an hour after we set off, we were driving though a wooded stretch of road when we were suddenly flung onto the back seat floor and the car stopped abruptly. My father killed the lights, turned to us and very deliberately commanded: "Do not say a word." He said those words quietly, making his message extra-clear.

Through the front windshield, Julian and I saw what terrified our parents.

Large men on horseback in white hoods and capes crossed the road. It was the Ku Klux Klan in full regalia, coming from where and going where, we knew not. And unlike the caped riders who a few years later would bring us religion and camaraderie in Millry, these horsemen had nothing we wanted. We, in turn, wanted nothing to do with them.

My parents were truly afraid; this was a back road somewhere in the state of South Carolina. Plain and simple, it just was not safe for a colored man to be driving a ritzy Hudson automobile in these parts in the dead of night. It was then that I experienced the contagious nature of parental fear, so we were frozen still. After the parade of riders passed—that probably took only 10 minutes, but it seemed much longer—we continued. Although my father believed we were now safe, he drove very slowly for about 10 miles. No headlights, no braking, no squeaks to betray our presence to the caped demons. This was the Madison family on a silent mission, with only the moonlight showing the way. But finally, we made it through.

After another 500 miles on two-lane roads, we arrived safely in D.C., and my father went happily to work. My mother was happy, too, and I soon made friends with other students who attended Monroe Elementary School, just a block from home. Life was good—and then it wasn't. While we made it out of the deep South for a better life, we couldn't escape economic reality. The Depression would eventually catch up with us and hit us hard.

But while it lasted, that first year in D.C. was actually one of our family's best. At the start, we were prosperous and riding high, at least so it seemed. I became best friends with Coleman Tucker, who also lived on Gresham Place. It was wonderful to live somewhere long enough to make a best friend. It's also amazing to me to remember the name of a best friend all these years later.

Tucker and I would peek through the fence at Howard Stadium to watch football games. One Thanksgiving Classic—Howard versus Lincoln—was played in driving rain, with a lot of mud. But the weather and field conditions didn't bother us. We had front row seats to a piece of sports history. The hero of that messy meeting was Martin Sutler, who later became a doctor and would attend to the care of my father for one last time.

Life was good but increasingly hectic. Though I started fifth grade at Monroe Elementary, I had to transfer to Morgan Elementary when we moved to 15th Street; then, within four months, we moved to Irving Street, putting me back at Monroe. So, even though we were "settled" in Washington, our frequent moves were like mini-migrations. And, I now recall, this was when we were in a stable situation, with my father working at a good job.

Though all this was unnerving, I graduated from Monroe No. 2 in the class behind Alvin Thompson, a good friend. His father, a college graduate like my father, had a steady job, too, working in the post office. Alvin and I also went through Garnet-Patterson Junior High School together, providing me some welcome personal continuity. We were the smartest in the class, and both of us were skipped ahead a semester. Alvin and I would reunite years later at Howard University and share the Freshman Cup Award for scholastic honors. Alvin would live a prosperous life as a very successful doctor in Seattle, Washington, until his death in 2012.

Despite such personal satisfactions and that promising first year, poverty was lurking, preparing to grind us down. This was the depths of the Depression, hitting home in a way no cold statistic or newspaper story ever could. I've heard it said that a recession is when your neighbor loses

A portrait of Robert J. Madison, Bob's father, circa 1928 during his tenure as an engineering professor at Selma University.

his job, and a depression is when you lose yours. I say that when my father lost his job—or worse, couldn't find any paying job—that was the Depression with a capital D. No matter how carefully he prepared his resume, the response was the same: No, we don't hire colored.

Despite all our hopes, my father would work as an engineer for only one year. When the hard times of the Depression hit, his situation unfortunately helped prove a cruel business axiom. When people discuss inventory or head count, LIFO, or "last in, first out," usually is the deciding factor. Since he was the last hired, he was the first fired. Over the years that followed, he could never come close to pulling himself all the way back up, financially or emotionally.

His life, defined by the civil engineering degree he earned from Howard University in 1922, became an unpleasant seesaw ride. What possessed him to become an engineer in the first place remains a mystery to me. But that dream of his was to become a clear inspiration for me.

He was a graduate of the crème de la crème of black colleges, one of the first African-Americans to earn an engineering degree, and the first black engineer in the War Department, the precursor to today's Defense Department. Ultimately, though, he couldn't make a steady career of his chosen field because of two factors, both beyond his control. He was born the wrong color—and he was born at least 20 years too soon. That combination would conspire to doom him.

I'm not sure what was worse—not being able to get and keep a job that he loved, that he was born and trained to do, or ultimately not being able to get any meaningful job. The first circumstance crushed his soul; the second crushed our family. Still, he was a man of high style and higher thought who did mighty things, stretching himself to the intellectual and physical limit. To paraphrase Theodore Roosevelt, my father "dared to dream big dreams," a trait I share with him. I loved him for venturing where no black American had gone before. I loved him for his ambition, his professionalism, his reach. And I love him still for his determination to keep going, and to inspire us to keep going, too.

The family frays

My father, who could recite from memory the hundred-quatrain-long *The Rubaiyat* by Omar Khayyam, was not alone in his predicament; hundreds of African-Americans with PhD degrees in physics, chemistry and engineering toiled in the post office or as Pullman porters on the railroad, working any jobs they could find.

From my seventh year until my father's untimely death 21 years later, I watched my father fight, lose, agonize, despair, fight again, lose again, question—and gradually decline. The Great Depression took from us food on the table, a car, nice clothes, all that and more. It took my father's job and by the time he lost that, he couldn't go back to the university. He was born and trained to be an engineer, and he was happy during that one year working for the government, but after that it was downhill.

My father went from being one of the most celebrated employees in D.C. to a jobless alcoholic with a wife and, with the birth of Bernard on August 13, 1932, four hungry sons. Our future was at best uncertain, and at worst, shameful and scary.

Although I was only eight years old when we lost the house because he couldn't pay the mortgage, I was old enough to know what was happening to my dad and to us. Soon, we also lost the car, that beautiful Hudson touring sedan.

It was only after my father lost his job as an engineer that he experienced the full effects of discrimination. Of course, my father was no stranger to the long arm of racism in America in the 1930s—no black man could escape those claws. It was mostly inconvenient and humiliating to be refused service in a restaurant or forced to use a separate drinking fountain. However, not being able to get a job that he was well-qualified for brought frustration and rage. But all those emotions pale next to the despair my father must have felt when he couldn't find a job—any job—no matter how he tried. And he tried, applying for any job available. It always ended the same way: He was too educated for the job. That must have felt suffocating. Our situation rapidly became a matter of survival for him and his family.

He did occasionally land jobs far beneath his capabilities. Once, he was able to work as an elevator operator. Imagine, a man who could design and engineer an electrical control panel was reduced to pulling door levers and pushing buttons. He also "earned" a job as a golf caddy for rich white boys whose fathers belonged to a country club. He must have felt like he was always going down.

But those types of jobs didn't pay enough to support a family of six, so, just as he had done in college, he worked at night, now as a taxi driver. Although we rarely saw him, when we did, we could see he was wearing thin. It was then that Julian and I realized the Madison boys had to help keep the household going.

In what would be the first of our many business ventures, the two of us gathered golf balls my dad brought home, dug holes in the backyard, acquired miniature golf clubs and told neighbors they could play golf in our back yard for 25 cents a round. This lasted for a summer until we were forced to move to live someplace cheaper, putting the Madison Brothers Country Club out of business.

For us, moving became a way of life. If we couldn't pay the rent, we were evicted. Twice, I remember coming home from school in the rain and finding our belongings on the sidewalk, sopping wet. Sometimes, all four of us kids slept in one bed, on the floor, in the homes of friends and even strangers.

In four short years, we moved a total of eight times. As I consider this today, that amount of upheaval was indeed unjust for developing young boys. We went from Park Road to this street to the next street to the next. People were very kind to us back in those days, however. They would see us on the tree lawn by the sidewalk and say, "Oh, let's take in the lady with the four boys." So somebody would give us a place to sleep, at least for that night. We would have to see what happened next, but because of that considerate person, we would stay together to survive another day.

It was against this backdrop in the summer of 1936 that Mother Julia had taken us to Alabama to give my parents some relief. Nevertheless, they had their hands full with Stanley and Bernard, my little brothers. More importantly, the underlying issues—racism, financial ruin, alcoholism, despair—dogged us as well. At least for a while, though, my parents had only two little mouths to feed. But even that wasn't easy, what with my mother running the household and my father struggling to find work.

Despite such hardships, I could handle our situation until I entered Garnet-Patterson, when the seriousness of our family's plight began to get to me. A very visible proof that couldn't be hidden or ignored was my appearance. Since I was the oldest, I didn't have many clothes; no hand-me-downs for me, not even something ripped or shabby. We needed to be creative and hands-on. To absorb the water that came in through holes in our soles, we put cardboard in shoes. Be careful and don't run around too much in the playground, and that cardboard might last the whole day so you wouldn't make new holes in your socks. We thought we were just being resourceful and solving a problem. Truth is, it was pitiful.

I was deeply embarrassed when kids started laughing at my overshoes—they were ladies' galoshes, probably my mother's. Lunchtime, too, was a sad experience, as I tried to conceal what was in my lunch bag: leftovers from last night's dinner, like mashed potatoes between slices of bread, or butter and sugar on a slice of bread. That was the way it was. No use complaining, because I knew my mother and father were doing all they could. I didn't like it at all, but the alternative was to steal, as some other kids did. But my parents forbade that, promising things wouldn't always be like this.

Times were really tough, and adolescents can be so cruel. One day in June 1937, after school had closed, Julian and I went to Garnet-Patterson to help the teachers clean classrooms. As we were walking home, some boys chased us up Sherman Avenue, trying to take the small rewards teachers had given us. A glass milk bottle one boy threw just missed the back of my head. I ducked just in time as I heard it whoosh by. We doubled back into a grocery store and hid like fugitives until we decided we were safe. To reach home, we took secret zig zag routes through alleys and backyards, breathless but happy to make it through another day.

I can't say we were the poorest family on Monroe Street—poor people don't share their misery—and everyone knew we were good people, so they did what they could to help. My father was still looking for a steady job, and in spite of his increased drinking he kept the pressure on us to do well in school. "Be the best," he would tell us.

But he couldn't remain his own best, and he began to change. He became irritable and moody when he was drunk, which was frequently. Can you imagine a college professor, an engineer, carrying golf bags for rich white kids who "couldn't solve the function of a complex variable"? His words. The thoughts behind those words, I'm convinced, drove him to despair and to drink.

Maybe worst of all, he started to fight with my mother, and the fights got bad. Nothing could have been more disorienting for us boys than to see our majestic father and sweet mother fight. Teammates for life, always on the same side, now screaming, scratching, fighting. One night, when I tried to intervene, he hit me quite violently. That incident marked the low spot for us.

Maybe through neighbors or friends, Mother Julia got wind of the situation and came to Washington. Her recommendation was that she take all of us boys back to Alabama. We'd be raised, maybe in Mobile, maybe on the farm of a relative around Millry.

My mother and her mother-in-law had a pretty chilly relationship in the best of times, but when presented with a slight or threat like this, the chill turned to ice. "Never," my mother yelled and, circling the Madison family wagon, my father took a break from fighting with his wife to back her up. Before long, though, Dad started drinking again.

One night, he flipped between arguing with his mother, and then his wife. Alternately, they would leave the house to sit on the front porch and pray. I was confused and angry and asked myself: Why did my father act like that? Was it something his sons did? What could we do to make it better? Only much later would I begin to understand that it was not our fault. It was not his fault either, really. And there was little any of us could do to make it better, at least in the short term. No matter how certain you are that you are not at fault, something silent and just as bad remains, sometimes for decades. We all felt stained by guilt.

Things were tough and getting tougher, but we all pitched in to earn money. No backyard golf course this time. Instead, I hauled my shoeshine kit to Georgia Avenue and U Street on Saturdays and shined shoes for 10 cents a pair. I also had two newspaper routes, and on Saturday mornings, Julian and I would pull our wagons to the grocery store to carry groceries home for women—not many people had cars in those days, and hardly any women drove—for 25 cents plus tips. But while we earned some money, we had no stability. We often didn't know where our next meal was coming from.

Sometimes there would be no meal. Going to bed without supper was not a punishment for bad behavior, but it felt like it just the same.

Yet we stuck together as a family; partially because we moved so often, we never had time to make friends. We were all we had, us against the world. Sometimes when people use that expression, it seems heartless and tribal. For us, it was about surviving.

And then something amazing happened: My father finally got a job as a surveyor, but that work would be some distance away, in Chesapeake Bay. On a job like that, several hours travel each way, it's not practical to make a daily commute. He would need to be on site for three, four weeks at a time. It was then that my mother effectively took over raising us. That's also when I became the male head of the household.

If I owe my ambition to my father, I owe my drive to my mother. My choice of profession and my faith, too. No matter how strong her drive or her ambition, though, sometimes they weren't enough to keep the bad guys away.

One morning, I went off to school as usual. I didn't know whether my mother knew the landlord was coming, but when I arrived home, once again on the sidewalk was our furniture, clothes, everything. Want to sample the ultimate combination of despair and embarrassment? Be on the wrong end of an eviction. I wouldn't wish that feeling of shame and helplessness on anyone.

Keeping the faith

As my father grew more distant, my mother worked very hard to keep the family on course. Of average height—5 feet 3 or 4—she was a good-looking woman, and like my dad, she knew how to dress. She was also the Christian type, and believed God would take care of us no matter how dire the circumstances. The church helped keep her together. It has long been a source of strength for me, too.

The St. John African Methodist Episcopal (A.M.E.) Church, which years later would make me its first official architect, has been a constant in my life. Going to church wasn't a question of like or dislike, it was just what we did. When you live in the ghetto where everybody else is going to church, going to church is not a choice. So we found a way to like it, of course, with Christian Endeavor, where young people would give talks, and teen-agers would come to St. John's Church Sunday afternoons. You'd get there in the morning for Sunday school, go to church, go home for dinner, come back for Christian Endeavor, then go back home at 9 o'clock. That was my routine. Time-consuming, but comfortable.

But the poorer we became, such pleasant and sustaining routines got harder to maintain. Thank God for Christian charity when we were evicted, and thank God my mother never lost her pride. People would say, "This lady is crazy." But my proud mother said, "I'm putting my boys through college." They laughed, either out loud and in her face or behind her back, snickering. Not sure which is more cruel. They didn't believe her, but she did just that. Turns out, less than 25 years later, every one of the four Madison boys graduated from college.

Guess she wasn't crazy after all.

Besides being a religious lady, my mother was also a worker. We all know, after all, that the Lord helps those who help themselves. Nettie Josephine Madison made sure we got the best we could possibly afford. During the Depression, she worked in the sewing circle. Back in those days of the W.P.A. (Works Progress Administration), she would go to Banneker School in D.C., where women would sew and she would earn money to buy us Spam, the newly introduced food staple.

The stress began to wear on us ever more, though. My father was so disappointed, so frustrated, so desperate. We reached the breaking point. Finally, it was time to break away from our current situation and, as a family, leave D.C. for good. While our time in Mobile and that late-summer country weekend in Millry did Julian and me a world of good, the world never did improve for my parents, at least not in the nation's capital. Still, my parents vowed that the world would be better for their kids. Getting us into a superior educational environment was critical.

So that summer, we learned that we would move again, this time back to my hometown of Cleveland. We were worse for wear— but at least we had a plan and a hope that we could make it work. And it had to work.

Within just a couple of years, we would begin to believe that our migration north was working. Turns out, though, that it probably paid the most dividends for the Madison boys, not our parents.

CHAPTER SEVEN
CLEVELAND CALLING

The 1930s were the first decade of the Great Migration, when blacks left the South for work in the North. As they moved, many of them switched their political allegiance from the party of Lincoln to the Democratic Party. My family was a participant in those momentous shifts, and at least for a time, we benefited from them. But they didn't last long enough for us to gain a foothold that would help secure a piece of the American dream.

Our personal migration, yet another journey, began when the Madisons left Washington, D.C., for Cleveland. Short-term economic advantages were certainly a factor in the decision to move. It would be cheaper to live with my grandparents in Cleveland than to remain on our own in D.C., where my father struggled mightily to find work. A stable and

▲

FirstEnergy Stadium, Cleveland, Ohio, 1999 | HOK Sports Facilities Group (now Populous), prime architect; Robert P. Madison International, associate architect
When the Browns' owner moved the team in 1996, the city of Cleveland endured three years of anguished anticipation before the franchise returned.

mostly free place to live, better job opportunities, and a less oppressive social environment were advantages we hoped to gain in Cleveland. But the key factor driving our move had nothing to do with short-term financial upgrade. The long-game opportunities in the North that would be life-changing for me and my brothers were related to education.

I had graduated from Garnet-Patterson in Washington, D.C., with a bang: Robert Madison, class salutatorian, second in his class. But as the June commencement drew closer, despite feeling great pride in that honor, I also felt ashamed. I was to give a speech to my classmates, and I looked forward to the honor. But I didn't have the right clothes.

Graduates of Garnet-Patterson were expected to wear cream-colored flannel pants and blue jackets at the ceremony. I didn't have any clothes like that, and my family couldn't afford to buy me an outfit that fit the bill. If I wasn't properly dressed, I wouldn't be allowed to deliver my address; a great honor seemed destined to turn into a great embarrassment. "You hear about that Madison boy? He's second in his class, but he can't give the speech, because he don't have the right clothes."

As was often the case, my mother came to the rescue. She had an idea. We traveled to a flea market downtown, where she bought an outfit that she could sew and patch. The result was a look good enough to allow me to deliver the salutatorian address to the graduating class. As I did so that same day, I'd officially gone as far as I could in the D.C. school system. And nothing my mother could scare up in any D.C. flea market could change that.

At that time in D.C., three high schools were available to colored people. They were tiered according to academic discipline and ambition. If you wanted to go into clerical work, you went to Cardozo. If you wanted to go to college, you went to Dunbar, the elite school. If you wanted to enter fields like carpentry or construction, you went to Armstrong.

Sadly, that educational arrangement shut me out. There was no place in D.C. for a kid who wanted to be an architect because that meant a combination of trade school and college-bound. My parents thought this through and settled on a solution: We would move to Cleveland so I could go to East Tech—if I could pass the entrance exam. In addition, maybe, just maybe, my father could find a job in the North. And so, in the summer of 1937, our expanding clan boarded a bus pointed toward Cleveland and a new life. The road and a new home were calling for the Madisons again.

Our family had tried its luck in Washington with much hope and some degree of fear. We gave it our best, and we were happy to simply have survived in the nation's capital, a place of great aspiration but also a place that could be unforgiving, even cruel.

Everybody talks about hindsight being 20/20, that it's superficial and pointless to rationalize the past. While I don't believe in dwelling in the past, I do believe in making a brief visit there once in a while to get a perspective to shape our future. Looking back on those seven years in D.C., I saw the city as a trial by fire, a crucible. Up North, I hoped, life would turn hopeful and things would be easier for me and my brave but troubled family.

A welcome home

That summer, when we moved back to my hometown, we lived in the Central area in my maternal grandmother's home. This was just a few blocks from the high school my parents had their eyes on for me. East Tech, a name that rang out for me, stood proud on the southeast corner of East 55th Street and Quincy Avenue.

We lived on the second floor of Grandma's house at East 59th and Central. It was a two-family home with a pot-bellied stove in the living room for heat. Sounds cozy, right?

Wrong. On the outside, at least, Central was buzzing.

It was a crazy neighborhood, with everything from a single watermelon stand to dozens of bars and clubs. One establishment was even a showcase for female impersonators. I could never understand much of the behavior I saw and heard in my neighborhood. It's hard for me to even remember what must have gone through my head back then, but Saturday nights sure were wild around there. This was the ghetto for colored people. It was almost like its own city. It was electric, and a far cry from downtown. Short Scovill no longer exists, except in the memory of the few of us remaining who lived through that era.

Walter Wills, the famous Cleveland undertaker, lived in a fabulous place up the street from us, and the area was known for its diverse professional make-up, including doctors, lawyers, preachers, pimps, and "ladies of the evening," as they were genteelly referred to back then. The Majestic Hotel at 55th and Central was a magnet for higher-class entertainment. Black entertainers, including such legends as Duke Ellington and Count Basie, top draws on the "chitlin' circuit," played the Majestic. Ironically, blacks couldn't stay in downtown hotels then, even though they could entertain their exclusively white guests.

The numbers racket was important, too. Every afternoon around 2, ordinary backyards were the unlikely site of this homegrown (and illegal) forerunner to today's lotteries. One day, the numbers game turned deadly; a police raid at the numbers site, shouting, pushing, everybody running to avoid capture. One man stumbles, he's trampled by the frantic gamblers—and just like that, someone's son, father, or husband is dead. A couple of days later, he travels to his services in the back of a great big black Cadillac, hundreds attend his funeral around the corner from the Baptist Church—and another Central resident's journey is over.

The numbers game produced superstars, too. Although I didn't witness it myself, I heard about Scatter's funeral. Everybody did. It was a sensation in the city.

On September 10, 1967, Herman "Scatter" Stephens, a numbers mogul and the owner of Scatter's Barbecue on the 105th Street strip, was fatally shot in an execution-style slaying. That September 21, over 3,000 people turned out for his funeral services at East Mount Zion Baptist Church, clogging two city blocks with custom, expensive cars. Scatter went on his final journey in an "$8,000 copper deposit, antique silver finished casket that contained the remains of one of the most colorful entrepreneurs in the Negro community," according to the Call & Post. Scatter was a celebrity both alive and dead.

Other horrific deaths haunted me. I became friends with twin brothers who lived across the street. One was shot to death, and the other went to prison for life. Seems like *Porgy and Bess* was a true story in that neighborhood. But that was the way Central was: wild.

Thank God for some order in my life. That fall, I was admitted to East Tech. It was great, because it was Cleveland's best school aesthetically, and even more important, academically. It was all boys, and you had to score very high on the entrance exam to be admitted. More than 3,000 students attended East Tech then, and only about 50 were colored. You could study anything, and you could achieve, with great teachers to guide you.

I remember a Mr. Cherubini taught me Latin and French. Mr. Davidson taught architecture to me and the other coloreds, Jesse Strickland and a guy named Rucker, who was the best student in our class. Perhaps it's a measure of the school, as well as how much emphasis was placed on education, that nearly 80 years later the names of teachers and scholars remain burned into my memory.

But that's to be expected. This was East Tech, the innovative Cleveland school where you could actually study technology—and at that point in history, you could help create technology, too. We had aeronautical engineering at East Tech in 1940—aeronautical engineering, while aviation was still in its infancy and the U.S. Air Force had not yet been conceived. Spanish, French, Greek, Latin—today, many universities don't offer that menu of languages. It was one of the best schools in the country. It was equivalent to a private school, and in those days we could compete with the elite, private Hawken School.

As for me, I was an excellent student. And even though I was too little and too small for varsity athletics—I stood 5 feet 8 inches and weighed 116 pounds dripping wet—I was a power at school. The movie committee, the National Honor Society and the Corinthian Club—I wasn't just a participant, I was a leader. And because I went to summer school to advance a semester that I had skipped at Garnet-Patterson in Washington, I began my career at East Tech a whole year ahead of my class. I was a tenth-grader at 14 years of age.

Much was expected of students at East Tech, and some educational practices that worked back then might not be acceptable today. I still think of one graduation requirement at East Tech: If you couldn't swim across the swimming pool, you didn't graduate. While I never really learned how to swim, I did make it across the pool—kicking, splashing, gasping for air, half-drowned, but I made it. Not sure that type of competency exam would pass muster with the school board today.

At East Tech, for those who worked and achieved, the rewards were there for the taking. I won a prize for best architectural design from Carbone Construction Company. Dominic Carbone, son of the owner, was in my class. Decades later, I would design a building for the Carbone firm. Such were the accomplishments and connections I would build upon later. I felt like my path to victory was opening up. For a while, that even seemed to be the case for my father,

My father gets a grip

Shortly after we moved back to Cleveland, my father found work mowing the lawns of those big houses in nearby Shaker Heights. An inner-ring suburb on the southeast border of Cleveland, Shaker Heights at one time had the highest per-capita income in the country. Even though it was only a few miles from where we lived, to me, Shaker Heights might as well have been the moon. And even though the landscape and homes in Shaker Heights were gorgeous, for my father, that city must have felt just as desolate as the moon. Cutting lawns, even Shaker Heights lawns, was barely a job; what a letdown after his distinguished academic and professional career. Still, it kept food on the Madison table even if at the same time it wore him down.

My mother, whose faith propped up all of us, made us join St. John's A.M.E. Church, and as she prayed a lot and cried a lot, we began to believe things might get better. They did for a while, thanks to some political connections of my father's. One was Charles Carr, a city councilman who, like my father and me, was a man of many firsts. He founded Cleveland's first black law firm, among other distinctions.

Carr, along with council colleague Lawrence Payne, arranged for my father to take an examination for the position of general foreman of dirt streets for the city of Cleveland. My father did not disappoint, scoring 106 out of a possible 100. His exam results were rated better than perfect. Had it been a different time—even 10 years earlier—he still might have been shut out. But his performance earned him the job, making Robert James Madison the first black engineer hired by the city of Cleveland.

In the winter, his responsibility was snow removal. In the summer, his priority shifted from plowing to paving those dirt streets. So life got

THOMAS, CARL
3255 East 48th Street
Gold Hi-Y
Homeroom Basketball
Homeroom Baseball

CARL THOMAS -

VAVRO, DAVID
10413 Crestwood Avenue
Student Council Representative
Varsity Swimming
Homeroom Basketball
Intramural Boxing

VITALE, MARIO
2187 East 106th Street
Library Committee
Corridor Committee
Homeroom Baseball
Homeroom Basketball

ZIMNY, JOE
4010 East 58th Street
Student Council Courtesy Squad
Annual Board

ARCHITECTURE

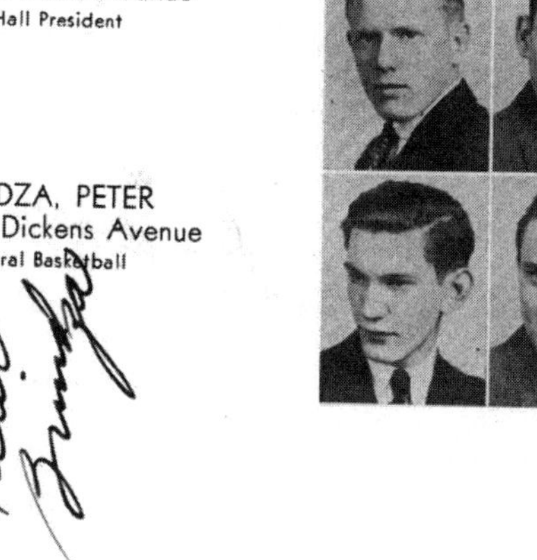

ANGEL, RALPH
10702 Dove Avenue
Study Hall President

BRINDZA, PETER
9713 Dickens Avenue
Intramural Basketball

COLLISTER, WILLIAM
10617 Bryant Avenue
Corinthian
Homeroom Baseball

EVANS, JOHN
1657 East 86th Street
Class Assistant Treasurer
Lost and Found Committee
Student Council Page Committee
Band
Corinthian

FITZGIBBON, BOB
1134 Dallas Road
Annual Staff
Corinthian

HEINEMAN, KENNETH
8210 Wade Park Avenue
Student Council Representative
Lost and Found Committee
Corridor Committee
Corinthian
Homeroom Basketball

MADISON, ROBERT
2168 East 40th Street
Student Council Noon-Movies
National Honor Society
Hi-Y Kappa
Corinthian
Homeroom Baseball

MORALT, JOHN
1096 East 77th Street
Corinthian
Library Committee
Intramural Baseball

PIERSON, JOHN
4369 West 52nd Street
Student Council Representative
Corinthian
Homeroom Baseball
Intramural Baseball

Bob's senior high school yearbook from East Tech, 1940. He was one of 11 graduates in the architecture program.

HI-Y KAPPA

Founded: 1939 Sponsor: Jesse Spight
Purpose: To promote the high standing of the Christian character throughout the school and community.
Row I: Nicholson, Mosley, Thomas, (v. pres.), Clayton, (pres.), Crable, Walker, (sgt. at arms), Lane.
Row II: Madison, Farrell, Alston, Hayes, Hall, Oldwine, Williams, (sec.)

One of the clubs at East Tech that Bob participated in during his senior year.

better in terms of being able to pay the rent and basic family expense, but by that time, the drinking had gotten to him. He just couldn't stop and he was smoking a lot, too, not a prescription for healthy living. He was never able to gain entry into the elite society of Cleveland, the city's professional class, which was devastating for him. At two universities in the South, he was Professor Madison, and he'd been on top. But here, they didn't know what engineers did. And they certainly couldn't grasp the notion of a black engineer.

So life at home was a struggle. In spite of my father's position with the city, he could not handle himself when payday arrived. We didn't know whether he'd come home or blow all his money at the Elks Club. That was a serious problem that affected the entire family, forcing us to move from place to place, just like we had had to in D.C.

My father's behavior also expanded the Madison family's side hustle efforts. My mother began to sell "fashion frocks" and Avon products door to door. The Madison brothers would contribute to make Mother's Day flowers from crepe paper for Julian and me to sell in local bars on Friday night. On Saturday, Julian and I would visit the grocery store with flowers we'd made from the proceeds of the night before. Our industriousness extended to Sunday, when we'd sell the flowers in front of church. We'd net $100 to $150 for those four days of work, not bad for a family in those days.

The lesson of East Tech

Thanks to my highly educated parents, I had a good sense of the importance of education before I entered East Tech, but that school in my home neighborhood sealed the deal, convincing me to pursue the best education I could find, wherever I could find it.

That lesson resonated through my later years at Howard University, Western Reserve University, graduate school at Harvard, and specialized instruction in France. However, East Tech is where it all began to come together for me, and I was in good company. Olympians Jesse Owens and Harrison Dillard were East Tech graduates, Owens in 1936, Dillard in 1941. Dillard was also a member of the 92nd Infantry Division, the Buffalo Soldiers, where I would become a second lieutenant.

At commencement time, East Tech conferred an award for the best student in mathematics. In 1940, the year I graduated, the school announced a tie between me and someone who may have been named Sinkovich. A tie? Really?

Bob, far right in the front row, with his intramural baseball teammates.

The two of us were subjected to an examination, which in reality was more like a contest. The winner would get the award, considered big-time in a school known for its math excellence. So one Saturday, he and I arrived at East Tech at about 9:30 a.m., took the exam and left. Two weeks later came the announcement that it was still a tie. Really? How was that possible? I believed I had won, but the matter was never resolved. I decided I would from then on beat them at their own game.

Too bad that kind of issue would come up every so often throughout my academic and professional career. A similar incident took place in 1941, at the end of my freshman year at Howard University in Washington, D.C.

I had five A's and a B that year. The next best performance was from a classmate who had four A's and two B's. Howard officials announced that we had tied for the Freshman Cup, because I was studying architecture and my classmate was studying pre-medicine—allegedly a much more demanding field.

I thought to myself, OK, this balances the award I didn't get at East Tech; I didn't get the award at Howard because the other guy's courses were deemed much more difficult than mine. But that's life, and I learned that you have to really excel. You have to really do it.

That meant working hard, and not just academically. It meant earning my way in every sense of the phrase. My father earned his way, too, working wherever he could. But as a man out of time and the wrong color, work itself never really worked for him.

Looking back on the Cleveland years, it seems that even though my father was my model and inspiration, the two of us slowly began to drift apart. While I began to map out a straightforward—and successful—trajectory, he stumbled, despite his occasional but transient professional achievements.

One day, he came home in despair, announcing he hadn't gotten a job as an elevator operator because he was overqualified. Still, he applied for every engineering position advertised in the newspaper. And time after time, he was told, "No, you can't fill out the application. We don't hire colored people."

Twenty years later, those very same phrases targeted me, not my father. Different time, same place: Cleveland. How the world turns.

CHAPTER EIGHT
SONG OF HOWARD

Like my father, I would shuttle between Washington, D.C. and Cleveland for quite some time. And, like my father, I spent wonderful years in D.C. at Howard University, first as a student and later as a professor.

I arrived at Howard, our premier black university, in September 1940, armed with an academic scholarship covering room but not board. This was the dawn of the war years, when I went to work as a waiter at a restaurant serving a government workforce that was beginning to employ lots of women. It was a time of great social change.

As a side benefit of that job, I earned tips and maybe even better, food. But sometimes, even that free food wasn't enough. I remember buying

▲

Ohio Theatre Proscenium, Cleveland, Ohio, 1921 | Designed by Thomas Lamb
For me, being a man of design also means being a man of the arts. I'm especially a fan of the performing arts: operas like Aida, concerts by the Cleveland Orchestra, Broadway plays like Hamilton. I attended hundreds of performances in dozens of concert halls and theaters around the world, and early on my attention was drawn to the distinctive framing of the stage's invisible "fourth wall." That framing, like the Ohio Theater's Italianate-style, separates artists from audience. But then the performance begins, the artists hold sway, and everyday life retreats.

day-old butter pecan rolls for a nickel apiece from Corky's Bakery on Georgia Avenue, a half-block from campus. To survive back then, a guy had to be able to improvise.

One day, however, my hunger got to be too much and I fainted. It happened when I was working as an errand boy in the school of architecture; a classmate of my dad's had helped me get the job. Luckily for me, a secretary in the school of architecture and engineering saw me prone like someone in the ring with Joe Louis. She alerted some of my friends, who picked me up, got me to drink some water, and I was on my way. That errand boy job lasted until I got hired as a busboy at a D.C. hotel. The pay was all I could eat, and I'd bring leftovers back to my classmates. Working there also taught me the kind of life lessons you can only learn in a restaurant; I think every young person should experience life in a job like that.

Overall, my stay at Howard was a great experience. This was my first time away from home except for those few weeks with my relatives in Alabama six years earlier. You don't really begin to develop your independent soul until you strike out on your own. Going away to college affords an ideal transition to adulthood—it's not like completely being on your own, but you have plenty of independence, and challenges to see how you'll fare in adult life.

I arrived at Howard with one-and-a-half suits—a jacket, two pairs of pants and, as I recollect, four shirts. I had packed all my clothes and belongings into one suitcase. I was assigned to share a room with a light-skinned guy with a long nose whom we called Pinocchio; I don't remember his real name. He arrived with four suitcases holding 20 shirts, eight pairs of shoes, and five suits, along with a lot of spending money. I had never seen so many clothes for one person.

"Where did you get all those clothes?" I asked. He told me he'd arrived from Little Rock, Arkansas, and benefited from a special educational grant called "out-of-state aid." That meant that if you were black and lived in the South and you wanted to go to a university, you could apply, say, to the University of Kentucky, but you couldn't go there because of your color. So your state would pay for you to go anywhere else you wanted, with the help of out-of-state aid. That was how this guy with all those clothes had

Bob refines an architectural drawing for a project at Howard University in 1941.

gotten to Howard. Every black in the South who wanted to go to college could pick a subject like engineering, which wasn't taught at black colleges in the South; out-of-state aid would effectively send that student north, affirming segregation by way of the notion of separate but equal education.

Imagine a typical conversation between a black student and a faculty adviser in the 1940s: "You say you want to go to the University of Alabama? No, you're not going there. What do you want to study? Engineering. They don't teach engineering at Morehouse College. So where do you want to go to school? Harvard. OK, here's the money. Yale? Here's the money."

In the South, there were convoluted ways to maintain separate but equal education. It wasn't guilt money, it was fact, and it was law. Many students from the South came to Howard courtesy of out-of-state aid.

But I lived in Cleveland, not Alabama, and I didn't benefit from out-of-state grant money. I had food and money from my work as a waiter. I also took in laundry. I used to wash and iron Pinocchio's shirts for a dime, sometimes a quarter. Thanks to my mother, who taught me how to wash and iron, I could do everything.

Bob, far right in the second row, at Howard University in 1940.

The joys of Howard

The Great Depression was just beginning to recede when I entered college, and Howard was emerging as an academic force, as well as a football powerhouse. If you talk about football, Howard University playing Lincoln University, another historically black college in Pennsylvania, was like Harvard and Yale. When they battled, everybody came to the game. All these successful guys arrived to see the game, a classic like you wouldn't believe. Doctors came to show off, parading their fine ladies in their fur coats.

As for myself, I finally began to step out, loosen up a little. I even joined a fraternity. I remember the brothers staged a dance, and they were trying to attract all the freshmen. I didn't have anyone to go with, so I arranged for a blind date, who turned out to be the least attractive woman I've ever met. We danced once, sort of—I couldn't really dance. I came out of St. John's Church, and we were very pious, so I did not dance. Not dancing did me good that night when it came to that girl.

At the same time, architecture and drawing came naturally to me, and eventually I would learn to dance; loving your dance partner helps. In the interim, I learned to love opera, and I still do. Many years later, I would be a trustee and longtime supporter of the Cleveland Opera.

All ears

In 1940, I was one of only six students in the design studio of the school of architecture at Howard. There was no television, no YouTube, no Netflix—none of that—but there was what used to be called wireless, also known as the radio. Don Peterson, a fellow student who was much older than the rest of us, had a radio, and that December he began listening to Metropolitan Opera broadcasts.

One Saturday, we're all drawing like hell, and this guy Peterson turns on his radio—to opera. "What the hell is wrong with this jerk? What's wrong with you? You're out of your mind. Where is Duke Ellington? Count Basie?" Don was patient and said, "Look, you don't have to listen to my radio." So, we did our best to ignore the broadcast.

This continued week after week—*Siegfried, Der Rosenkavalier, Tosca*—until we couldn't stand it. We contrived a plan to disrupt the next broadcast, and we were ready. But when the time came, the announcer said the upcoming opera was about a beautiful princess from Ethiopia who was in love with an Egyptian warrior who had captured the princess' father, the king of Ethiopia.

"Wait a minute," I said. "Did you guys hear that? It's a story about beautiful black people from Africa. It's called *Aida*."

At that time, Hollywood studios were producing films like "Birth of a Nation," "Tarzan" and "Gone With the Wind," and there were radio programs like "Amos 'n' Andy" and "Jubilee," a show presented by Bill "Mr. Bojangles" Robinson. There was a great deal of blackface imagery denigrating colored people, along with cowboys and Indians movies where the cowboys always won, of course.

But this seemed different. We were stunned. We sat quietly and listened to the whole opera and, at the conclusion, decided that this Italian guy Giuseppe Verdi, who wrote the operas *Aida* and *Otello,* was truly sensitive to the lives and stories of people of all races, religions and cultures. This was a revelation to us, and we concluded we wanted more. So, no more complaints from us to Don about opera on his radio.

Years later, when I went to fight the Axis powers in Italy, I got exposed to much more opera. In Italian villages, I heard young boys singing "La Donna E Mobile" from Verdi's *Rigoletto,* and many other songs from popular operas. I was sold on it, and I visited great opera houses in Rome, La Scala in Milan, and small-town ones in La Spezia and Civitavecchia. I became acquainted with true opera goers and became one myself.

In Italy, if the soprano missed the high note in "Un Bel Di," that great aria from *Madame Butterfly,* she was pelted with tomatoes and eggs, almost as if she expected it. This was like real life. I loved the whole experience, and years later, when Cleveland Opera asked if I was interested in joining its board, I was delighted.

I adore opera. But that's not all. I also like Lena Horne, Ella Fitzgerald, Billy Eckstine, Duke Ellington, Count Basie, Erroll Garner—listening to them preceded opera for me. As for people like the Supremes, Marvin

Gaye, the Motown catalogue, I liked it, but I wasn't enthusiastic about it like I am about opera. Call me eclectic.

When I got to Italy to fight the war, listening to opera was all we did—besides trying to stay alive. Kids would run up and down the street singing opera. I went to opera houses, while many other guys went to many other kinds of houses.

Above all else, however, war was indeed hell.

CHAPTER NINE
THE WAR YEARS

Fighting for the United States in World War II taught me about leadership and respect. It also taught me again—as if I needed a reminder—about racism.

In 1941, the conflict with Hitler and the Axis powers began consuming the attention of America. What finally compelled the United States to enter the war was the December 7, 1941, bombing of Pearl Harbor. The war would consume my father and me for the next several years but in very different ways and with radically different outcomes.

Where I would become a second lieutenant in the Italian campaign, my father never got the opportunity to cross the ocean in service of his country. As a member of the Army Reserves, he was likely to be called

▲

American Jeep, Willys-Overland, Toledo, Ohio, 1940

The origin of the word "jeep" is commonly associated with a slurring of the acronym "G.P." Some say G.P stands for "general purpose," others claim it as an abbreviation for "Government Property." Still others tie the term to the Popeye comic strip character, Eugene the Jeep. No matter—for me, a jeep will always mean the go-anywhere, do-anything vehicle that replaced the horse in the U.S. Army. More than one-third of a million jeeps were manufactured for the war effort; my life nearly ended in one of them in 1944.

Bob Madison in military uniform during training at Camp Croft, South Carolina, in 1943. Note the label "Monk," Madison's lasting nickname.

up early for a major campaign. When the call came, he was ordered to active duty at Fort Huachuca, Arizona, as a first lieutenant. This would be his chance to serve his country and put his education and training to meaningful use.

At that time, it was customary to promote college graduates in the Army Reserves with engineering degrees to the rank of major or lieutenant Colonel. But the Army was still segregated and would remain so until July 1948, when President Harry Truman desegregated it. My father was kept at the rank of lieutenant. Just as he was caught in no man's land when he was judged overeducated and overqualified for all but the most menial jobs, now he was trapped both by his color and by Father Time. He was black and over age in grade and thus not qualified to lead troops in battle or design bridges to cross rivers like the Arno, the Seine or the Rhine.

Even though my father went through additional training in California with the Blue Helmets of the 93rd Division, he would effectively be kept on the sidelines of battles he was qualified to wage and even lead. But he soldiered on even as he settled into the long, slow slide that would come to define the rest of his life.

So, while my father would face cruel, closed doors during the war years, circumstances were different for me. At least I had a chance to use the early 1940s as a time to advance. What people call the Great War also made me a man of the world.

Because I was on scholarship at Howard, it was mandatory for me to enroll in its Reserve Officers' Training Corps. I was joining an illustrious program: More than 50 percent of blacks holding commissions at the beginning of World War II graduated from Howard's ROTC.

I slowly acquired the combat skills a soldier needs from the ROTC program at Howard, as well as various basic and advanced training assignments in the South and Southwest. At Camp Croft (Spartanburg, South Carolina), Greensboro Training Center (North Carolina), and Fort Benning (Georgia), I evolved from a soldier into an officer and a leader. After I graduated as a second lieutenant in May 1944, I was assigned to the 92nd Infantry Division—the Buffalo Soldiers—in Fort Huachuca, the same Arizona outpost where my father had been stationed.

I graduated in May 1944, and my father retired from military life just two months later at the age of 45. Seeing a photo from a family gathering marking that milestone is bittersweet. Both my father and I are in uniform, but while I was a man ready to head overseas to engage the enemy and lead troops to victory, my father never had a chance.

That August, I departed from Hampton Roads, Virginia, on a troop transport ship bound for Italy.

I found myself in the heat of battle almost as soon as I landed.

Taking pride, taking command

Serving in the 92nd Infantry Division was a full-time occupation for me in the first half of the 1940s. As a member of the 92nd, I wasn't a student or an aspiring architect, I wasn't an ROTC enrollee—I was a soldier. And I proudly wore a patch on my uniform that signified I was a special soldier, a Buffalo Soldier.

The Buffalo Soldiers were formed by an act of Congress to organize and recognize the black cavalry who fought in the Indian Wars, mostly in the mid- to late-19th century. In fact, it was the Indians themselves who gave the Buffalo Soldiers their names. To the Native Americans, the black cavalry they faced on the wintry plains, their adversary, looked like buffaloes—their dark complexions blended in with their coats made of buffalo skins. The term eventually became synonymous with all African-American regiments formed in 1866, and was passed along in the culture of the segregated U.S. Army. I was a Buffalo Soldier first, an officer second. A term that began as a case of mistaken identity became a source of pride for me in my military career.

The beginning of that career found me in military intelligence. That beginning was anything but smooth—in fact, it was downright bumpy.

Just two days into combat, on September 1, 1944, we were on the south bank of the Arno River just north of Pisa. As battalion intelligence officer, I was the only black officer at headquarters, so I had some authority. How I used it proved tricky.

We had been ordered to make a midnight reconnaissance to assess German troop strength. I got into an argument with the battalion commander, a white guy, about the plan to have black soldiers cross the river without artillery support. That reckless order came straight from Mark Clark, the commanding general.

That directive frosted me to the point that I screamed at the battalion commander, demanding to speak to General Clark.

"Get me Mark Clark on the phone!" I shouted.

The nerve! A 21-year-old black second lieutenant questioning the decision of a West Point graduate, the commander of the Fifth Army?

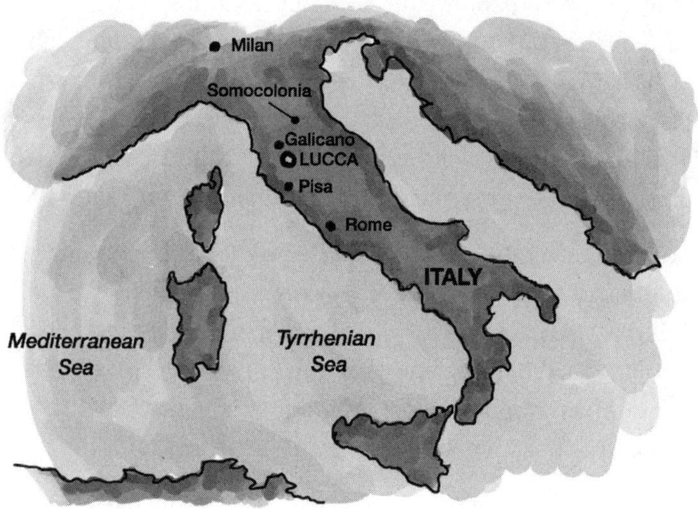

The northern Italian region where Madison served as a Buffalo Soldier in World War II.

Fortunately, that fateful phone call was never patched through. Matters simmered down, and I headed to the front line to tell the company commanders and encourage the troops to cross the river. The all-black 92nd was flanked by the 88th Division, all white, on our right, with the 442nd Battalion on our left. The 442nd is best known for its history as a fierce World War II fighting unit composed primarily of second-generation American soldiers of Japanese ancestry.

After uttering a brief and somber prayer, the battalion chaplain joined me in wading into the Arno to start the reconnaissance. A full moon exposed us like ducks floating on a pond. It was scary.

After wading about 10 yards out, we realized none of our troops were following, so we whispered and waved our hands to persuade the squad to cross behind us. I was furious, convinced that the plan was to deliberately let our black soldiers suffer during their first engagement.

I was so upset that it wasn't until I was halfway across the Arno River that I remembered something very important: I couldn't swim. Making my way across East Tech's pool in gym class was a far cry from surviving this, a midnight river crossing in full battle gear.

Luckily for us, early on we discovered the Germans had already pulled out and redeployed. So, I flailed away in the water well enough to make my way back to shore with the rest of the troops. We then returned to our base. I reported our findings to battalion headquarters—and was promptly reassigned to platoon leader. Even though my call to General Clark hadn't gone through, my approach had ruffled some feathers in the battalion.

So, in a way, I guess, I lost that battle; my reassignment meant less responsibility and maybe status. Perhaps my reassignment was a subtle way of communicating the importance of chain of command. But I also felt I had won the war, the long game of earning the respect of the combat team and even commanding officers. We had to keep going, moving forward to victory on our front. But we had to make smart decisions.

Being on the winning side of combat means being in the right place at the right time. Sometimes, it is important to have a bit of luck, too.

The last man standing

That Arno River incident paled next to what I experienced the day after Christmas that same fateful year. It happened in the village of Gallicano and effectively put an end to my combat career.

On December 26, 1944, after a great Christmas party the night before, I was in the Serchio Valley on my way to Sommocolonia, a hilltop village just east of Florence. The Germans knew the Americans would be celebrating Christmas Day, so they launched the Battle of the Bulge on Christmas night.

I was due at battalion headquarters at 11 that morning, but, when I went to wake my driver, I saw he'd had at least one too many at that Christmas party at Contessa Laura Ferrari's villa in nearby Lucca. He was in no shape to drive—in fact, he was in no shape to even roll out of his cot. So I took the wheel into my own hands, and off I went up the mountain road, negotiating its treacherous curves.

As I approached Gallicano, the Germans got me in their sights and launched an 88mm shell from a rail-car gun. Shrapnel shredded the passenger seat where I usually sat. Thank God my driver's hangover put me in the driver's seat. Thank God for my driver as well, blissfully unaware and asleep in his bunk.

Even though I didn't suffer a direct hit—which would have been immediately fatal—the howitzer blasted me violently out of the jeep. The driverless vehicle continued on, tumbling down the side of the mountain. Shrapnel penetrated my stomach and nearly severed my left foot. I was losing a lot of blood.

A couple of soldiers from an observation post jumped into action, picked me up and brought me to a battalion aid station. Later that night, I was transferred to a field hospital in Civitavecchia. I soon learned that the German Panzer division had overrun the company of Buffalo Soldiers. Only a few survived. I learned later that, if my jeep had not been blasted from beneath me, I would have driven just 100 meters further, straight into a Nazi stronghold. It took me a while to appreciate what happened. Thank God those Germans fired on me, and thank God I was wounded—I guess.

My limp is a souvenir of that frightening encounter. So are my three battle ribbons and my Purple Heart.

The Germans, who considered blacks subhuman, had received very blunt orders: Take no prisoners. In many ways, at least some of the white American soldiers, our alleged brothers in arms, shared that same attitude. American soldiers often called us black soldiers "monkeys with tails," even though the Italians called us "liberators" when we beat back the fascists.

Years later, I read a newspaper story that told it straight: "If black soldiers were wounded in action and required emergency blood transfusions, only the plasma of other black soldiers could be used to save their lives," said a *San Francisco Chronicle* article detailing that assault on Sommocolonia, a village near Gallicano.

"The segregated units in which the majority of black enlistees served were commanded by whites, many of whom regarded their men with contempt and limited them to duty as gravediggers or mess hall workers," that account, which was published in 2000, continues.

Actually, the 92nd was supported by Senegalese soldiers, Hindu soldiers, and Japanese soldiers. Maybe that's where I got the idea for my own architectural firm, which became a kind of United Nations in itself.

As for our white officers—everybody with a title of captain or higher—they came to the 92nd because they were misfits who couldn't cut it in a white division. They were rejects, sort of like those in the movie, *The Dirty Dozen*. Even their own kind hated them, not just us.

The hostility in the 92nd was palpable.

The battlefield phenomenon of troops turning on their own officers is nothing new; accounts of fratricide go back to ancient Greece. While I can't say I witnessed any incidents, I've learned of ones in World War II where troops killed an officer whose incompetence threatened everyone's lives. Happened in Anzio, happened in many other places. And I heard of incidents where some of these black soldiers shot officers who were white. Those whites didn't like us. They didn't want to deal with black folks, and the feeling was mutual. To get a sense of that tension, you might want to check out *Miracle at St. Anna*, a movie produced in 2009. I was honored to serve as a consultant for director Spike Lee on that film.

As for me, my wounds in that holiday incident near Gallicano didn't end my combat career, but the collateral damage that followed as a direct result did.

After the shrapnel was removed from my abdomen and ankle, I spent about four weeks in the hospital recuperating, and I took the opportunity to pick up a new skill: I learned how to play bridge.

Once I recovered, I was ready to rejoin my platoon on the front lines, but when I did, a new kind of affliction surfaced. My tonsils blew up, I couldn't swallow, and my temperature spiked high. The field ambulance roared in and returned me to that same Civitavecchia hospital for a tonsillectomy. My tonsils had been touchy before, so doctors said they had to go. Fairly routine surgery, then I'd be back at the front in a week, right?

Not quite.

A young doctor's botched tonsillectomy left me bleeding. When he tried to sew me up, the needle broke. I bled for a week, until noon one day I finally collapsed. They rushed me back to the ward and found I had lost a fourth of my red corpuscles. I stayed there for another three weeks and eventually stopped bleeding, but by the time I recovered, my combat career was over. That's because on May 8, 1945, Victory in Europe Day was celebrated.

At first, the end of the war in Europe brought great, if not complete, relief to soldiers there. Our joy was tempered by the likelihood that we would be shipped east to the Pacific Theater to finish the war; victory in Europe was not complete victory. As it developed, most of us were kept stationed in Europe to provide a variety of necessary administrative and relief duties. Europe was liberated, but it was a messy, chaotic, and impoverished continent. Roads, bridges, water and food supplies, almost anything needed to allow people to live in a civilization, were in tatters. The U.S. military had the presence and the matériel, and the U.S. government had the will to do what it could. Because of that commitment, Americans who traveled in Europe were greeted warmly by the French, the English, the Dutch, the Italians, and even the Germans. We had not only helped win a war—we committed to building a recovery and to peace, even with our enemies. Sounds strange today, I know, for a country to not only cease hostilities, but to actually turn an enemy into a friend. Every war must end.

But in my life, the war lingered on far after the official armistice with both Germany and Japan. Every December for the next 30 years, I would become quite ill for no apparent reason, forcing me to take to my bed for a week. Was it the stress of the holidays, an allergy to food or maybe pine trees?

That annual illness didn't cease until a psychiatrist friend diagnosed the true cause of my affliction as silent trauma resulting from my experience in the Italian campaign. Turns out posttraumatic stress disorder (PTSD) existed back then; it was labeled "battle fatigue." It wasn't until the matter was diagnosed and I received treatment that I became truly cured and the sickness passed for good. Still, the reminiscences remain vivid.

My survival in Gallicano was the climax of my wartime experience, though I endured plenty of other skirmishes. That dangerously close call left me feeling singled out, even blessed. It gave me hope, fanning the flames of my architectural aspirations.

As it played out, I wouldn't leave Europe for another year, and, as I've said, war is hell. But there also were times—and characters and situations—that could help make even a world war more bearable and even fun.

On December 28, 1945, the Swiss Alps provided the setting for post-war recreation and downhill skiing instruction for Madison and two other U.S. service members.

CHAPTER TEN
ITALIAN NOBILITY

Danger was a constant companion during our Italian campaign, so it could be easy to become complacent. But when danger came too close, it was uncomfortable and brought out feelings and attitudes you didn't know were inside you. Consider one night in 1944, as I led my platoon of about 30 men toward the front line north of Lucca. We were looking for a place to sleep when we came across an old farmhouse. It was late afternoon, we'd eaten our supper rations, and I decided it was time to pray. We got on our knees.

As we implored God to help shelter us safely that night, a tremendous crash jarred us from prayer. We looked up at the farmhouse and saw an unbelievable, almost surreal sight. With our ears still ringing and

▲

Villa Ferrari, Lucca, Italy, 1944

Located in the city of Lucca in the province of the same name, this villa is in the heart of Italy's famed Tuscany region. The residence of the Contessa and her family was surrounded by acres of cultivated land, storehouses, horse stables and lodging for the servant class. Cobblestoned and tree-lined streets, a wonderful climate, beautiful food, wine, and companionship, combined with a blissful end to a horrible war...what's not to love? On December 25, 1944, I met Contessa Laura Ferrari the first time.

our sight clouded by dust, it was hard to reckon what happened, but we saw that some sort of armament had penetrated a second-floor wall of the farmhouse. We crept up the steps to the top only to discover a large, unexploded German shell, eight feet long and about two-and-a-half feet around. It had pierced the wall at a shallow angle. Had the shell carved a trajectory just a few degrees steeper, its plunger would have depressed, triggering the detonating cap. This was a very large ordnance, more like a rocket than a shell, and had it blown, we, along with everything within 50 feet, certainly would have been decimated.

We got out of there in a hurry. We didn't want to be hit by another shell, and there were spies all over the place who could direct fire at our coordinates. To keep safe, we scattered some distance away in a field to sleep under some trees. It was as peaceful an ending as possible to a too-close-call day.

Wartime experiences aren't always that threatening, though—if they were, even the most hardened soldier wouldn't last a week. The mental stress would kill you, even if the enemy didn't. You had to find relief wherever you could. Some encounters could be amusing, even tender.

The deeply amusing arrived a few weeks later, somewhere between Lucca and Gallicano, when our battalion stumbled upon this enormous estate. We wanted in, so I told my troops that, as commanding officer, I would speak to the owner first.

So I knocked, and a servant opened the door. He was very submissive and told me to come inside.

Suddenly, I was no longer in a wartime environment. I was in the grand foyer of a magnificent, centuries-old estate, looking up in wonder at an elegant, circular stairway. The servant bowed, and practically scraping the floor, finally called the master of the house. Soon, a very stylish gentleman wearing a smoking jacket appeared at the top of the stairs. He looked to be about 65 years old, and his white hair flowed to his shoulders. I felt like I was in some sort of movie.

The man looked at me, our eyes locked, and he slowly descended the stairs, never shifting his gaze. At the third step from the bottom, he stopped.

"Do you know who I am?" he thundered. "I am Giuseppe Garibaldi, duke of such-and-such, and commander of the Italian navy."

"Do you know who I am?" I countered. "I am Robert Prince Madison, commander of the first platoon, and I have my troops outside this building, armed, awaiting my orders. I ask you, sir, where is your navy?"

He got the message. Literally and figuratively, Garibaldi stood down, and commanded his lackey to find a villa on the grounds for our platoon. I think this duke was actually Giuseppe Garibaldi II, the grandson of Giuseppe Garibaldi, a popular Italian general who in the 19th century played a big part in Italian unification.

Lt. Madison in Italy, 1945.

Despite (or perhaps, because of) his pedigree, this Italian nobleman was absolutely arrogant and likely a bit delusional. As for his navy, I guess it was AWOL.

A different world

Naturally, my wartime European engagement meant combat above all. But for me, there was another, far friendlier meaning to the term. Remember how that howitzer blast nearly killed me the day after Christmas?

On Christmas night—the night before the Germans nearly wiped out the 92nd —that division's officers went to a party at that villa just north of Lucca, in central Tuscany. The party was designed for the junior officers ranked captain and lower, all the "colored" soldiers. How the invitations got around, I don't know. Word spread there would be plenty of girls at Contessa Laura Ferrari's villa, but first the girls had to be rounded up.

I can't recall how I was identified as the motor officer from the 92nd, but somehow I became the guy who commandeered the truck, so I brought the truck to the Villa Ferrari. I'd never been there before, and I'd never met the contessa, who knew all those village girls. She got in the truck, I drove, and we went from farmhouse to farmhouse to pick up these ladies. I brought a literal truckload of them to the party.

Here I was, completely and happily out of my element. I'm a black lieutenant from inner-city Cleveland, driving around the Italian countryside with an Italian countess sitting next to me in the cab and about 20 giggling girls in the back. The party started at 5 p.m., the officers came, and we had a great time. But all good things come to an end, and I had to take people home. Laura—by that time, she had taken to calling me "Roberto"—was there to guide, because I didn't know anything about driving from village to village, so I had my driver do it. When we got back from dropping off the girls, I took Laura herself home; it was about 3 in the morning. For a while, I sat and talked with this woman, Laura Ferrari, who was very nice. It was too late to return to the barracks, so I slept on the couch. The next day I got out and went to this place called Gallicano, where I got hit, and the word got out. You know the rest.

Woman to woman

During my tenure in Italy after the war, I dated the contessa, who was a few years older than me. I could speak her language, I was an officer and a gentleman, and I had a keen appreciation of opera. Maybe that's what made me appealing to her. I treated her well, too. Many American soldiers were not that kind to people over there.

I had never met a woman quite like Laura, a northern Italian blonde who was confident and cultured. We shared more than our interests.

We met her friends, dukes and counts and other nobility, and I accompanied her to holiday parties and concerts. We became very close for a year, parting about a year after the war ended and I went back to America after my tour of duty was over. Even though this was a wartime encounter, it was far more than a fling.

I look back at my time with the contessa with affection. She was one of the first of several strong women who would influence my life as I grew into a young man of 23. Along with my mother, Mother Julia, and Grandma Land, all these women believed in themselves, were people of faith, and possessed an air of confidence no man could breach.

I met Laura Ferrari in Italy, toward the end of World War II. I met a woman I was briefly engaged to in Cleveland shortly after I returned from the war. But before any of them, before the war, I first met the strong woman I would eventually marry in Washington, D.C., when she was studying to be a math teacher and I was preparing to be an architect at Howard.

While they had their commonalities, they also were very different. One, however, really saw something in me, and I think that's what put us together. I've told Laura's story. Now it's time for the stories of Coretta and Leatrice.

CHAPTER ELEVEN
SMOOTHING THE SQUARE

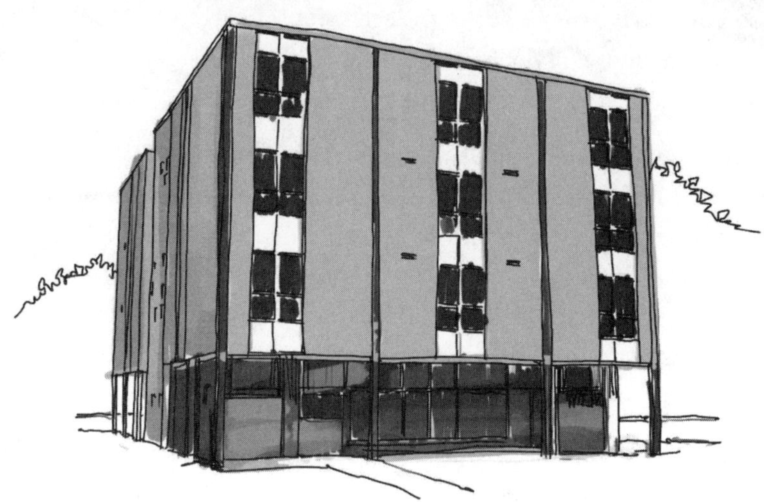

The 1940s was the decade in which I became a man. Not only did my combat in World War II toughen me, the war also left me far more worldly, and eager to connect with a woman who would be my soulmate until time itself ran out. The contessa taught me so much—about another way of living, about a wonderful culture that has endured for centuries. But many factors were at work that made it clear to us that, while we had enjoyed a special relationship, the contessa and I were not destined to enjoy a lifelong one. So, when I left Europe, I left with the reasonable expectation that I'd never see Laura again.

By the time I arrived back home in 1946, I was a well-rounded man, far from the square I was when I entered college six years earlier. That

▲

Medical Associates Building, Cleveland, Ohio, 1960 |
Designed by Madison Madison Architects & Engineers

The Medical Associates Building was the first multi-story medical facility for doctors of color built in the state of Ohio. Society has changed and the need for segregated facilities no longer exists. I am pleased that the current owners in 2017 created a new purpose for the continued usefulness of this structure. Its official title is the PNC Glenville Arts Campus, but most neighbors simply call it the Madison Building.

unfortunate blind date at Howard University may have been a fiasco, but at least it resulted in one positive outcome: my more formal engagement with women. Becoming comfortable with the fairer sex didn't come easy for me, though. Mostly due to my mother's strict and pious upbringing, I was so näive that, when I got to college, people called me "Monk." Some of my close friends still do, and that's OK. While some might shrink from a nickname like that, to me it's kind of fun.

When I arrived on campus at Howard in September 1940, I was the poster child for what was known as a "square," something I wouldn't realize until much later. You know, all straight edges and socially clumsy, that was me. Maybe I was that way because we changed neighborhoods and elementary schools so often, I never had time to form healthy, steady relationships. Another factor was poverty: I couldn't afford to take girls out on dates.

That pattern continued even at Garnet-Patterson, Washington's best junior high school. And because East Tech in Cleveland was an all-boys public school—unique then and virtually unknown now—I didn't have many opportunities for regular, casual contact with girls my age.

In more ways than one, though, my college experience before the war had already begun to round me out.

Stretching the square

My metamorphosis didn't happen all at once. At Howard, guys would be drinking, but not me. Smoke? I didn't smoke. These guys would say, "This guy has got to be in the monastery. Look at this guy, Monk. He doesn't drink, he doesn't smoke, he doesn't run around with women."

First thing I actually tried my hand at was smoking. Seemed easy enough. To start, you put a pipe in your mouth. Someone said, "Why not put something in that, like tobacco?" So I smoked the pipe, and it was cool. I was trying to grow up like the rest of the guys.

But the nickname, "Monk Madison," came first, and that is what I've been known as ever since: Monk. I was pious, I really was. I used to go to chapel every Sunday. Most tellingly, I didn't know the first thing about girls.

Bob, first row, third from left, with other pledges to the Alpha Phi Alpha fraternity at Howard University in 1940.

In Washington, D.C., I was still a novice at socializing, especially with the opposite sex. Things didn't improve immediately, though my social circle widened when I became an Alpha Phi Alpha pledge and went to a fraternity dance with a friend, Lucretia Lindsay. That date was an education all its own. Whoever said socializing "Monk" Madison would be smooth?

We took a cab, because I couldn't drive, and when we got to the dance, she said, "Where is it?"

"Where is what?" I said.

"Where's the bottle? The booze?" Now she turned cold.

I came up short and dry, and she didn't have anything to do with me for the rest of the dance. I began to wonder about Howard girls.

Branching out

I called my friend Jeff Rogers and said, "Jeff, I'm having a tough time with these chicks."

Ever the fixer, Jeff said to me, "Bob, I've got the right woman for you," and he gave me a phone number. He had told her about me, so when I followed through, she was expecting my call. My experience with women gained perspective when I met Leatrice Lucille Branch, who was on the other end of that phone line. She was studying to be a math teacher at Miner Teachers College across the street from Howard.

Leatrice turned out to be quite a talker. I'm not; back home, we were on a party line, and there was no time to be windy. Anyhow, we talked for about five minutes, and I said I'd like to come see her. She had no objections. I walked to her home, about three blocks from campus, she let me in, and she introduced me all around.

At my house, there was my mother, my father, me and three brothers—five males and one female. At Leatrice's that night, I met her two sisters, her mother, her grandmother, and her father—one male and five females in her house.

As I sat in the living room waiting for her, the Branch family was screaming up and down. I had never seen such a busy household, and I didn't know what to do. I noticed a canary in a cage in the corner, so I started talking to the canary.

I'd never been in a household like Leatrice's.

I loved Leatrice from our first meeting, though I may not have realized that then. In 1943, as commanding officer in the ROTC Army Specialized Training Program, I even staged a parade for her. That parade was really something—at least I thought it was.

Leatrice was home that Thanksgiving because her grandmother had passed away. I told her I was going to do something special for her. So I gave an order to the ROTC battalion that we would be passing the field at 1600 hours. I told Leatrice about it, so she came up and stood right behind me. I shouted to my troops, "Pass in review!" On cue, they saluted me, and both the parade and my show for Leatrice were over.

It doesn't take hindsight for me to realize I was full of myself. At just 20 years of age, already in charge, I tried to take advantage of my position to win over Leatrice. One hitch to my grand scheme, though—the girl of my dreams was not that impressed. I told her to wait for me while I changed into civilian clothes, but I returned to the parade stand only to discover that another fellow had walked her home. Still, we dated for a year, and, when I left for officer candidate school in Fort Benning, Georgia, in 1944, I told her I wanted to marry her. She didn't say yes, but she didn't say no, either, and I was OK with that. Maybe that was because of the optimist in me, or maybe the vision of Leatrice and Bob, together as husband and wife, burned so brightly in my imagination. As I readied myself for a brutal war, I just knew that a wonderful love would be mine when I returned.

She gave me a picture of her before I left; I carried her photo in my wallet throughout the war. When I was wounded, and everything was taken from me, that picture stayed with me. And even though our correspondence was one-sided, she was never far from my mind.

I always thought Leatrice would marry me. I just knew she was right for me. I felt it in my bones. But in the back of my mind, in training camp or in Italy, I couldn't help thinking that Leatrice hadn't given me a "yes."

Finally, the war was over. For me, so were Europe and the Contessa Ferrari, whom I grew so close to toward the end of that conflict and for some time after. I was ready to go back to America and, above all, to Leatrice. But when I got home, I found out I would have to bide my time for that woman.

About two weeks after I returned to the States in 1946, I went to see Leatrice at her home in Washington. She smiled and greeted me—but I could tell something wasn't quite right. Then, she softly told me some startling news:

She was engaged to be married—to another guy. Not me.

Wow.

Even though I was shaken on the inside, for her sake and mine, I held it together on the outside. I was a returning, decorated soldier; got to be strong. Got to be a gentleman. I hid my shock behind a smile and managed to say, "I'm sorry to hear that and I wish you the best, but I still want to marry you." And although I wasn't aware of any script to follow on how an officer and a gentleman should act when a lady rejects his wedding proposal, I spoke what was in my heart. Believe it or not, I really meant that. When she said she was sorry but she was already taken, intuition led me to think she wasn't all that convincing.

Something's going on, I thought. But I couldn't stay stuck in the Leatrice situation. I had a design for victory as an architect, and that meant getting my degree in that demanding field.

CHAPTER TWELVE
BREAKING THROUGH

When I returned stateside from the war, I was determined to establish myself as an architect. Since Western Reserve University had an accredited architecture program, enrollment there in Cleveland, with a goal of building on my previous studies at Howard, was a natural for me.

It also was natural for me, a 23-year-old returning veteran, to be interested in women, particularly as Leatrice Lucille Branch was engaged to another man. Maybe I needed to move on. To move that process along, I decided it was best to not go it alone. Time to solicit help from I guess what today you'd call a "wing man." I was fortunate to have made many close friends, and one special buddy helped me spread my social wings. He told me of a place on Woodland Avenue worth checking out: the Friendly Inn, a home for female students on work-study programs. These teachers-to-

▲
The Peter B. Lewis Building, Case Western Reserve, Cleveland, Ohio, 2002 | Designed by Frank Gehry

Universities evolve over decades, yet typically their missions remain very similar. As buildings are needed to meet new demands, it is important that their form reflects the architectural aesthetics of the time. Frank Gehry's building on campus is his own unique interpretation of the current international aesthetic.

be would alternate a half-semester working with a half-semester at school. One of my friends told me there was going to be a dance there, so we decided to drop in; we were cruising, looking for a good time.

Meeting Coretta

I saw one woman there whom I really wanted to meet: an aspiring singer and very cute young lady named Coretta Scott. We soon became quite close.

Coretta was a young lady from Marion, Alabama, who was studying at Antioch College in Yellow Springs, Ohio. Over a few months of dating, we became more than good friends. It was very proper, but we were very much in love. As a matter of fact, I gave her my Alpha Phi Alpha pin, and I expected to marry her after she graduated from Antioch in 1947.

Remember, this was a very different time. Our relationship was not sexual. It wasn't with Leatrice either until we were married. At that time, even holding hands when you went to a party was considered "hot."

Coretta and I did so much together. We went to the movies, dancing, concerts, and we talked—a lot. She was impressed that I was an opera buff, that I'd been in Italy and knew so much about opera. Before the war, when I was at Howard, I was a square. Then came the war—and the contessa—so by the time I met Coretta, I was sophisticated.

But Coretta and I weren't engaged for that long, maybe three months; things began to fall apart as her graduation approached. I wanted both a family and a career as an architect. She wanted to be an opera singer. I told her those careers were incompatible, so it wasn't going to work.

I told her it would be hard for both of us, seeing as how at that time neither profession was open to blacks. Besides, I thought she'd have a hard time singing opera, not to mention the need to be on the move. An entertainer's life on the road doesn't fit well with maternal responsibilities.

We talked things over for about a week. Then we cried for about two weeks. She gave me back my fraternity pin, and that was it. Sad times.

Years later, Coretta and I would reconnect, but for now, my focus would be my chosen field. After Coretta and I broke up, I set my sights firmly on my career. Since my ultimate goal was to establish my own firm, I knew I

Coretta Scott and Bob Madison at an Antioch College dance, 1947

had to further my education. So I turned my attention to Western Reserve University, a very prestigious institution in my hometown.

Western reserved

Armed with my expectations and perhaps a bit naïve, I was blindsided by how hard Western Reserve worked to keep me out; I guess you could say I eventually talked my way into the program. Not long after I was formally accepted there, I began to realize that acceptance was not an unalloyed victory. It took extraordinary measures and a willingness on my part to carry a heavy burden, both academically and psychologically. And if getting in was tough, in many ways getting out was even more challenging.

I approached Western Reserve after completing two-and-a-half years at the School of Architecture at Howard University, followed by two-and-a-half years in the Army in World War II. I had a lot of life and experience under my belt, or at least so I thought.

But when I met with Francis Bacon, dean of the School of Architecture at Reserve, to discuss my admission to the architecture program, I saw just how well my prior experiences had prepared me for his answer. Dean Bacon was blunt: The school had never admitted any "colored boys," and he doubted it ever would.

As for me entering architecture school there, his answer was "no," because allowing me into the program would mean I would take the place of a white person who could benefit more. How could a white man benefit more than someone like me, who committed himself to architecture when he was just a boy?

Two days later, after stewing over that rejection, I devised a plan. No sense meeting with the dean of architecture—he was a blank wall. Instead, I decided to meet with another Western Reserve official: the dean of admissions. To prepare, I outfitted myself in my dress military uniform, complete with Purple Heart and combat medals, and I shined my shoes like my career depended on it.

I counted on appealing to a sense of fairness, reason, and maybe even a bit of shame. I stated emphatically that I had fought and almost died for this country, and that, with the GI Bill of Rights, I could pay in full for my education. I demanded to know why I could not be admitted.

After lengthy discussions and review of my material from Howard, we agreed I would sit for a test every Saturday morning from July to September—on any subject, without preparation—and that the dean would consider my admission.

I like a dare, but I like winning even more. Those tests were brutal, and looking back, not truly fair. But I took them anyway, in steamy summer classrooms, and after Labor Day, I waited for the result.

On September 14, 1946, I received a phone call telling me I had made it into the Western Reserve School of Architecture. I was elated but skeptical because of the attitude of Dean Bacon, who, it seems, didn't quite know what to do with me. I was ready, though.

On the ship back home that very month, while my fellow soldiers were playing poker or bridge, I was studying *The Wonders of Italy*, a remarkable book about classical Italian architecture. Little did I suspect that knowing what was in that book would come in so handy in Cleveland.

It was clear Dean Bacon didn't like me, and the feeling was mutual. The dean also taught the history of architecture, a required course for me. Although I did not want to take his class, I didn't want any confrontation with him, either.

One day, I asked to have a word with him. In his office, I said, "Dean, I'm really excited about studying the history of architecture in your class. I just wanted to talk to you a bit and find out how I could get prepared to study for the class next semester." He was very accommodating, and I said, "Well, Dean, I just want to let you know I've been doing some thinking about this, and I want to ask you one question: I can't remember whether it was Donato Bramante or Filippo Brunelleschi who designed the gates of paradise on that cathedral in Florence." He was startled, and spent a few seconds collecting his thoughts.

"Well, Mr. Madison, we don't need to discuss it now, but you're excused from taking my course," he said. "I think that you will be all right without it." I thanked him. That was how I got out of taking the history of architecture. That amuses me to this day.

But when one hand giveth, the other often taketh away. So it was no surprise to me that Western Reserve saddled me with exams in physics and French, calculus and differential equations, courses most architecture students fail. I guess there was consensus among the faculty that I would either drop out or flunk out.

Not a chance for either. I'm methodical. I'm also determined. Some recognize that drive, even if grudgingly.

One of those key "flunk-out" courses Western Reserve threw at me was physics. That class was also one of the biggest, taught in an arena-type auditorium packed with about 300 students. The professor would go to the front of the room and start with equations that related to that day's study.

I remember thinking this was going to be very boring, but decided I would listen very carefully anyway. One day, the professor gave a lecture and said homework for the rest of that week would be on a certain page, and we would be talking about static electricity or something like that. I said to myself, maybe I should get started on this today because this may be something that he's going to stress. At the very next class, the professor stood behind his lectern and for the first time in weeks addressed his pupils.

"Now I want to have one of the students come to the blackboard, and we're going to find out some more about this subject today," he said. "Robert Madison, would you please come to the board?"

I was stunned but, without thinking, said, "Yes, sir." I went up to the board, and he said, "Mr. Madison, we have here a particular formula which leads to this conclusion. We should begin solving this problem."

Much to his surprise, I had the solution. I had done my homework the previous night and I was ready for him, so I went to the blackboard and started drawing all these numbers and letters and symbols. After about 15 minutes, he said, "Well, thank you very much, Mr. Madison. Go back to your seat." That was the last time he called upon me or even spoke to me, and I am sure now that that set-up was part of the ambush the administration and faculty had in store for me. They were continually scheming to rid the school of me.

On another occasion, I was studying architectural specifications, and the professor was explaining how one must be very careful because "in specification writing, we have to be alerted to apparent conflicts, and this is the real nigger in the woodpile."

Of all the metaphors he could have selected, he chose that? Really? To explain my feelings when I heard him use that expression, I'll use my own expression: I saw red. I had never heard anything like that before, and to hear it spoken by a professor in a lecture in a college classroom that had me as a student made me so angry. I sat and asked myself, "What do I do now?" I could get up and walk out—but I calculated that was probably what they expected and wanted me to do. I could shout some words back at the professor—also what they probably expected me to do—and give them a reason to dismiss me. Or, I could take the approach they didn't expect or want. I could just sit there.

That's what I did. For the remainder of the class, 20 minutes or so, I didn't hear a word the professor said. Fury overwhelmed me. I may be stoic and patient, but that doesn't mean I lack for emotion. But that was how it had to be for me at that school. Keep in control. Smile, don't shout. Study, survive. And keep going.

Toward the end of my career there, I found out that Western Reserve had slated me to graduate in 1949, as I had begun classes in 1946. I was very eager to graduate, though, and had to find a way to accelerate the process. First, I approached C. Merrill Barber, a professor who taught structures of wood, steel and concrete. I asked for permission to audit his course; sure, he said. As fate would have it, years later Barber would become a structural engineer for me.

At 8 each morning, I'd walk to his class, find my seat—and proceed to sleep through the entire period. That's because late into the night, I studied lessons in a frenzy to catch up to the rest of the class, which had started in September. It was now March, and I needed to cram in nine months' worth of material to prepare to successfully take the exam in just three months.

At the end of the year, Barber agreed to let me take the final exam. Three days later, I learned the news: I passed that class and earned promotion to the next grade.

Another significant class was design. I was to be an architect, after all. As part of the curriculum for that, all our projects were to be submitted to the Prix de Rome. Originally established in 1663 during the reign of Louis XIV of France as a scholarship program for painters and sculptors, the Prix de Rome expanded to cover other artistic disciplines and students outside of France. Our projects were subjected to a special process for all Beaux-Arts schools of architecture. All designs on this particular scale were submitted to Rome. It happens that the one submitted by the team headed by Robert P. Madison, working with a landscape architect, a sculptor and a painter, had a special mission: to stand out, to make a mark.

From Rome, Italy, to Cleveland, Ohio, and Western Reserve University, we brought home an honorable mention from the Prix de Rome. And Robert P. Madison was the designer in that class.

Despite such recognition, Western Reserve was still trying to get rid of me. The fall and winter of that 1947-48 academic year, I was required to take 11 subjects in addition to researching and writing a thesis. I was also working that winter to make money to support me and my family, but I still took all those courses. When June rolled around, I learned that the faculty had voted to graduate me. I began to realize I would be in the class of '48 instead of '49. I was very happy about this, proving I could do it, even though they didn't think I could and just wanted me to go away.

Racism wasn't confined to campus or the classroom, either. Thank God for Western Reserve friends brave enough to stand up for me.

In June 1947, the class before me scheduled its final outing at Lake Shore Country Club in Bratenahl, a wealthy village incorporated in 1905 after breaking away from poorer, more populous southern Glenville. All architecture students had been invited for a day of golf, tennis, swimming, dinner and dancing. I paid my fee and arrived at 6 p.m.

After the club manager greeted my classmates, he summoned me to his office. Joining him there were the dean of architecture, two members of the faculty, two students and several club members.

The manager seemed somewhat apologetic, explaining that club rules prevented me, as a "colored person," from eating in the dining room. I had nothing to say, and I was sad that the dean and the professors remained silent. The manager kept talking about the club's members and how important it was to adhere to the rules.

He then said, "Madison, we will be able to seat you in the kitchen with the help, where you can eat, or we can give you a bag with your dinner in it to take home, or we can give you a total refund of your money."

I said nothing. I just stared as if I didn't understand. Sometimes the best response is no response, then see how the matter unfolds.

Finally, Philmore J. Hart, a white classmate who graduated with me along with Hal Retzler and Jerry Doyle, said, "If Bob doesn't eat, I don't eat, and if I don't eat, nobody eats."

When he said those words, it was like a controlled bomb had been dropped. Simple, controlled, but straight to the heart of the matter. No turning back now. Stunned silence.

After some awkward throat clearing and shuffling of feet, the manager spoke. He said, OK, I could eat but I could not stay for the dancing. I agreed—I didn't have a date anyway—and then left almost immediately so as not to cause further discomfort. This was an embarrassment for the school, and I learned much later that after the dance, the faculty met and agreed I was a troublemaker; I had to go. But they couldn't flunk me out. They couldn't shame me out. "Graduate him as soon as possible" was their solution, the agreement they cooked up. By the time I made it through, fortunately other parts of my life were beginning to fall into place, like my relationship with Leatrice.

I never did know who that other man was or how Leatrice pulled out of her engagement to him. What I do know is that Jeff Rogers, who had introduced us years back, called with momentous news. It was near the end of spring 1947, just after I had broken up with Coretta Scott, that I got a call from Rogers, who'd been invited to Cleveland to pastor Mount Zion Congregational Church.

He told me Leatrice was free again. So I called her, and when I went to Washington for the wedding of a friend of mine, I went over and chatted with her. It felt comfortable. We picked up right where we left off, and I invited her to come to my commencement the following spring.

She came, staying at the Rogers's house in Glenville. That summer, I went back to D.C. and, during a walk in a park, stopped and said, "I'd like to marry you." This time, there was that same smile, but also a direct answer. She said yes, her father gave us his blessings, her mother was agreeable, and her sisters approved.

I was a very nice guy, a little square, but also ambitious. I think they saw that. Besides, Leatrice, at 26, was the oldest child; a younger sister was already married, and people were worried that she would end up an old maid.

I finally graduated with the proper pomp and circumstance. The ceremony for all Western Reserve colleges and schools was in Severance Hall. In the audience was family—after all, this wasn't just an honor for me, it was validation for my parents, and I hoped, an example for my three brothers. As I looked at the program book, I saw that the graduates of the school of architecture were last in line. As for me, I was the very last graduate that day to receive my diploma. Still, I was happy—at least until I heard the parting words Dean Bacon spoke to me.

"Well, Madison, I guess now you can get a job in a lumberyard."

It was the first time he'd spoken to me in two years. I said, "No, Dean. I'm going to become an architect," and I walked out.

CHAPTER THIRTEEN

BEATING THEM AT THEIR OWN GAME

I was proud to be the first African-American to graduate from the Western Reserve School of Architecture in 1948, but that distinction turned bittersweet. It dawned on me that Western Reserve had excused me from taking courses in electrical systems, mechanical systems, building equipment, and the history of architecture. It seems faculty had banked on my never becoming an architect, so why would I need to know about such things? I guess the calculation was, spend time teaching students who will work as registered architects, and don't waste time on students like me who will never even take the state architectural examination.

Despite that flawed academic strategy and the resulting omissions in my education, I was recognized at graduation. The Jansen Book Prize for excellence in thesis was awarded to me. My thesis centered on special de-

▲

Robert A. Little office, Cleveland, Ohio, 1950

I arrived at this modest-looking office in downtown Cleveland as a fresh graduate. When I started working for Bob Little, I had no architectural registration and earned no salary. Three years later, I left with my architectural registration, experience on several high-profile projects, wonderful friends, and a new determination: to form my own architectural firm. How appropriate that my architectural dreams were shaped there, on an avenue named "Prospect."

4.29.87.

ROBERT A LITTLE • DESIGN & ARCHITECTURE •
5 PEPPER RI... LEVELAND • OHIO • 44124 •

The 120th Charter Day Convocation
Howard University
conferred upon
Robert Prince Madison
The Degree of
Doctor of Humanities
Honoris Causa
February 27, 1987

dear bob :

congratulations on the latest of your many honors and distinctions

i am very proud to have been a small part of the extraordinary career that you have made — i remember the early days when none of it was easy

just in case the impressive successes should go to your head, i am reminding you here of your 4th day at 1303 prospect ave

yours bob.

Years after he left the firm, Bob's first architecture employer, Robert A. Little, sent this playful congratulatory note on the occasion of Bob earning an honorary doctorate from Howard University. In closing, Little writes: "Just in case the impressive successes should go to your head, I am reminding you here of your 4th day at 1303 Prospect Ave."

sign and construction considerations for contemporary churches, so I designed one for the A.M.E. Church. I was also elected to Epsilon Delta Rho, the honorary architectural fraternity at Western Reserve.

Turns out that the hurdles of getting through Western Reserve were nothing compared to those I would need to overcome in building my own architecture practice. Even though it seemed as if my achievements were beginning to speak for themselves, racism continued to rear its ugly head.

Working it out

I had my degree, I was excited, but I needed a job. I went to several architecture offices, walked up to the desk and said I would like to fill out an application. "You can't have an application because we don't hire colored people," I was told. This was exactly what Dean Bacon had predicted: There are no jobs for you. I was probably going to have to go to work in a lumberyard drawing up two-by-fours, work like that, like Dean Bacon said. But I vowed no, that wasn't going to happen.

I decided I would go, unannounced, to the office of Robert A. Little, my professor in that Prix de Rome design contest where my team had made such a mark. I presented him with a bold—some might say desperate—offer: to work for him for nothing for two weeks. We talked for a while, and he said he'd let me know in a week or two.

Sure enough, he asked me to come down to his office at 1303 Prospect Avenue. I will never forget his call. "You can work here for a month and then the young man who works for me will be coming back and I'll have to let you go," he said. I told him that was fine, and I began doing what I had been educated to do—work in an architectural office.

That was the most sophisticated office I had ever been in, with four professionals and a secretary. There was Bob Little, of course, the owner and a very reserved and high-class guy. There was his wife, Ann Murphy Halle Little, the daughter of Sam Halle of Cleveland's legendary and high-toned Halle Brothers department store chain.

Then there was Ed Hodgman, a man with roots in England who years later would join my firm. And there was Mort Epstein, a wonderful guy. Mort and I would become very good friends.

So you had in this office Bob Madison, a black; Hodgman, a white Congregationalist; Epstein, a Jew; and Robert Little, an aristocrat of the highest order. It really was a wonderful work experience, and people there were kind.

I remember one time trying to place files in these multiple cabinets and the case flipped over and all the files fell onto the floor. People helped me clean up the mess and put everything back in order. Twenty years later, Bob Little drew a cartoon for me based on that incident. It was a collegial, friendly place.

There I was: 25 years old, a decorated war veteran, eager to learn, driven to work hard and anxious to experience the next phase of life.

I was impatient, too, and I had become a lot more social. No more "square" for me. That's because I had a life outside of work, hanging with friends and meeting women. One woman in particular was never far from my mind—Leatrice Lucille Branch, who would become my partner for more than 60 years. Even while Coretta Scott and I had been far more than an item, Leatrice kept calling to me. She and I were different, for sure, but we were deeply complementary, and alike enough to make our bond seem predestined.

My better half

Leatrice was educated, like me, but our parents were very different. During the Depression, her parents had jobs and steady paychecks. Mine didn't, even though they were college-educated. Her parents didn't have a college education, but they worked in a laundry and in jobs like that. Leatrice had a chinchilla coat. I wore an ill-fitting, borrowed overcoat. The difference between our families was night and day.

Leatrice certainly had her own challenges. People in Washington didn't treat her right because of a hierarchy driven by skin color and profession. Black society in Washington, D.C., was vicious. You belonged to the elite because you were light-skinned, a professional, or both. Light-skinned people tended to be in a separate, highfalutin and disdainful group. Although Leatrice was light-skinned, her parents were neither educated nor wealthy, so she was snubbed, angering her. Because she felt she had something to prove, she pursued higher education.

In D.C., there was a kind of parallel between white-on-black discrimination and black-on-black discrimination. Still is.

Leatrice's father was quite dark. Her mother was very white, so you know some miscegenation had gone on there. The lightness of her skin didn't give her an advantage, though. Leatrice needed to rely on her brain, though her brain didn't get her invited to all the right parties and social functions. Point is, Leatrice was very resentful because she was not invited to parties and stuff like that despite her powerful intellect. She went to the University of Chicago—on the train, by herself—to get a master's degree. Her father had only a sixth-grade education. Therefore, when she married me she was determined that together we were going to be somebody.

She told me later she'd only agreed to that other engagement to please her mother, by the way.

As I think back on it, Leatrice was pushing me and I was pulling her, and I was pushing her and she was pulling me. We came out of the same milieu of wanting to prove to people we were somebody. Leatrice, when she married me, was determined that she, her life and her children were going to be elite one day, and that we would put that together.

Maybe that's one of the reasons we lasted so long and worked so well together: Both of us had something to prove—to ourselves, above all, but also to each other, and to society at large.

For now, there was work to do at Bob Little's office.

Thank God for Friday

In 1948, the world was black and white, and Cleveland remained largely segregated. Even though I went to work like everybody else, Little and Hodgman would go to lunch at nearby restaurants, while I would have to bring my lunch to work; most restaurants didn't serve black people. Epstein, who was very sensitive to this, decided he'd bring his lunch to work too. So I very rarely went out to lunch, and with Epstein hanging around, I enjoyed the gift of his company.

A couple of times I dined at the Forum Cafeteria, where black people were allowed to eat. But more often than not, Epstein and I ate our lunch and played chess in the office, and some games went on and on. Little came in once after lunch and saw us playing chess and even though we didn't stop, we arrived at a point where we could put the game on pause. He knew we would work until 7 or 8 o'clock if it was necessary for us to catch up.

I was in a pleasant, professional routine at Little's office, and having a great time learning and contributing. But time passed quickly, and the month that Little said I could work was coming to a close. Soon, that guy Little was expecting would show up to claim his job—and I'd be out on the street.

But at the end, Little had decided I was a pretty good draftsman because I had mastered some things; he said later that I was the finest draftsman he'd ever met.

Of course, Little didn't know that my father was a civil engineer who had taught me how to draft. My studies at Howard University and at the University of Pisa at the end of the war also helped. So I kept my job.

It wasn't until nearly 70 years later, when I nearly completed gathering accounts for this book, that I learned an interesting postscript. A gentleman named Jim Gibans was "that guy" who Little expected to return. Gibans would go on to become a wonderful architect, colleague and friend years later after he and his wife, Nina, eventually relocated back to Cleveland from San Francisco, where he began his career.

All in all, Little was very good to me, helping me become a true professional. As a member of the American Institute of Architects, he wanted me to join, so that September he submitted my name to the AIA. But as is often the case, an obstacle needed to be overcome, and a precedent had to be set.

The AIA really didn't know what to do with me because there were no rules or protocols for permitting black people to join the Cleveland chapter. They had all kinds of emergency meetings about that matter but kept me in the dark. Meanwhile, Little asked me to give a lecture to the chapter about what young architecture graduates should expect from the offices in which they work.

Leatrice Branch and Robert Madison on one of the signature days of their relationship: the couple's engagement day.

Sure enough, I went home and prepared for this and gave a lecture on what such graduates should be. This was just after the war, and there were only four graduates from the Western Reserve School of Architecture, the only school of architecture in Cleveland. In Ohio, there were others at Kent State University, Ohio State University, and the University of Cincinnati.

That year was really busy, with commencement, my new job with a high-powered firm, and reconnecting with Leatrice. What I found out about her even before we got married was how single-minded she was—for both of us. To her, it wasn't enough for me to have a good job. What really mattered was for me to own my own business, to lead my own architectural firm. Now that we'd decided to join forces, it was time to seal our troth and design victory together.

Tying the knot

On April 16, 1949, Leatrice and I exchanged vows in Rankin Chapel at Howard University. The chapel was very poetic, a beautiful building where Howard Thurman, a leading theologian who greatly influenced Martin Luther King Jr., was the dean.

The ring I put on Leatrice's finger was beautiful, a simple, white gold band with diamonds all around. I bought it in Italy after my combat was over. It was a great ring. I worked at Bob Little's office until I married Leatrice. Little sent us a very nice wedding present, a form-fitting, ultra-modern Eames chair. That was quite a classic. And Leatrice and I started our life together.

Like Coretta Scott, who struck out any mention of the wife obeying the husband from vows she exchanged with Martin, Leatrice displayed the mindset of a strong woman, independent before her time. Our wedding ceremony sealed the deal, but long before, I knew Leatrice and I would be bound for life. Mr. and Mrs. Robert Madison honeymooned in Niagara Falls, our first trip in a marriage that would last 62 years.

When Leatrice and I got back to Cleveland, I already had a job with a high-profile architectural firm, but I had not yet acquired all the education I needed. So Leatrice said that because I had to register with the state to practice architecture, we had to study for examinations.

Every day after dinner, we would study at the kitchen table for at least an hour. We did that for at least six months. My goal was state registration as an architect, and Leatrice was preparing for the teacher's licensing examination.

The next stage

Here I was, ready to practice architecture, to build on all my education. Little did I know it would be several years before I opened my own practice. It turns out there was more learning to absorb, trips to take, languages to learn, and a family to raise, a cultured family. A key next step was becoming a true professional.

Architecture is one of a handful of fields that require rigorous testing, certification and registration in order to practice. In January 1950, after eight months of postgraduate study, I got in my car with three other men—white classmates from Western Reserve—to go to Columbus to take the final examination. I already had some stature working for Robert A. Little, a descendant of Paul Revere and one of the first white architects to hire people of color. Stature, however, doesn't score points on the test.

Phil Hart, two fellows and I drove down to Columbus in my little car on a Sunday. When we arrived, I dispatched them to the Fort Hayes Hotel while I went to the YMCA, the only place in the Ohio capital I knew of where black people could stay.

The exam began at 8 in the morning on a Monday. On Tuesday, we labored for 12 hours to 8 at night on design. We had to make sketches and draw them up for working drawings. It was very intense.

We ate lunch in. We took exams in the history of architecture, on structure, on mechanical, and on electrical. Before that, at this YMCA, there was all kinds of noise, while I was trying to study. A weird-looking guy just walked into my room. There was a basketball game almost every night; I'm trying to study, and cheerleaders are screaming. Not an ideal situation for someone whose professional future depended on quiet study and passing a brutal test that would last for five long days.

Phil Hart was sympathetic. "Why don't you come to the Fort Hayes?" he said to me. So when I picked him up in the morning to take him to our examination site, I asked the hotel attendant if I could get a room there. He said, "Well, we're all booked, but you can stay with these guys if you want to, because they can bring in a bunk in their room." The hotel was empty, but I guess it was full if you were black. I continued to stay at the Y and, after finishing the exam, returned to Cleveland and worked in Little's office.

One afternoon, months after that trial by fire in Columbus, an unexpected and pleasant visitor stopped into the office. It was Leatrice, come from home, envelope in hand and a smile on her face. I had passed the state test on my first attempt; only two others had done that. It took Bob Little three tries. He was genuinely happy for me, and sent out for cigars and a bottle of Cognac to celebrate. To think that just two years earlier, I was the first African-American to receive an architectural degree in the state of Ohio. In the summer of 1950, I became the first African-American to become a registered professional architect in the state.

Leatrice had come to Little's to inform me that I had passed, but she also was doing what she would continue to do all of our lives: paving the way to our dreams. Leatrice and I were well on our way, in love, in harmony over career, both of us ready to take on a rapidly evolving world. It hadn't been easy up to his point, and it never would be. But every step we took together would be very satisfying and rewarding.

CHAPTER FOURTEEN

FINISHING SCHOOL PART 1

Leatrice and I shared a respect for learning, hard work, and for high culture. Both of us also had an appetite for the finer things.

Perhaps I developed my taste for such things in Europe after my combat career ended. Maybe it was my time with the contessa. It might have been reading that architecture book, which I bought in the University of Pisa bookstore, on the troop transport ship.

Reading that book about Italian architectural style during that ocean crossing back to the States made me realize that, even though I was well-versed in the general subject, I was woefully ignorant about many aspects of my chosen field and didn't know much about the history of architecture

▲

Shaker Tower East, Shaker Heights, Ohio | Designed by Walter Gropius, 1969

This was the first Ohio commission for Walter Gropius, my instructor and mentor at Harvard University. Signature elements of Bauhaus sensibility are evident in this building: oversized structural elements that ground the design and sturdy yet delicate concrete detailing, especially framing the windows. Special for me? The Tower, the last major project Gropius completed, is less than one mile from my home. Every time I pass it, I think of the man who taught and inspired me.

in France, Germany or England. That part of my education was neglected, but at least I got through by studying on my own.

So, even after I earned my architecture degree from Western Reserve and passed the state exam to become the first African-American architect registered in Ohio, I felt a need to spread my wings even further. I thank my own ambition and my wonderful wife.

Leatrice—she really was my cheerleader—said, "Well, it's time to do more studying." She said, "I've got my master's from the University of Chicago, and you should get yours. Why not Harvard?"

I said, "Harvard?" She was one proud lady, and her spirit was infectious.

Leatrice Branch had taken the train by herself to Chicago to study for her master's. I thought the least Robert Madison could do was drive to Massachusetts to get his.

Looking back on Leatrice and Coretta Scott King, I realize the two ran in overlapping circles. Both of them were deeply involved in family and civic matters. Leatrice was devoted to civil rights, like Coretta; in fact she headed a Southern Christian Leadership Conference in the 1960s.

Leatrice was resolute from the start, earning a bachelor of science degree cum laude from Miner Teachers College. In 1947, she secured a master of arts degree in guidance and personnel from the University of Chicago, where she studied with the famous child psychologist Dr. Bruno Bettelheim.

While I was in Italy fighting with the Buffalo Soldiers, Leatrice was teaching in public schools in D.C. Then, between 1954 and 1960, while I was building my practice, she taught in Cleveland public schools, virtually supporting my young enterprise. Finally, once Robert P. Madison, Architect, was on a firm footing, Leatrice retired from teaching, devoting herself to motherhood, making a home—against great odds, at times—and being a civic activist.

Back in the early 1950s, Leatrice knew there was more to learn, more rounding of the square to accomplish before I opened my office in Glenville. Time to venture forth, to leave the familiar behind.

Cambridge calling

Leatrice didn't want to be the only one in the Madison family with a master's degree; my turn. As it happens, I had the GI Bill of Rights from the war, which provided the money to go to school. Whether Harvard would accept me, however, was another matter.

When I told Bob Little I was going to apply to Harvard, the school he had graduated from, he told me he didn't know if I could make it in and said I might "have to re-bach." I had no idea what he meant by "re-bach," until it occurred to me that when Western Reserve awarded me that architecture degree, I had not completed about half the required courses. Because of those gaps in my education, Little thought I would have to go back and complete a bachelor's degree, or re-bach, at Harvard before I could gain admittance to graduate work there. This would be especially likely since I was enrolling in Walter Gropius's elite master's class. I'm talking about Walter Gropius, founder of the famous Bauhaus School in Germany.

Gropius, however, was aware that I was already a registered architect. Why would a registered architect need an additional bachelor's degree? So he decided Harvard should admit me. I'm also sure Gropius wanted me in his class because he had fled Germany, where all sorts of atrocities were committed on Jews and black people because they were believed to be inferior. Gropius knew differently.

Still, I had to bide my time. Although Gropius wanted me in his class, I could not be admitted that September, so I had to wait until January of 1951. Leatrice and I spent the fall of 1950 making preparations to leave Cleveland for my studies at Harvard, and many people from different aspects of my life gave us nice going-away parties. Still, I encountered some resistance to the move. For one thing, I had a good job and some stability right where I was. All that, contrasting with the uncertainty of such a move, led my mother-in-law to say, "You must be some kind of a nut to leave your good job."

I guess she was right—I am some kind of nut—but off to Harvard we went anyway. I studied with Gropius in the master's class, where I was the only black. Two students were from China and one Russian made the trip

Robert Madison with the 1951 Graduate School of Design of Harvard University. In the middle is Walter Gropius, founder of the Bauhaus, arguably the most influential and distinctive architecture and design school of the twentieth century.

for study here. We always had joint projects so we all worked together frequently. It was quite a diverse class. It was also quite wonderful.

Gropius was one of the first world-renowned architects to strongly advocate for quality public housing. I think Gropius was committed to being an architect for people all over the world. But I was curious why he always placed me on the same team with students from Alabama, even Georgia, people you'd expect might have a hard time with me. One I've never forgotten was Nellie Long. She was a landscape architect from South Carolina, and she had a tough time; she just couldn't hack it. Gropius paired us up to write a special paper, but Nellie never showed up. So I wrote the paper by myself, got an A, and she thanked me by mail. Never, ever in person; because of guilt or misplaced pride, I guess, she couldn't bring herself to do that.

Gropius was quite a humanitarian and a warm person. His goal was to make architecture more than bricks and stones; for him, architecture could be very much more. Quality architecture that could enable beautiful but pragmatic buildings could be a vehicle for social change. That's why many of our projects dealt with housing for the masses. The goal of one design project, for the Michael Reese Hospital, was to create mass housing in the South Side of Chicago, where mostly black people live.

What was funny about that Chicago project was that the people in charge couldn't figure out what black people wanted, so, of course, they turned to me as an expert. I figured I'd have some fun.

"Bob," they said, "we're trying to develop a good program for the South Side of Chicago. What do black people want?"

"That's a good question," I said. "In baseball, black people want first base to be 90 feet from home plate. In football, black people want the goal lines to be 100 yards apart."

"Bob, that's the same things white people want," they said.

"That's right," I said. "That's right." True story. I cracked up—even though I couldn't be sure my message got through. When Gropius heard about it, he just laughed himself to death, because these students were so serious and so out of touch. They thought there was some basic difference between what black people and white people want.

Wrong side of the tracks

That spring, we lived in the home of Satira Bennett, a lady referred to me by the bishop of the A.M.E. church. I was a regular attendant at St. John A.M.E. Church in Cleveland, and when the bishop found out I was attending graduate school at Harvard, he put out the word to people he knew in the Boston area. He was referred to Bennett, who said she would be delighted to have us stay in her place. Little did I know the kind of apartment I would find on my reconnaissance.

I drove to Washington, D.C., to drop off Leatrice with her parents so I could go to Massachusetts to find out what was going on and get us settled in. I left the car in D.C. On the train from Philadelphia—and this was a truly remarkable coincidence—I discovered that the lady sitting next to me was Satira Bennett herself. We eventually realized I was the student who was going to live at her house.

Bennett was from the Bahamas and a very arrogant lady. She was sophisticated, too, but that didn't help. She thought I was fortunate to be able to spend a semester living at her house.

When I arrived there just before Christmas of 1950, I found out that the space Mrs. Bennett had rented to us was actually the attic. It looked like someone had tried to close in the rafters and make a decent room of the drafty, dirty space, but whoever tried to do that hadn't succeeded. What's more, the layout was inconvenient—we had to descend a dark, creaky staircase just to use the bathroom. To use the kitchen, we had to tromp down another staircase to the first floor. So that was where we would stay, in this one room. I was not looking forward to sharing this news with Leatrice.

When I went back to D.C. to pick up my wife, I did not explain the conditions of the place to her. I just said it was in Cambridge, off Massachusetts Avenue about two blocks from Harvard, so I could walk to school. When we drove to Cambridge and moved into Mrs. Bennett's house, Leatrice called the place "very interesting," and Mrs. Bennett showed her where the stove was. Leatrice was just happy because we were finally at Harvard.

Too bad her good feelings only lasted a few hours.

After a very long day, we went to bed, but woke up abruptly around 2 a.m. What popped us awake was what sounded like a tremendous roar. We looked out the window and saw a passenger train rumbling behind our yard. The train and the noise made me realize this neighborhood was where all the colored folks lived in Cambridge, Massachusetts.

Leatrice was fed up, saying she couldn't stand this situation and we had to find another place. So she looked in the newspapers and found all kinds of apartments for rent. Once, she knocked on a door and the owner took one look at her and said, "We have nothing to rent here." Even after she showed him the rental notice in the paper, he said, "We have nothing to rent here, nigger. Get out."

We realized Cambridge was not a very nice place. Still, we lived in that attic for the rest of the semester, and we managed. We even made some friends there, and some classmates became friends for life.

Our attic home life lasted from December 1950 to June 1951. As summer break began, we returned to Cleveland and Leatrice decided she wanted to spend time with her parents. So she went back to her parents' house in D.C. while I went to live with my family on Orville Avenue in Cleveland. This was a long-awaited chance to help my father with his surveying firm—Father and son, working in the business together.

But that was not to be. By that time, my father was too far gone, his body riddled with cancer. He died that August.

I was just 28, holding my father's head in my lap as he gasped his last breath that Saturday. On the death certificate the cause was listed as cancer, but I believe that's only because "despair" is not a medically recognized cause of death. I was sure he had simply given up; he had fought as long as he could and his body was plain worn out.

The Monday before, he had called me to be ready to go out on a survey we had scheduled for that day. But at 10 a.m., he collapsed, and we put him in a makeshift bedroom on the first floor of our home at 10713 Orville. The doctor came over at about 2 p.m., shook his head in resignation and gave us an important order: Call for his mother.

Julia Craig—his mother, my grandmother—came quickly, arriving from Mobile on Wednesday. The next day, my dad asked me to get him a pint of whiskey. I was at his bedside along with his wife—my mother—my brothers Stanley and Bernard, and my dad's mother. Not everyone could make it, though; time was literally our mortal enemy. My wife was in Washington, D.C., while Julian was stationed at Fort Leonard Wood in Missouri. We called the ambulance to transport my father to the Veterans Hospital, but he died at home before it arrived. We buried him the following Wednesday from St. John's A.M.E. Church. By that time, my wife, my brother Julian and his wife, Mildred, had made the sad visit.

I was relieved for my father's sake when he passed, because he had suffered for so long. He was in so much pain, surely the reason he asked for that whiskey. Through it all, my mother denied all this was happening, but she, too, had suffered, and with great anxiety. God's will be done.

At the same time, I was very angry. Angry because he was a truly remarkable man years ahead of his time, a fighter and pioneer who died too young to enjoy the fruits of his labor or see any of his grandchildren, let alone witness his business become a success. I have spent my life keeping promises I made after he expired:

I would vindicate his name and bring honor to his heritage.

I would never let my family suffer from want, and provide my wife with the finer things my mother never enjoyed.

I would never let my children worry about receiving the best education available.

I would enjoy my children and grandchildren in a manner never available to my father.

I would work, and work, and work, because that was the only avenue available to achieve these things.

I would live the kind of life my father strove for but could not lead.

My time, of course, was different, though it would prove no less challenging. Still, I was determined that his past would not be my prologue. And life went on.

Cambridge encore

In September, Leatrice and I went back to Harvard University for my second semester in Walter Gropius's master class. We found an apartment in Roxbury, a largely black neighborhood on Boston's west side.

Leatrice, meanwhile, had gotten a job at Harvard's Graduate School of Design. While she was working there as assistant librarian, she came across a circular in which the State Department was advertising Fulbright fellowships for study abroad.

So, in her usual fashion, Leatrice came home and said to me, "This is a Fulbright Award to study anything you want to—why don't we go for it? Let's go see about studying with Le Corbusier in Paris." I said, "What are you talking about?" This was in October of 1951.

Sure enough, we sat down, filled out the application forms, and Leatrice made sure to file them with the state department. Not only did

Leatrice provide the initial push, she saw things through. As for me, you could say I was cautious; my brother Julian, he was a go-getter. As for Leatrice? "Let's go get it." Still, both had to have a base, a rock, and, when I think about it now, I'm successful because of Leatrice, my mother, my father, Julian and Mildred, Julian's wife. But I've always been the rock. I keep the ship steady.

In the meantime, I finished that semester, and my classmates elected me president of that master's class. There were 15 students, eight the first semester and seven the second, after one dropped out. I was just the third African-American ever to study with Walter Gropius at the Graduate School of Design at Harvard. I earned my master's in February of 1952 and was offered a job to teach at Howard University. We soon found out Leatrice was pregnant with our first child. Life was busy indeed.

But even during the busiest of times, a random encounter can bring unexpected joy.

I remember walking across Boston Common and hearing this sweet, musical voice call out "Bobby!" I looked up and smiled at the delightful young woman who reached out to hug me. How great it was to run into my old girlfriend, Coretta Scott. As we caught up and she told me about the wonderful young man she had just started seeing, I couldn't help recall falling in love with her six years earlier.

But just as I would renew my bond with Leatrice, the woman who shared my dreams, Coretta would eventually find her own soul mate, the extraordinary Martin Luther King Jr., whom she met in Boston. Coretta was a voice student at the New England Conservatory of Music while Martin studied at Boston University.

After that wonderful encounter in Boston Common, Leatrice and I had Coretta over to our house in Cambridge, and I tried to hook her up for a date with some guy from the school of architecture. But that connection didn't happen; who knows how history might have changed if it had? That's because next thing I knew, she was dating Martin quite seriously, and soon after, they were engaged to be married.

We were invited to their wedding but we couldn't attend—which I regret, considering what a historic couple they became: Martin and Coretta.

Down the line, I met Martin on various occasions, including several times in Cleveland, but I was not part of his inner circle. I also saw Coretta several times in Atlanta after Martin was assassinated in 1968, leaving her to carry on with his mission. Coretta was a strong woman.

I could see that Martin was exceptional from the time I watched him rally a crowd for the Poor People's March. There was a lot of debate during the early 1960s over who should lead the civil rights movement, Malcolm X or Martin Luther King Jr. Now, I'm not much of a marcher; I prefer a different kind of expression, and I sided with Martin, not Malcolm. Martin also helped later with Carl Stokes' campaign for mayor of Cleveland, a campaign in which I was deeply involved.

Martin made several Cleveland appearances in 1967, at churches and high schools. That April, he gave Glenville High School students this advice: Blacks must "develop within ourselves a deep sense of somebodiness. Don't let anybody make you feel that you are nobody."

CHAPTER FIFTEEN
FINISHING SCHOOL PART 2

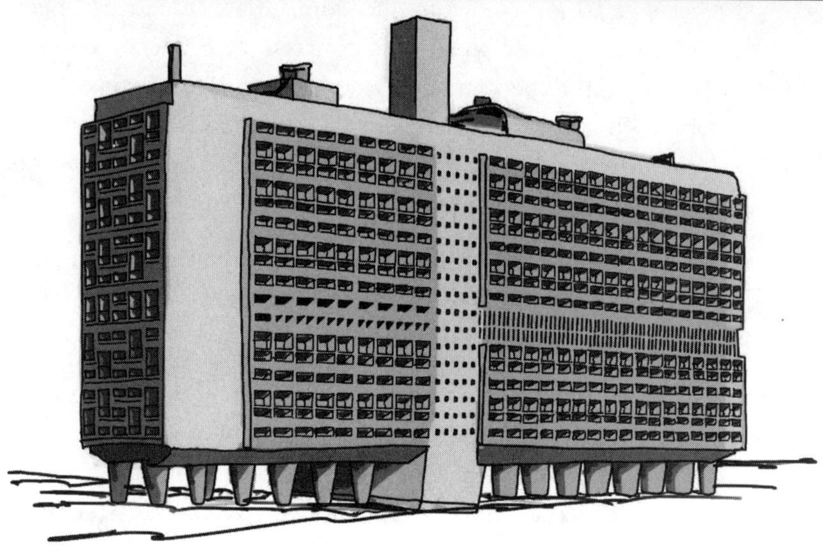

What a summer. After my commencement at Harvard, Leatrice and I moved back to D.C., found an apartment, and I began teaching at Howard. While many periods of my life were terrible due to various circumstances that conspired against me, others were wonderful because it seemed that all the stars aligned to make my life beautiful and bright. Even my mother, who often was hard to please, was happy, though she would have preferred me back in Cleveland. Unfortunately, because Leatrice was expecting, she couldn't travel to my commencement, which, as you might imagine, was a very big deal for me.

So I drove to Cleveland, picked up my mother, and we drove up for the commencement exercises at Harvard University on June 1, 1952. The address was given by John Foster Dulles, a long-time American diplomat; he would become Secretary of State six months later.

▲

Unite d'Habitation, Marseille, France | Designed by Le Corbusier

The famous architect Le Corbusier started to design this innovative apartment building in the late 1940s. Completed in 1952, it is considered a prime example of Brutalist architecture.

The next day, we drove to Washington to reunite with Leatrice. Momentous events continued to shower our life. On July 17, 1952, Jeanne Marie Madison was born. Just to complicate things, Jeanne's birth came fast on the heels of a momentous notification. In late June, I had been awarded a Fulbright to study prestressed concrete with Eugene Freyssinet at L'École Nationale Supérieure des Beaux-Arts in Paris, France. I was floored. It happens that I was selected because I had studied with Gropius, could speak the beautiful language of French and understood the power and possibilities of prestressed concrete technology.

Let me recapitulate that summer of 1952: I got my degree from Harvard in June. That same month, I was granted a Fulbright award, and a few weeks later, in July, our first child, Jeanne, was born.

So there we were with our first-born in one arm and my Fulbright to Paris in the other. We were excited, even overjoyed, and we were eager for the adventure. But my mother-in-law—again—put up resistance, just as she had when we moved to Massachusetts for the Gropius master class. "You know what you are? You're a damn fool," she said to me. That's the first time I'd ever heard her use a phrase that coarse.

"You got a baby who is one month, and you're going to a country where you've never been before. You can't really speak the language, and you're going to take this newborn baby?"

It was time to talk things over with Leatrice.

We had three choices. I could decide not to go. Number two, I could go by myself and leave Leatrice and Jeanne at home. Number three, the three of us could go together. We mulled these over for less than an hour, and Leatrice said, "I'm going, we're going." So we started to pack up to get ready to cross the ocean on the Île de France, the most celebrated ocean liner of its time, after the Queen Elizabeth.

Before we booked the ship, however, Leatrice discovered she had trouble breast-feeding, so we packed a carton of Carnation milk along with us for our two-month-old baby, going to a place we'd never been before, a country with a language we were not fluent in, even though a professor at Howard tutored me in French during special classes that summer. But speaking French on a French ship, or later, on the streets of Paris,

Bob and Leatrice Madison and their infant daughter Jeanne sailed to France on the storied ocean liner, *Ile de France*.

would be so different. When we finally set foot on that huge ocean liner, I realized everybody spoke nothing but French, and it wasn't schoolboy French; still, I could say things like "Comment allez-vous?" and "Ça va?" making conversation just like we do here. I always get along.

So, even though I was giving up my job security and incurring my mother-in-law's wrath, we set out for France. Friends drove all the way from Cleveland to wish us a good trip and a good stay in Paris. I was very eager to learn about the latest in architecture from two men who were so in the know, they were far ahead of their time: Le Corbusier and Eugene Freyssinet.

Settling into Paris

For Leatrice, me and Jeanne, the trip to Paris was a very big deal. It also was a big deal to my Cleveland friends Kenny Clement and Martin Sutler, who drove all the way up to New York to wish us bon voyage. All this fuss!

The ocean voyage was relatively uneventful. We sailed tourist class, and Jeanne was the youngest passenger. Our room on the lower decks was

ÉCOLE NATIONALE SUPÉRIEURE DES BEAUX-ARTS

CARTE TEMPORAIRE D'ÉLÈVE No 2462A

NOM : Mr Madison Élève de Mr Perret

Prénoms : Robert P.

Né le 28-7-1923 Cleveland

Domicile

Paris, le 7 - 11 - 52

Signature du Titulaire, Le Directeur de l'Ecole, Membre de l'Institut,

N.-B. — Tout élève doit être porteur de sa carte qui ne peut être prêtée sous peine de confiscation.

Bob's student ID card for L'École Nationale Supérieure des Beaux-Arts in Paris, France.

comfortable, the shipboard food was excellent, and the seven days passed quickly. After disembarking at Le Havre, we took the train to Paris, then a taxi to our hotel.

We arrived midday—and Jeanne promptly got sick. Fortunately, before we left we'd gotten the names of some French doctors, so I called one and he came right over on his bicycle. Neither of us had a thermometer; it seems every French family has one so doctors didn't carry them. Anyhow, we used sign language well enough to determine that all Jeanne had was a little cold.

Once we settled into our hotel, I began looking for an apartment. We also became regulars at a nearby café, where everybody fell in love with Jeanne. We had a basket shaped like a large shoe, with loops on either side, and Leatrice and I would swing the baby between us, to the delight of the neighborhood.

We finally found a large apartment on the Avenue de Neuilly, just north of the Arc de Triomphe. It was great, with a huge master bedroom, and it was perfect for visiting friends. No trains barreling through our neighborhood. No landlords saying no to our color. Quite a difference from our experience finding a place to live in Cambridge just a year or so earlier.

I think it's amusing that we needed to cross the Atlantic Ocean just to rent a good apartment.

Learning in the City of Light

My Fulbright got me enrolled at L'École Nationale Supérieure des Beaux-Arts, where I received instruction from the great architect Le Corbusier and did research with Freyssinet, a pioneer of prestressed concrete.

When I wasn't taking classes, the Madisons took in Paris—and more—with Jeanne in her stroller, of course. We saw the Louvre, Rodin's museum, the Champs Elysees. I remember very clearly that every now and then a French couple would invite us to some small party because we were Fulbright scholars, and the party was very well done. The French were sticklers for the process of who knows who and how you should act and what you should and shouldn't wear. We went to several parties, and the last one I remember was called the Réveillons de Noël, which was held on Christmas Eve. We went to the Cathédrale de Notre Dame for Mass

Bob, Leatrice and Jeanne toured Europe while Bob was on a Fulbright Scholarship. Their circuitous tour began in Paris and ended in London and included stops in eight countries in just under 12 months.

that midnight, then came back to the house of our guests for a wonderful dinner party that lasted through the night.

We did some major sightseeing that spring, too. We rented a car and decided to visit the châteaux. By that time, I'd begun wearing a beret and spoke French pretty well. Because I was black, people thought I might be from the Côte d'Ivoire, then a French colony in West Africa. I didn't contradict them; in fact, I started posing as someone from Côte d'Ivoire, which enabled me to spend less money on my driver's license than I would have as an American tourist.

We drove to Château de Fontainebleau in the south of France, where the king spent some of his time. It was magnificent. We eventually wanted to make it to Italy; that was the plan. Getting there was another trip in itself.

Uptight in Italy

First, we traveled to Switzerland, using the Simplon Pass that connects it to Italy. This is a high, twisty two-lane road, and I can tell you, I was very nervous.

But we finally made it to Milan after several stops along the way, including a two-night stay in Geneva. We got into Milan too late to stay in the hotel we'd booked, so we bivouacked in the parking lot and slept in our rental car.

I remember getting up a little after dawn to go into the hotel to get water to boil and sterilize so we could make formula for Jeanne, who was in the car. There was Leatrice, joined for a few days by her old friend Caroline Tempio, and the baby, and I was out there pumping up this portable butane gas stove. I walked through the hotel lobby looking like a hobo, a bucket and a pot in my hands, to get this done.

That was nothing compared to the next day, when we toured the city of Milan, marveling at the great cathedrals. While traveling in our rental car, Leatrice said Jeanne needed feeding. I said no, not here, not in the middle of the city; we'd cause a riot. That made Leatrice mad at me, so I started driving as fast as I could to the outskirts of town, finally parking on the side of a road where the only thing I could see was a fence enclosing what I figured was an estate. I couldn't see a soul. Too bad I couldn't see even farther.

Jeanne and Leatrice in Paris, 1953.

Bob in Paris, dressed as a Parisian in a classic beret.

I got out, unpacked my folding table, and started pumping up our stove. What I didn't know was that I had parked on the edge of a boys' academy. One young man apparently saw us and disappeared only to return with a horde of people—and then even more people started coming from all directions. Can you imagine this, way out in the middle of Nowhere, Italy?

Here this black man gets out of a car and starts pumping up fire with this little stove. Here's his woman in the car, a baby, and a white friend—they couldn't believe this, nor could I. I had told Leatrice we would create a riot if we stayed in Milano, and sure enough, we did.

At any rate, so many people came up to see Jeannie—"Ooh, baby," they cooed; they thought she was the most wonderful thing they had ever seen—that Jeannie got really frightened and even Leatrice got scared, with all these folks pressed up so close to us. One old woman with no teeth who looked like a witch particularly frightened Jeanne. We got in the car and raced away as fast as we could, and things finally simmered down.

After a few blissful days on Venice's Grand Canal, we drove south to Florence, finally arriving in a small town whose name I don't remember. Maybe I've suppressed it because that place frightened us, too.

We arrived there in the middle of the square on a Sunday, encountering nothing but men. There we were, a black man driving up in a car, with the wife and the baby and Caroline, Leatrice's white friend. We were made to feel very uncomfortable, and we left in a hurry.

We ate dinner outside Florence, then headed toward Rome. We saw the Vatican, did all the other things sightseers do, and I even managed to fit in some education when I saw firsthand the fabrication of prestressed concrete building components. Freyssinet had arranged the logistics of that amazing factory tour.

I also executed a much more personal mission, bringing a very special relationship to a close. My young family and I visited Laura Ferrari in her villa, as I'd promised the contessa I would just after the end of World War II. I had told her I'd be back, and an officer and gentleman always keeps his word.

Following our visits to Venice and Rome, we drove up to Lucca to see Laura. I brought my wife, her friend, and our baby daughter with me. People thought I was crazy to have them all meet, but I thought it was great.

After Laura greeted us and introduced us to her mother, all of us gathered for conversation in the living room. Laura and I left to take a walk through the fields, we came back, and then we said goodbye. That was the last time I saw Laura.

All in all, the year I spent in Europe was profoundly educational, both through classroom work and through travel. The educational agenda was loose, in a way, as the teaching and learning were continually being adjusted and recreated. It was also demanding and, above all, stimulating.

Even though I had no classes formally scheduled with Le Corbusier, I was determined to meet him. Le Corbusier was a tremendous designer known for his use of reinforced concrete, so when I got to L'École, I made a point of looking him up. I was there as an official student of Eugene Freyssinet, who was a Frenchman with no particular flair; he also didn't speak that much English. Le Corbusier, however, was something else, a figure I absolutely had to seek out.

Meanwhile, the powers that be at L'École were so impressed that I'd been a student of Walter Gropius, they wanted me to teach.

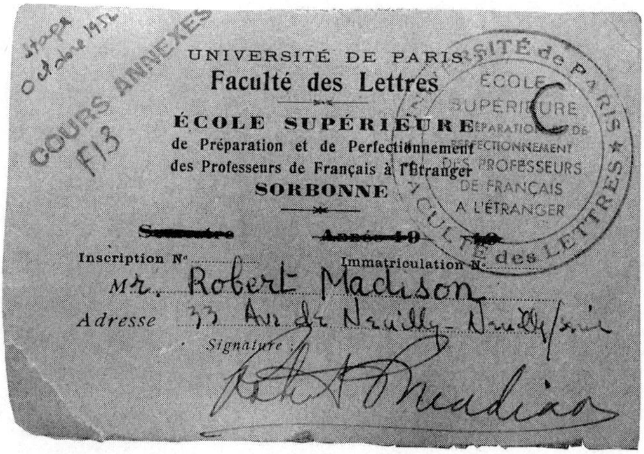

The student advances: Bob's teaching identification card at L'École.

"Thank you very much, but my French is not that good," I told them. Still, I was tickled; I wound up teaching a class, but not before I learned a whole lot about prestressed concrete, a field in which Europe was way ahead of America.

To comprehend how prestressed concrete works, it's best to first understand typical concrete construction. Say you're going to pour a concrete floor. What's typically done is to first construct a wooden framework, then put some concrete down. Then you install iron reinforcing rods and pour more concrete on top. It's a bit like pouring batter into a cake pan, with a wire rack in the middle.

With prestressed concrete, however, you're creating a high-tech, extra-strong cake. You stress the rods first by stretching them so they flex upward in the middle. They then flatten out with the weight of the top layer of concrete as it's poured, providing more resistance to pressure. The result is an architectural element that's stronger, lighter, uses less material, and requires less labor—all factors that make it cost less. And because prestressed concrete construction can be formed into novel structural shapes that wouldn't otherwise be possible, that type of design seems built for success.

The powers at Fulbright selected me because of my interest in prestressed concrete, so I sat in on Freyssinet's lectures weekly. He also sent me on a trip, up to Scandinavia and then down to Italy, to look at prestressed concrete procedures and report on them to him. There was one point in my Scandinavian trip in which I learned as much about my color as I did about concrete. I ended my Fulbright year delivering a lecture—in French—on the Italians' use of prestressed concrete to engineers, including Freyssinet, at L'École des Beaux-Arts.

Le Corbusier, by contrast, was extraordinary; an aristocratic and handsome Swiss gentleman. He also was quietly inspiring and while where Walter Gropius was a man of the people, Le Corbusier was more of a solitary person. Le Corbusier was also a bit arrogant, although very eloquent. His friends gave him the nickname "Corbu," a play on the word corbeau (raven) and a nod to his raven-like features.

I finally arranged a meeting at his office, which was located in a slum. To get there, I had to make my way through all sort of obstacles before opening this door—and then I was in a new world. I don't know why he worked it that way, but that was Le Corbusier. His place was inconspicuous on the outside but beautiful on the inside. Modern art and sculpture marked Corbu's workplace, which was very clean and simple and uncluttered.

We started speaking in English, but when he realized I was speaking American—not the King's English—we switched to French. Corbu wound up giving me letters of introduction to present at places he'd designed, including a great apartment building in Marseille.

In Corbu's Marseille building, the elevator stopped at every third floor and the apartments were on two levels. With apartments running the width of the building, ventilation flowed all across each suite. The 12-story building, made of rough-cast concrete, has a flat roof and is supported on pilotis, a type of pillar that "suspends" the structure. The building is part of the Unité d'habitation project, which some say launched the Brutalist style of architecture. Beautiful concept. I designed that kind of building when I returned to Cleveland, but couldn't get it past plans.

That was Le Corbusier. I was not with him continuously, just on occasion, to talk about his work—in French, of course. He was impressive.

Meeting of the minds

By a wonderful coincidence, my great teacher Gropius happened to be in Paris when I was there on that Fulbright. When we met for lunch, he

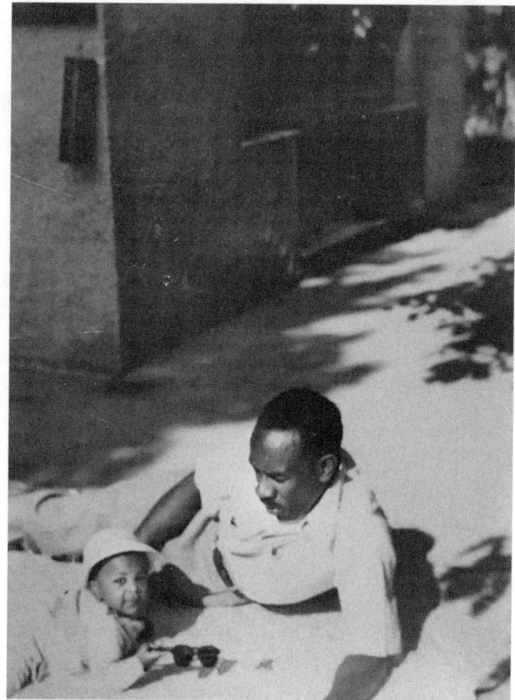

Bob and Jeanne on the French Riviera in 1953.

told me he and Le Corbusier had allied with Mies van der Rohe and other architects, including the Brazilian Oscar Niemeyer, to form the Congrès Internationaux d'Architecture Moderne, an organization dedicated to solving urban problems. Being in the vanguard on such information proved to me that I was keeping illustrious company.

Such men were the pillars of architecture just after the war, when everything had to start over again, everything had to be rebuilt or built anew. Gropius was very much involved in trying to bring people together, whether at the Bauhaus or at the Congrès; he had Jews, Russians, Slovaks, whatever it took. He had the same program at Harvard.

I would eventually strive to do that in my firm, too. Like Gropius, I made sure my company would be inclusive in color and culture and geared toward affordable projects, and I never worked for a rich patron. My work was good but not flamboyant, because we couldn't stress the extras. My projects don't go over budget. I'm not like a noted architect I've worked with, who is said to have once remarked, "A blank check is never enough."

The classes with Freyssinet honed my expertise in prestressed concrete. The conversations with Le Corbusier sharpened my appreciation for architectural risk-taking, for thinking ahead not just as an architect but also as an agent of social change.

A winterlude

That trip up north in the winter of 1953 to further my knowledge of prestressed concrete took me to Copenhagen in Denmark and Oslo in Norway. It also landed me in Elverum, a town in Norway on its border with Sweden, where I was scheduled to catch an express train to Stockholm.

I couldn't speak or read Norwegian, my family didn't know where I was, and I felt very much on my own. When I got off the train from Oslo, I was the only passenger to disembark. The Kongsvinger station was lovely and functional, with room for about 50. Eight people were there when I arrived, and the train wasn't due for an hour and a half.

It was near midnight, but, because I had time to kill, I ordered a cup of coffee and a sandwich at the snack bar. The gracious attendant took my order, then excused himself to make a phone call. A few minutes later, five teenagers entered the place, looked around and left. It was

Two pages from Bob's extensive scrapbook chronicling the European Fulbright trip.

midnight. Ten minutes later, more people showed up, including many little children.

The crowd grew, furtive glances were exchanged, and the stares intensified. Not a word among all these people, mind you. Every time I took a bite, someone would mimic me. I couldn't figure out what was going on. Why are all these people, especially those sleepy little kids, gawking at me?

Finally, it dawned on me: They were there to see a black man, probably the first to stop in this tiny village in many years—if ever. Now I realized what kind of phone calls that clerk had made. Things felt strange.

I smiled at one kid. He smiled back. I called him over, shook his hand, and said "Farvell," which is Danish for "farewell." That broke the ice, I guess. All the people formed a line and, one by one, approached me with hands outstretched. As we shook hands, they looked to see if my color would come off.

All left as quietly as they had arrived, joy in their faces. Joy in my heart, too.

It was time to go, time to board the express to Stockholm. The villagers of Kongsvinger waved me goodbye as the train chugged out of the station. Snow was falling. I have never forgotten the color of that white night.

Taking leave of Europe

My European year with my very young family was an experience none of us would ever forget. Even today, Jeanne swears she remembers lying in the back of our car looking up at the starry French night.

But finally, it was time for my Fulbright-sponsored learning to come to an end, time to return to Cleveland. Time for one more trip, too, before getting on the ship home. In June of 1953, we boarded the SS Mariposa so Jeanne could return to the States as an infant rather than a one-year-old, which would have cost us a lot more due to ticketing rules. But before we left, we spent a week in England, experiencing food that in no way measured up to the culinary delights of France and Italy.

What England lacked in cuisine, it made up for in pomp and ceremony, however. On June 2, 1953, we were in London for the coronation of

Queen Elizabeth, with all the decorations and celebrations on the streets. It was a wonderful spectacle. Who knew we were witnessing the beginning of a reign that would last for over 65 years? And who knew that 65 years later, I'd reflect back on that trip so fondly, with so much to share?

I owe so much to my experiences overseas. When I was in Europe the first time, I was a soldier, fighting to keep my country free. Now, on my second tour of Europe, I was a different man. I was nearly 10 years older, married, a father, a registered architect, a Fulbright scholar, student and colleague of most of the storied architects of the century. But even though I was now a civilian, I was still fighting—to be the best architect possible, to bring honor and economic liberty to my family. My year there made me truly worldly—and made a difference in who I am to this day, 65 years later.

Still, we were eager to return. It was time to head home, and time to start teaching at Howard.

A pencil sketch from Bob's European scrapbook.

CHAPTER SIXTEEN

LAUNCHING THE HOUSE OF MADISON

After my Fulbright, when I joined Howard University as the youngest member of the architecture faculty, it seemed I was destined to advance there, maybe even becoming dean of the school of architecture. I was a Harvard guy and a Paris guy, after all, and I'd studied with Walter Gropius and Le Corbusier.

But that year at Howard was tough, even though it began with such promise. When we returned to the U.S. in the fall of 1953, Jeanne was a lovable and active one-year-old, and I had high hopes. Although I had a wonderful time teaching, I soon felt a chill from other faculty.

I was a popular teacher with a stellar work ethic. After class at Howard, I would go home and make models of buildings and design a city, design

▲

1335 East 105th Street, Cleveland, Ohio, 1954

To have an architectural business, we needed to have an office. Why pay rent when we could own our own building? So we scraped together "friends and family" financing, bought the property for $4,000, and proceeded to turn a residential house into the "House of Madison." We built the first African-American-owned architectural firm in Ohio, and only the 10th in the country, right in the heart of Cleveland's Glenville neighborhood.

a factory, and the students wanted to learn from what I worked on, study with me, learn with me.

I think they appreciated that I was a hands-on professor who stayed late and made himself available on weekends. When the students were working in the studio, I was there, too—there for them. Architecture thrives in company.

The rest of the faculty was much older; in fact, two members had taught me when I was a student more than 10 years earlier. A few of them became quite resentful of me; maybe they felt threatened or intimidated by my success and studies at Harvard and in Europe.

Howard Mackey, the dean of the school of architecture, had an interest in two architectural firms, and other professors had similar arrangements. But nobody there said, "I'm going to make my living exclusively practicing architecture." Nobody was willing to take the chance and step outside that academic comfort zone. I was.

I had other ideas and aspirations: to create great designs, bring great buildings to life, and create jobs and opportunities for black architects. I had to start with creating a job for one important black architect—me. "Somebody's got to do this," I said. "I'll do it. I will start a practice of architecture." My mother had been talking up this very scenario since I was only six years old: "You will be an architect."

Other Howard faculty members were secure in their jobs, and couldn't fathom the real risk and consequences of failure. Mackey warned me if I struck out on my own I could starve to death. I said, "Sure, I could starve to death, but somebody has to do it." The more resistance I encountered, the greater my resolve to go through with this.

Another factor in my decision to strike out on my own was a meeting during which I wondered out loud why Howard couldn't commit to dedicate a design studio in which students could create. That prompted Dean Mackey to convene a faculty meeting where the design studio issue was raised. The other full-time architecture faculty did all they could to prove that my proposal wouldn't work. I felt they were wrong. I still feel that way.

My premise was simple: spend more time with students. Today, I believe some degree of jealousy was in play here. After all, I'd studied in

Instructing young employees in the 1960s.

Cambridge and Paris. I had met and collaborated with the likes of design greats like Mies, Corbu, and Gropius and structural giants like Freyssinet.

What that all added up to was they were becoming increasingly uncomfortable with my popularity with students. I felt like a pariah. Some other path had to open up, even if I had to blaze a trail myself.

When I was coming up, everybody told me there was no such thing as a black architect who could actually make a living from his own practice. I made it my mission to create a business of my own, to making architecture more than an academic project for blacks.

So, in the second semester, I started saying to myself, "Why are we teaching these students architecture but when they graduate there's no real place for them to work? And they don't know anybody in the field?" I was willing to be a mentor and a role model to make a difference in their careers.

I was really disappointed when the faculty didn't even consider my advice on how to better teach these kids. Then, when the discussion moved beyond our profession and became personal, I said, I've got to go. That's when they became rather hostile toward me.

But I never even considered staying. What's the purpose of studying architecture if you don't have a job to work at? Somebody's got to give you opportunities.

It wasn't until years later that I realized that my own attitude and even my wording inadvertently resembled my response to the harsh warning of Western Reserve's Dean Francis Bacon years earlier. But while Bacon's words were driven by prejudice and disdain, the thrust of my inner dialogue was practicality and purpose. This was something that had to be done.

So I talked this over with my wife, and, not surprisingly, she said, "Let's go." She promised she would work to bring in the money we needed to get the Madison architecture firm going. My Leatrice, my business partner, my partner for life.

With Leatrice's support in place, I submitted my resignation. Ironically, the school had actually wanted to promote me. It seems that somewhere in the recesses of the Howard mind was the notion that I would be the next dean of the school of architecture there because I was young, I was a Fulbright scholar, and I had a master's degree. But I was also determined to create my own practice—and to create jobs for other black architects.

When I officially announced my plans to start my own practice, my relationship with Howard's architectural faculty essentially ended. As a matter of fact, just before the Madison family departed D.C., they never even gave me a farewell party, which was the custom in that department. The only acknowledgment came from some terse words from the dean who informed me, "Well, you know, you can starve to death." That wasn't much different from Dean Bacon at Western Reserve mocking me at my graduation about my likely career in a lumberyard. My reply to a disparaging comment was now more measured. I calmly said, "Thank you very much, Dean Mackey." Long past time to move on to the next phase of my career—and my life.

Getting going

Before I could do anything else, I had to make money, and I earned some of the most gratifying commissions of my career designing houses

Exterior of a Froe house, Washington, D.C.

in the nation's capital. The source of these projects was a referral; someone connected me with a black contractor named Froe whose business was just beginning to take off. The Froe brothers asked me to design a house for them; they served as both builders and developers. So I designed a modern, four-bedroom house unlike any they had ever worked with. It was so advanced, people couldn't believe what they were seeing. People were fighting over it. So Froe invited me to keep going, and I did four houses for that company within two months.

I didn't get a lot of money for the Froe work—maybe $250 a house—but those homes were selling like hotcakes. This was modern architecture, advertised as designed by "Walter Gropius' design setter." These were pretty elaborate homes for black people, and they were sizeable, at 3,000 to 5,000 square feet. They were scattered in different neighborhoods of D.C., particularly in the northeastern part of the city.

I have to credit the work I did for the Froe brothers in Washington for laying the foundation of my reputation. Would I be able to do the kind of work I did for the Froe Brothers in Cleveland? I was eager to find out.

My hometown start

So we packed up. My mother was really excited about the move when I told her about our plans. Leatrice was behind me all the way, which in a

Interior of a Froe house showing extensive use of glass, wood and the judicious allocation of space that would figure in many early Madison projects.

way was the seed funding we needed to get the firm off the ground. Thank God for family support.

When I talked to Julian about starting the firm, I found out he was on board, too. So in early June of 1954, we bought a house at 1335 East 105th Street in Cleveland's Glenville neighborhood. We converted the first floor of that two-story house into the first Madison architecture firm office.

We spent June getting everything ready to go for our opening on July 17, 1954, Jeanne's second birthday. The office of Robert P. Madison, Architect was the first one owned by a black man licensed to practice architecture in the state of Ohio. There were all sorts of celebrations and hoopla, and the *Call & Post*, a wonderful newspaper that largely served the black community, did a lot of good things for me, like running articles about Madison the architect. I slowly began to practice in Cleveland, building on knowledge I gained from work I did during my last year at Howard. The only person missing at our wonderful opening that June was my dad, who had died just two years earlier. He never saw this dream come true—at least not its official beginning.

We literally began below ground, remodeling basements for people who wanted recreation rooms. We also converted second floors to living suites in houses in the Glenville area, where, at that time, most of the black people of means lived.

Our beginnings were certainly modest. At our first office, we started with some remodeling, primarily to get fresh paint on the walls. I put a sign out: Robert P. Madison, Architect. I used the first floor for an office, and we rented out the second. We needed all the money we could bring in.

Leatrice never had an official role at the company, but—put it this way—she was the financier. When I came back to Cleveland, I made $400 as architect my first year. Leatrice taught at Miles Standish Elementary, a public school in Cleveland, starting in 1949 when we got married. She retired in 1960, when we moved to Cleveland Heights.

Julian joins in

For the first two years, Julian worked at NASA during the day and did whatever engineering work I needed done—at night. In 1956, he became a registered engineer in the state of Ohio and joined full-time

Julian, far left, Bob and a deacon at Mount Hermon Church grand opening.

in 1957. Changing the name of the firm to Madison Madison marked Julian's spot in the firm.

Julian and I made a great team. Julian was a very aggressive guy who had no fear of calling people he didn't know to turn them into clients who would pay us. Hop in a car or on a plane to travel to a new place—Julian was the guy. When we were having some difficulty getting work, Julian said we could try for some in Abu Dhabi, and he went there to try to scare that up. Later, in the early '70s, we were invited to participate in a national competition to design the University of Abu Dhabi. I studied the Koran and realized that the sexes had to be separate, which raised substantial design considerations. We won an honorable mention, but that's as far as we got. We didn't get the job, but it wasn't for lack of trying or preparation. What we learned by preparing for that competition and from people we met while bidding on other projects would help us grow. Even if we didn't win the projects, that knowledge was all part of the design for the success of our enterprise.

It's a cliché, but truly Julian could sell ice to the Eskimos, and he had quite a professional and personal network. Because he went to Howard, he was very comfortable in the black community. I went to Western Reserve, Harvard and Paris, and I was very comfortable in the white community; together, we could do anything. He could be the lead for blacks, I could be the lead for whites, because whoever the client, at least one of us could make things happen.

Besides, Julian going to Howard for four years meant he had a lot of classmates and a lot of people knew him. These people were spread all over. Julian could call a classmate in Texas and prospect for work. I couldn't do that; all my classmates were white, and they were not the kind of people I could easily call and say, look, I need a favor or a referral.

We built on black business initially, remodeling places first in Cleveland, and secondarily, churches all over. We did churches all over the country—in Niagara Falls, Cincinnati, and Columbus. Howard graduates Julian knew in these cities attended and even led churches, and their A.M.E. connections eventually led to the appointment of Madison Madison as official church architects. The A.M.E. church is both my faith and my business foundation.

Not even the design and development skills of Bob and Julian or the rendering talent of Bernard could ensure that all Madison designs became reality. This $2.5 million project, first proposed in 1959 for 931 East Boulevard in Cleveland, would have brought to life a multipurpose structure modeled after Corbusier's critically acclaimed Marseille apartment building. Nearly 60 years later, the site's land remains vacant.

From left, Bob, Julian, and Bernard Madison along with childhood friend Jesse Strickland at the Medical Associates Building site in Cleveland.

As the business rumbled into life, Leatrice and I also had family concerns. Today, I guess they'd call it a matter of work-life balance. Early on, we arranged for Jeanne to be in daycare at Karamu House, a local multicultural facility that largely serviced the African-American community. But when we moved to Cleveland Heights, Leatrice wanted to be home when Jeannie and our younger daughter, Juliette, came home from school. That would be years later, well after my firm had made its mark.

Fortunately, most of my clients had some familiarity with me from college days, and many were doctors who had a great need for their own offices. These had to be designed to clinical specifications so the doctors could practice much as they could in a regular hospital. We took houses in the Glenville and Central areas, gutted them, and built offices according to what these doctors wanted. They were very happy with us.

In 1957, we won the Mount Pleasant Medical Center job, designing a building for black doctors who couldn't rent offices from whites and didn't

Bob, far right, at the groundbreaking of the Mount Pleasant Medical Center.

have privileges to work in segregated hospitals. The small facility we built at East 139th Street and Kinsman Road won an award for best building design from the AIA.

That same year, I entered Madison Madison Architects into a design competition sponsored by the Ohio Home Builders Association. One of my entry panels received an honorable mention, and another won third prize. There were 250 entrants. Not bad for a black architect no one had ever heard of.

I finally felt professionally validated, because, when I came back to Cleveland, there were a lot of doubters, and not only white people. Whoever heard of a black architect? Me, for one. And my family.

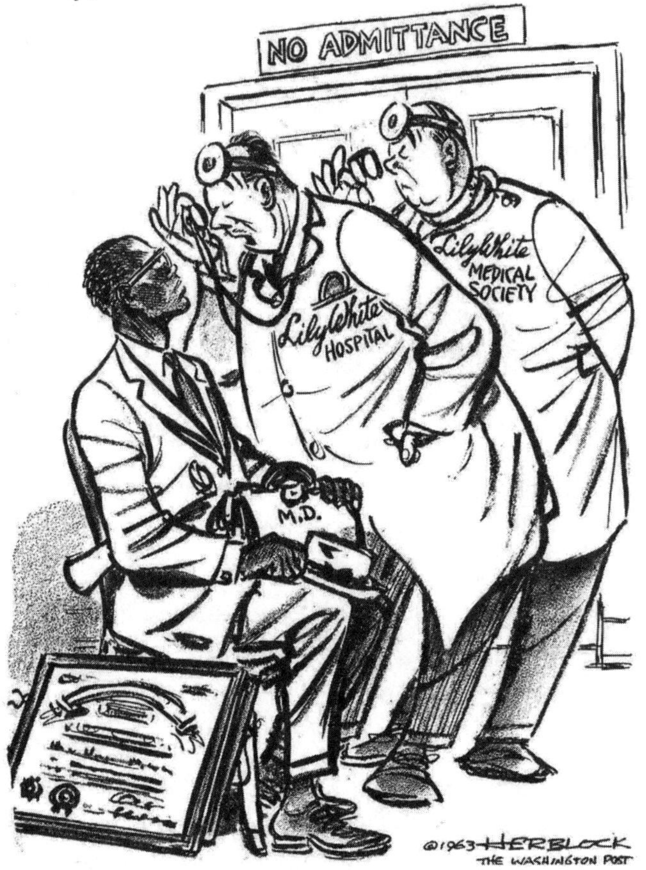

This cartoon by legendary *Washington Post* artist Herbert Block appeared the same year Madison's firm designed the Mount Pleasant Medical Center and just before the Medical Arts building in Glenville. Block's cartoon illustrates the stubborn bigotry black professionals like doctors and architects encountered in the 1960s.

CHAPTER SEVENTEEN
SCALING THE HEIGHTS

As the Madison firm grew, so did my family, and toward the end of the 1950s, I decided it was time to move out of our house on Willowmere Avenue in Cleveland. Our Glenville neighborhood was becoming so crowded, our kids would have had to go to school according to a practice called "relays." While the term sounds dynamic and maybe even like fun, Leatrice and I wanted no part of it for our children.

I did some schooling of Jeanne myself, though it wasn't exactly the academic variety. I think of it as a wildlife lesson.

There was a groundhog that was plaguing the neighborhood; everybody was terrified of this beast. Jeannie and I tracked its habits and eventually discovered it lived under a platform, really just bricks and a wood plank, where we kept the trash cans. Since the groundhog hid underneath

▲

North Park Boulevard home, Cleveland Heights, Ohio, 1960 |
Designed by Madison Madison Architects & Engineers

Nearly 60 years later, I can look back on the house and let go of the hardships and humiliation we had to endure. When I drive or walk by, I try to only see our family, our life, and the joys this house brought to us.

that platform, our first job was to determine how to get it to show itself. This called for teamwork. We had a plan.

Jeannie went upstairs and out onto the second-story porch. Her job was to throw bricks and rocks on the cans to scare the groundhog out. She was up to the task.

After a few bricks came crashing down, the groundhog was roused from its safe space. Ready for action, wearing my Army shirt, I felled the creature with one shot from my .45; as an officer, I was allowed to keep that firearm after my discharge. As for Jeannie, she wasn't repulsed or upset, even though the fatal shot left a basketball-sized bloodstain on the street. I guess my reputation grew. Shooting that critter dead made me the talk of the neighborhood and made Jeannie a street celebrity on her own.

Looking back on the bigger neighborhood picture, the groundhog incident was little more than a diversion. The key issue continued to be education—or its lack.

Students in Glenville schools forced to operate under the relay system only spent a little over half the time on learning. That's because half of the student body was in school from 7 a.m. until noon, the other half from 11 a.m. to 4 p.m. Lunch rooms were crowded and rushed; 20 minutes, back to a classroom crammed with 40 or more students—and harried, overmatched teachers.

The quality of public education was in jeopardy all over the city, but especially in Glenville, one of Cleveland's most densely populated neighborhoods. That's why we decided to make the move. While our decision was all about banking on the future for our children, it also reflected my own past. After all, it was my father and mother who about 25 years earlier decided to move us from the overcrowded schools of Washington, D.C., to the excellence of Cleveland's less crowded public schools.

We wanted better and demanded better. It was time for deliberation and research. We investigated several local communities in search of a better school system for our girls. Following the lead of many of our friends, we considered enrolling Jeanne in an elite private school like Hathaway Brown or Laurel School, both in upscale Shaker Heights.

But after agonizing discussions, Leatrice and I came to this conclusion: Why not move to Cleveland Heights, where Jeanne could walk to a neighborhood school and make friends with kids who lived nearby? In fact, Jeanne later would be enrolled at Roxboro Elementary School just up the street from our house.

We needed better educational opportunities, not to mention room to breathe and grow—and I wanted to design my own house. Achieving all those goals was especially complicated for an upstart black architect like me, no matter how credentialed.

On the rise

Building my house on North Park Boulevard in Cleveland Heights required a stealth operation. Living there, at least at the start, was a stealth operation, too. As we were looking for vacant land on which to build— nobody would sell us an existing house—I ran across two open, contiguous lots. They looked like they would work for me and my friend Charles DeLeon.

We knew we couldn't buy the property, at least not openly, so we called upon a lawyer, who was Jewish and a good friend of Charles'. This fellow bought the land, so his name was listed on the title—but only briefly.

A view looking southward at the Madisons' North Park home.

We didn't know whom to trust except this friend of Charlie's. We also didn't know, initially, that there were two lots involved. The interior lot was bought at a church raffle, and the other was bought at a sheriff's sale. Each lot was purchased by a different buyer, and each buyer was white. To build on that property, we would need to find a way to take ownership of the land. We nevertheless proceeded to design both houses, and just as we were ready to build, we had a quit-claim deed prepared. So when I went to file for a building permit, with a simple procedural filing it became our property. That's how we got the land.

Another hurdle was access to city water; we soon discovered there was no waterline on that corner of North Park Boulevard. Fortunately, there was access to water on another corner and on Delaware Drive nearby, so I gave Charlie an easement in perpetuity to my property to secure water rights for him.

I never actually walked on the site before I built on it; I didn't want to be seen on it because if neighbors saw a black man walking there they'd become suspicious. For historical context, this was years prior to the 1968 Fair Housing Act. Culturally and legally, it was then acceptable to bar blacks from living in certain neighborhoods.

My only option was to drive around the place and sneak a look at it, then sit in a parked car on the street and make sketches to guide the design Those lots were tough; there were boulders, all kinds of large rocks carried to the site by the last ice age. In short, the site was a dump. We had to be creative to build there. And determined.

I put a lot into my new home and there were things about it that I appreciated. But I never could be completely satisfied by that North Park house, even though I lived there for 40 years. When we finally moved away in 2000, Leatrice and I were empty nesters and I was tired of trying to find somebody to pick up the trash, stuff like that. It was time to move, first to Shaker Square, then to Shaker Heights, where we lived until Leatrice passed.

Still, North Park holds all kinds of memories; after all, it was where we raised our kids, and we had a great friendship with another black family, the DeLeons, who lived next door. I designed my house to meet whatever the city fathers in Cleveland Heights required because I didn't want them to turn me down by saying the house wouldn't work. I couldn't let my design stand out; that was how you had to look at it. It's got a pitched gable roof, like all the other houses in the neighborhood. It blends in. It was designed to get by.

But long before we moved in, we had to clear the way. And I'm not just talking about just boulders or waterlines. I'm talking about racism.

The Madison mission

All I wanted was for my family to move from our overcrowded neighborhood in Glenville to North Park. Moving from the ground floor of our inner-city duplex meant my girls would get a better education. We felt hopeful about the move, which on balance turned out to be a good one. But the neighborhood sure was different—and better.

In our old neighborhood, the guy across the street had a Cadillac he washed and polished every day of the week. That was his prize, his pride and joy. Nothing against him—he was a nice guy and seemingly a good husband and father—or any other neighbors there, but, for the sake of ourselves and our children, we aspired to more.

We sought something different, and we were running to something, not running away. We weren't satisfied with where we were so we were on the hunt for higher things. If that ultimately meant the need to compromise with Cleveland Heights over the design and construction of our house, so be it.

We looked forward to a new beginning at a time when everybody was talking about integration. We were hopeful we could inspire a conversation about race that would lead to positive social change. I fought for that then; always have, always will. We were on a mission. I still am.

I would like my girls to go to school here, I told the city of Cleveland Heights, so I promised to build whatever city officials wanted me to build, and that's what I did. In a different time and place, I would have had the opportunity to design and build a house I loved unconditionally. But I needed to stake my claim in a new community. So I designed the house to comply with whatever those people wanted so they couldn't say, "Oh, this

Everyday family life inside the North Park home.

house has been rejected" because the property owner was me, Robert P. Madison, that black architect.

I finished the drawings with Charlie, my next-door neighbor, took them to Cleveland Heights City Hall—"Oh, thank you, sir. This is very good. We'll put them in a file and get to them pretty soon"—and then I left.

A couple of weeks later, I called, and someone from the building department said, "Are you Mr. Madison?" I said yes. "Could we see you, please?"

I went to City Hall and identified myself as architect Robert Madison representing Mr. and Mrs. Robert Madison.

"Is that you?" "Yeah."

"We didn't know you were building this."

Despite this expression of doubt and surprise, the building permit process got underway, keeping me in suspense for four weeks. Still, once I'd written that easement so my neighbor could hook up to the waterline, and after we had those unbelievable rocks cleared—I'm sure they're the reason nobody had built there—Cleveland Heights finally issued the permit.

Crossing the color line

It happened that right across the street was a professional named J. Byers Hayes. Hayes was one of the best architects in town at that time, and he was a good guy, a member of AIA who backed me when I pushed to get in. Byers also supported me in landing my first job out of Western Reserve. "That boy is going to go far," I overheard him tell Robert A. Little. "He's a unique guy."

Just after I opened my office in 1954, Byers told me that following these three rules was essential to practicing architecture:

1. *Get the job.*

2. *Get the job.*

3. *Get the job.*

At North Park, my job—both as architect and father—was to get my house built. I preferred to do that discreetly; the last thing I could afford was to make waves. Not a chance. Despite my efforts, boy, did I become big news in that neighborhood.

One day, Byers called me up and said, "Bob, I hear that some black architect bought land and is planning on building right across the street from me."

"You say a black architect?"

"You know anything about it?" he said. "Yup," I said.

"Who is it?" "Me."

"Why didn't you tell me?"

"Why should I?"

"Because 20 years ago, another black fellow tried to build a house on the street, and people got together and bought him out. I'm going to have a meeting soon, and all the neighborhood's going to come by."

I was puzzled to hear this from someone who'd been in my corner earlier, or so I thought. Our conversation was friendly but perplexing. With hindsight, I see that maybe Hayes was testing me or putting in place a plan I couldn't understand. No matter—our exchange felt like a weird rite of passage. That feeling only intensified the day before the meeting, when Byers asked me to give him my buyout price.

"I don't have a price," I told him.

"Come on, Bob. Everybody has a price," he countered.

I said, "OK, $250,000 per house." So it was on the table: $500,000 in exchange for walking away and not building two houses on that property. Armed with both that information and résumés from Charlie and me that he had requested, Hayes shook my hand and said we'd have to see how things turned out. A few days later, I heard the story of that meeting.

First, Hayes told everybody "We're going to have some new people living on our street. One's a very good architect, with two little girls. And the other is a medical doctor, a big psychiatrist at the university, with three children." The neighbors at the meeting laughed and said, "Oh, we don't need more doctors and architects." Their jokes seemed like self-congratulation for living in such an elite neighborhood. Hayes told his neighbors that Charlie and I were true professionals and our wives had college degrees, too. Everybody said that was wonderful. Hayes then delivered the kicker: "One more thing about them—they're colored."

"There was just silence," Hayes told me. "You could hear a pin drop." Finally, somebody said, "Buy him out."

Hayes explained our buyout terms. More silence. No offers. They decided they didn't want to spend all that, proving that even prejudice has a price ceiling.

I felt that Hayes had set up his neighbors and smoothed our move into Cleveland Heights.

Welcome to the neighborhood.

CHAPTER EIGHTEEN
WELCOME TO THE NEIGHBORHOOD

Now that the city of Cleveland Heights and the neighbors had finally given me the green light, I was eager to get my house built. Clearing the land was a pain, but fortunately, the issue of race was no problem for me, at least not on the construction side: Kares Construction was the contractor. Frank Kares, who was white, knew me from our work together on Mount Hermon Baptist Church on East 40th Street. The church, which I designed, is in Cleveland's Central neighborhood.

Kares had no issue building my house. That took about eight months, and, at every step of the way, I did everything I could to conform to what was in the neighborhood already so nobody could say, for example, that I

▲

Mt. Hermon Baptist Church, Cleveland, Ohio, 1958 |
Designed by Madison Madison Architects & Engineers

As an architect, your buildings are like your children. You dream of them, they're conceived, nurtured, and all along you agonize—did you take the right approach? Will they have a full and productive life? If an architect and a father is fortunate, he's equally proud both when his creation is new and when it's mature, standing proud, still productive, still beautiful. As both the architect of Mount Hermon, and the father of two amazing women, I'm quite fortunate.

used the wrong kind of brick. We didn't want to give anybody any reason to reject the house.

If I'd had my way, I would have built a larger home—this one came in at about 2,500 square feet—and I would have built it taller, with the garage on the lower level and the living space on the upper. That configuration would have enabled us to more fully appreciate views of picturesque Doan Brook winding through the Shaker Lakes into Rockefeller Park. That sight is beautiful in all seasons.

We did have an open floor plan with large expanses of glass on the back and an interior courtyard we could enjoy without being seen from the street. The house's design placed a priority on privacy. I guess you could say it looked both inward and over its shoulder.

The house couldn't shield us from who we were, however; it didn't change our color. Over the years, we endured expressions of racial violence, from threatening phone calls to a neighborhood woman refusing to use the sidewalk in front of our home. Once, during construction, someone even tried to burn our house down.

Homeland insecurity

You don't realize what you're taking on when you move, especially if you're the first black in an all-white community. You attract a lot of hate.

Our family was so radioactive that every time this one lady reached the lot across from us, she turned right around and walked back to her house. She didn't want to be anywhere near us, didn't even want to admit our existence. Every day, when she walked her dog, she'd cross the street so she wouldn't touch our sidewalk.

We also got letters. One from the Ku Klux Klan began, "Niggers go back to Africa."

The first two years were tough, for sure, but that's the price you pay when you push. We weathered it all, even though I admitted later we didn't know what we were doing and what we were getting into. This was new territory. We were trying to do what we thought it meant to live the American way.

A Madison family portrait with matriarch Nettie Madison at the center, circa 1958.

Homeland security

Actually, once we moved in, the house itself was kind of cool, especially after dealing with those big rocks, either by clearing them or working them into the landscape.

Seeing our North Park home being built was special. As an architect, I had marshaled the progress of scores of buildings, from blueprint to excavation to checking off the final punch list items and declaring the project complete. But this was much more than a project. This was our home.

I especially appreciated the work of artisans in the building trades. What I remember most about one guy who installed the floor is his great rhythm in laying the tile. Watching the way he moved when he troweled the mastic in swirling motions reminded me of the rhythm of dance.

The Canadian redwood I specified for the ceiling was beautiful, too. As for the palette of the walls, I purposely painted with anything but white—white isn't the most calming color—so there was a bright orange wall, a blue wall, and a lot of natural light. I wanted this house, my official entry into white society, to feel as open as possible even as it guarded our privacy. A lot of strategically placed glass in the house allowed in light and wonderful views, but at the same time, it was designed to mask the hostile eyes of strangers.

I made a number of fixtures specifically for that house, like little trays for pencil leads to hang in front of the stereo speakers. Jeanne and I even made furniture together. Although she was only eight when we moved in, she learned how to drive a nail straight, how to blunt a nail point to avoid splitting wood, the difference between a Phillips and slotted head screwdriver—she learned skills while making all kinds of things.

I also taught her why our Knoll furniture and Eames chairs are so distinctive. And I told Jeanne something I learned early on: Architects and conductors live a long time because nobody gives them their greatest commissions until they are older. Architects and conductors are often in the vanguard, too. They are all about advancing their fields— and, in my case, about social change. Not only were Leatrice and I in the right location for that, we were in the right position. We were the perfect couple for an imperfect and difficult but necessary job.

Becoming comfortable in our new home took some time. Fortunately, many parents in the neighborhood tried to be friendly, and we cultivated friends. We also joined organizations we thought we could help in driving social change.

More than friends

First, Leatrice joined the PTA and eventually became its president; after all, she'd been a schoolteacher. She soon became a prodigious civic leader, serving in such organizations as Case Western Reserve University, the Cleveland Heights/University Heights Curriculum Committee, Harambee: Services to Black Families, Planned Parenthood, Cuyahoga County Juvenile Court, Women's League AIA, Blue Cross of Northeastern Ohio, Karamu House, United Way, the Cleveland Orchestra and the Western Reserve Historical Society. Years later, I was very proud to nominate Leatrice for a citation from the University of Chicago, particularly considering how modestly she began.

In 1994, her alma mater honored her by proclaiming that Leatrice Branch Madison had "given time to more than eighty-five committees and thirty-five agencies. ... Her commitment to human rights is evinced by her involvement in the Urban League, the NAACP, and the Cleveland Heights Citizens for Human Rights."

While Leatrice was doing her part, I plunged into involvement in the community as my work life allowed. I was proud to be asked to join St. Paul Episcopal Church. An imposing architectural landmark with a bell tower soaring nearly 100 feet, St. Paul's is home to a large and influential congregation. I became an usher. Our children took part in that church's Christmas pageant and everything was going well. I would go to church every Sunday, and I met all kinds of people. Our engagement there was one reason Cleveland Heights began to feel like home. I had high hopes for St. Paul and wanted that church to help me realize them, particularly given the tone of the times.

One Sunday in 1968, while Cleveland's Hough neighborhood was still burning, I was particularly eager to hear the message the preacher would deliver. Would he instruct us on our duty to help promote peace and civility? Would he work to broaden and unite the community?

No. Instead, he started talking about a sculpture of the hands of grace some British artist had given the church. I sat there for an hour, waiting for him to say something about the Hough riots. Even though the Rev. Dr. Martin Luther King Jr. had spoken from that very pulpit five years earlier, this preacher didn't say a word about what was going on a few miles away.

Nothing.

So I wrote a letter to the bishop telling him that, while Hough was burning, the preacher was talking about some gift from England.

Nothing. I never heard a word. In the same way that a threat can be just as destructive as an action, "nothing" can be the worst response of all. To be true to myself, I knew I had to do something. So I rescinded my membership in St. Paul's to return to my old church, St. John A.M.E. I wasn't bitter, just disappointed that lasting change takes so long.

Consider the slow change of complexion in Cleveland Heights, which had a black population of 1 percent when we moved there—and only 2 percent even 10 years later.

Inch by inch

I continued to do my part, attending meetings of people working to do the right thing, and there were bridge clubs and discussion groups. Pretty soon, it became clear that few of our neighbors had credentials to match mine and Leatrice's, let alone our educational achievements. Also, I had my own firm for many years and grew accustomed to not needing outside direction or approval.

Slowly, we began to be invited to places we had never been, and most of the time, we were the first people of color to be asked. We belonged to a group called Living Room Learning. This group's members, from both the black and white communities, invited us to meetings where we talked about the challenges and opportunities associated with integration.

I didn't just feel like a token; that's because I actually was one, at least at first. But being mere tokens was not our goal. Leatrice and I had vowed that neither of us would settle for that. Instead, the special couple that we were would be a worthy, accepted part of greater society even as our qualities set us apart. We would do what others did, yet argue and fight for what we believed in. For example, the opera association used to be all-white and largely Italian, but a Jewish guy who owned a mattress company invited me to join. His wife even asked me to dinner at the Union Club. She said, "Bob, I want you to join the opera board." She knew I loved *Aida*. She knew I would contribute.

It didn't matter that I was black. I was an opera association donor, and I knew and loved opera. Association members really wanted to have people who were knowledgeable. They would have these black-tie opening nights where we'd go to dinner just like anybody else.

Madison family portrait, 1963.

After I had spent about 10 years as a trustee of the Cleveland Opera, the Cleveland Orchestra was looking for somebody to join its board. I joined because I liked it; I also felt it was time such boards be more representative of our country. Funny how society opens up in these small but important ways.

I decided we could be useful in such roles, and as we were invited to join one group after another, we decided to become involved in places where we would have the greatest impact. After the PTA, Leatrice joined the Women's League of the AIA and ultimately became its president. In addition to serving on the opera and orchestra boards, I became a trustee of Case Western Reserve University—nearly three decades after Western Reserve refused me admission because of the color of my skin. Sometimes, society progresses inch by inch rather than by giant steps.

Not quite neighborly

No matter the environment, the biggest concern for my wife and me remained our two children. For example, some guy called us up the day before we moved into North Park and said, "You going to walk your kids to school?" A veiled threat like that is an assault in and of itself. My wife stopped teaching so she could be home for the kids and monitor their safety.

At the same time, many people were quite welcoming. There was a group called Parents for Justice, and we would meet with white people at different houses in the neighborhood. We'd talk about socialization and how we could make things better.

I'm sure my daughters would agree that Leatrice and I led serious lives. Not that there was never any fun—we took family vacations every summer—but we were thinkers, we were serious, we weren't about small talk. The environment in the house was very intense, with a lot of discussions about civil rights, politics, the environment. Neighborhood gossip was not on the menu.

We didn't just sit around the dinner table and say, Oh, you know the Joneses down the street just got back from Jamaica and that's so fun. Wouldn't it be great if we could all go on a beach vacation? We didn't talk about that. We might talk about how the Joneses just supported this referendum that's going to be bad for the city, so what are we going to do about it? We led purposeful lives. I worked all the time, and Leatrice had an office at home in North Park where she would write notes and record minutes, come up with ideas and call people for meetings.

Leatrice would read the newspapers every day and we'd watch the news on TV three times a day. This was all about keeping up, keeping our mission of social change going. Always having to prove ourselves could become tiring—it's no way to live—but it was necessary. One way to do that was to keep up with what was happening in the world. Do that and you won't be caught off guard.

We tried to integrate. We tried to be both welcome and welcoming. We joined a bridge club that met every month. But even though the sailing was relatively smooth for Leatrice and me, the children had a more difficult time. Jeannie was called names, and worse. She got it from all directions.

When it came to high school, we wanted her to attend Cleveland Heights High. Now, we lived on North Park, which was upper-class. Black kids made it clear they didn't like Jeannie because she was from North Park Boulevard. Sometimes they even beat her. And the white kids didn't like her simply because she was black. Such dynamics explain Leatrice's decision to stay home during the day. Somehow, though, the kids got through.

To this day, I feel badly about Jeannie and what she had to endure. When we realized how very unhappy she was, we transferred her from Heights High to Lutheran East, a private school a few miles away. I was disappointed that the reason we moved east—the public schools we so badly wanted to believe in—had failed us. The move to Cleveland Heights, at best, was problematic. At least for the first few years.

Juliette had an easier time when we enrolled her in kindergarten in the Cleveland Heights public schools. Since the main reason we moved there was the city schools, Leatrice and I decided we needed to give that one more shot. Quickly, Juliette became friends with a white classmate, a little girl named Martha McCorkle, who lived nearby. Martha's parents were doctors, and they had friends of all kinds. They welcomed us.

Martha had to walk by our house on her way to school, so she'd pick up Juliette. They did that all through Heights High, so Juliette had a kind of protection. She's still best friends with Martha.

Jeanne and little sister Juliette in their North Park home. Jeanne is a socially engaged businesswoman and actress who lives in Cleveland, Since 1979, Juliette, an artist who works in ceramics and fused glass, has lived in D.C., where she creates schematic layouts for property renovation. The playful joke between Juliette and her father is he tells her she should have been an architect.

Six years earlier, Jeannie had it a little tougher. But times change, and, when Martha said she would be happy to walk Juliette to school, the offer was genuine and welcome. Maybe change was actually happening.

Tough enough

The end result of our daughters' exposure to racism was this: Jeanne and Juliette stand up to anybody, white or black, because they had to in school. Back then, many black high school graduates wanted to go to historically black colleges. But since our girls already had confronted and overcome adversity in public schools, Jeannie went to Western Reserve and Juliette decided on Boston University.

And despite earlier reservations and tribulations, we liked our place. We had a nice house across the street from a park we could explore, and we got to know people in the neighborhood, like Bob Morse, the president of Western Reserve University. I would visit him at his house before I was appointed a trustee of Western Reserve.

I was trying to be a good citizen. Not trying to be quiet, just trying to be a good, engaged citizen. I think if anything is to come of telling my life story, it's that we lived, or tried to live, an exemplary life. I was also trying to be a good neighbor.

When challenges bubbled up and we didn't know where the hostility was coming from, we just said that's how some people are. And we kept on going.

Sure, we faced genuine challenges, but we were so busy living through them that's it's only now, 60 years later, that I can fully appreciate that era. Moving to Cleveland Heights taught me that being a good neighbor and being a good citizen can be the same thing.

Moving ahead

We joined all kinds of organizations, because we wanted to make a statement: that our people could do anything anybody else could. Slowly, seeing people of color participate in every aspect of society, occupying every social and professional position, was becoming the norm.

As citizens, we thought we had to make a contribution. That's what citizens do. My mother always said you've got to lead, and you've got to try to make a path for others to follow. We did that. We tried very hard to be representatives of who we were. After all, some of the Americans we met in Northeast Ohio had never interacted with a black person until they met us.

At that time, blacks and whites were far more segregated than they are now, one of the reasons the '60s were so combustible, particularly in the inner city. Literally combustible.

The Madisons moved into Cleveland Heights well before the Hough riots of July 1966 and the Glenville shootout that followed two years later.

Closer to home in the Little Italy neighborhood? I didn't dare venture there. Go down Mayfield Road during the hot mid-August evenings for the Feast of the Assumption back then, and you wouldn't see a single black face. Ironic that only 20 years earlier in Italy, this black man was treated as a hero, a friend, and more. Back home in America, though—different story.

I remember one time when I was a student at Western Reserve and six of us went to a legendary restaurant in Little Italy for dinner. My friend, Phil Hart, said he wanted a table for six. "I count five," the maître d' said. Six people walked out on that guy. Society may have not progressed far enough from that incident or when I was snubbed at Lake Shore Country Club, but the support of friends and colleagues was encouraging.

On North Park, I could at least communicate with other professionals. Some were very hostile, some were preoccupied and just didn't care. Others were genuinely eager to help America become what it could and should be. Still, we all had a long way to go, particularly in those turbulent '60s.

CHAPTER NINETEEN

1968

If things were brittle on North Park and dicey in Little Italy, they were nowhere near as tense and violent as they were in the city of Cleveland lower down, just over three miles from the Glenville home we had left. I remember a killing at the top of Cedar Hill in July 1968. The victim was Tedd Browne, a black folk singer on his way home from a meeting with his lawyer. The shooter had carved an "N" on his gun, signaling his intent to shoot "the first nigger to come up Cedar Hill." Browne, who was said to be a good friend of Cleveland Mayor Carl B. Stokes, was murdered while sitting in his car.

No way could I have known it then, but 1968, a seminal year for all kinds of people and all kinds of reasons, was not quite the halfway mark in my career. At that time, my company was known as Madison Madison, reflecting my alliance with my brother Julian, the engineer whose structural and mechanical expertise ensured my designs would become reality.

▲

Medical Center Courts, Detroit, Michigan, 1964 |
Designed by Madison Madison Madison

As an architect, you never know exactly when or how your next project will find its way into your office. In this moderate-income public housing urban renewal project, a former client for a church design was our champion.

Early in our careers, Julian and I worked together on churches, houses, a bank, even an impressive funeral home for a leader in the community. But in the late '60s, our work entered a different, more impressive phase. Signifying that was the commission we earned to design the U.S. Embassy in Dakar, Senegal. This was a prestigious, complicated project that was put on hold until the latter part of the '70s, when the Vietnam War finally ended, freeing federal resources.

Which brings me to reflect on 1968, a momentous year not only for me and my firm but for the country as a whole. That was the year in which both Martin Luther King Jr. and Robert F. Kennedy were assassinated. It also was a signature year in the ongoing escalation of the Vietnam War, which I was against from the start.

Closer to home, there was the Glenville shootout in late July, when gunfire in one of Cleveland's poorest neighborhoods left seven dead, including three Cleveland policemen, and launched several days of riots. The city still bears shootout scars; that bloody stretch may have marked the depths of racial discord here. Besides, the Glenville riots marked the beginning of the end for Carl Stokes, Cleveland's first black mayor, a very exciting man whose campaign I championed early on.

Hard to believe in 1968 I was 45 years old and not yet in the prime of my career. That was 50 years ago. Hard to believe today I'm 95.

During 1968, that tangled year, Julian and I worked to get projects in the South, going after the Atlanta airport project and several others. Going through an airport and getting on a plane, seeing the tension of people in the shocked aftermath of the King and Kennedy assassinations, was quite uncomfortable.

I remember visiting Tuskegee Institute in Alabama to design its Engineering and Nuclear Facility. The way down was tricky, though, especially for a black man. While I could sit anywhere in the Atlanta airport, I had to sit in the colored section when I transferred at Pensacola. That era was fraught with all sorts of anxieties.

I recall feeling that all the progress that had been made—Carl Stokes' election, the ascendance of black mayors in Gary, Indiana, and Newark, New Jersey,what seemed like real empowerment for African-Ameri-

Cities that represent the Madison firm's expansion (corporate offices and locations of field offices at major projects) in the United States from the 1960s through the 1980s.

cans—had ground to a halt. All of a sudden, with the King and Kennedy murders, it seemed there was a significant segment of the country that didn't believe in all these advances. Rather than build our country and society up, they were willing to tear everything down. Still, we just kept going, because keeping going was the only choice. Always is.

Yes, we had made progress in civil rights, with passage of the Fair Housing Act of 1964, the Voting Rights Act of 1965 and the Freedom of Information Act the following year.

The inroads black professionals like me were making were encouraging, too. But continuing, legal segregation like I experienced in the Pensacola airport were maddening reminders of how far we still had to go. It wasn't easy to keep the faith that deadly spring and summer.

A frozen moment

On April 4, the day of Martin Luther King Jr.'s assassination, I was in Washington, D.C., designing the Industrial Bank of Washington. Vice President Hubert Humphrey had convened a meeting. I'm not sure what group it was, but I was there that Thursday. Anyhow, at 7 p.m., just as the meeting was slated to begin, Humphrey stepped up to the platform and said, "Ladies and gentlemen, Martin Luther King has been killed."

When Humphrey said King had been assassinated, the room went silent and sorrowful. The gathering, stilled by the awful news, represented a coalition of political people; we all tried to get Humphrey elected president—black and white, men and women, everybody.

There must have been 250 people there, and after hearing this stunning news, we stumbled out of the room in shock.

That same night, Juliette was in our North Park home watching the news when the announcer interrupted to say MLK had been shot. Juliette could tell that this was important and ran upstairs to tell her mother. But Juliette didn't break the news to Leatrice. She had already learned of the tragedy from me.

"Oh, my God," Leatrice said. "Oh, my God!" She was a nervous wreck but she composed herself long enough to tell me I had to come home. A few hours later, I was glad to see Leatrice and Juliette when they came to pick me up at the Cedar Road train station. We stayed in the house that night; it was all we could do.

Life goes on, however. Leatrice and I had scheduled a vacation in Jamaica for that month, putting us there when King's funeral took place. All of Jamaica mourned the loss of MLK, with parades and bands playing in celebration of his life. But the feeling was more bitter than sweet.

When just a couple of months later Bobby Kennedy was gunned down, it was, like, "What's happening to this world? Is everybody crazy?" I was in Cleveland the Wednesday Kennedy was killed. It was incredible; we couldn't believe it. That's when John F. Kennedy's widow, Jacqueline, married this Greek guy, Aristotle Onassis—to get her kids out of harm's way. They were killing Kennedys, she said.

Despite these horrors, I felt—no, I believed—that a power shift was in the works.

The view from midway

There I was, 45 years old, and my company was nearly 15 years old. Little did I know that the best was yet to come.

When Carl Stokes beat Seth Taft to become mayor of Cleveland, it meant that blacks—finally—had power, and not just the political kind. Soon, we could see that a lot of work was in store for Madison Madison.

Over the next few years, with the election of other black mayors, there was a sense that power was slowly being transferred to minorities. There was fresh confidence, backed by reality. We could go to Newark and have an audience with the mayor or development director, something not possible before. And in Atlanta, there was Mayor Maynard Jackson, whom I knew from socializing with him at Western Reserve. Stokes, however, was the first to give us power and lead the way.

The Stokes effect

There was a heady sense of arrival when Stokes was elected mayor of Cleveland on November 7, 1967, the same day Gary Hatcher was elected mayor of Gary. All of a sudden, it seemed, blacks were in charge of some very important cities.

When Stokes decided to run for mayor, it was quite an event. Up until that time, African-Americans, colored people—whatever you want to call us—would not participate actively in the government of our city because black people just couldn't get elected. And they were worried about the racial divide.

As a matter of fact, at that time, black people typically didn't go beyond University Circle going east. The city of Cleveland was where nearly everybody lived who was black. African-American lawyers, architects, engineers, even salespeople, lived in the city because we couldn't move elsewhere.

The West Side was pretty much all white, the East Side pretty much all black, with the Cuyahoga River as the dividing line. Some progress had already been made: Charles Carr was a councilman, Lawrence Payne was a prominent black lawyer and ward leader, and a number of colored politicians began to get elected to council. African-American architects, incidentally, were not even on the radar—yet.

So when Stokes decided to mount his first run for mayor in 1965, we said, why not? He was a charismatic person and we had nothing to lose. Stokes narrowly lost that first bid to incumbent Ralph Locher, so we said, don't give up. After all, he had made a good showing, partially thanks to a substantial black turnout.

When we began to mobilize for his second run, in 1967, I was prepared to leave my company and work in the Stokes administration as its public housing specialist. Both Stokes and I had once lived in Outhwaite Homes, Cleveland's first federally funded housing project for the poor. Both of us had risen far, and it seemed we shared a point of view.

I told Stokes I could write all his urban renewal material and be his adviser on public housing. Urban renewal was hot—not to mention a hot potato—at that time.

In the mid-'60s, urban renewal was a program that aimed to tear down dilapidated slums in the inner city and build other, better kinds of buildings. Whether those new buildings would be for the current residents or somebody new was not the issue.

The timing of Stokes' second mayoral run was perfect: After the 1965 election, the Locher administration's poor management of urban renew-

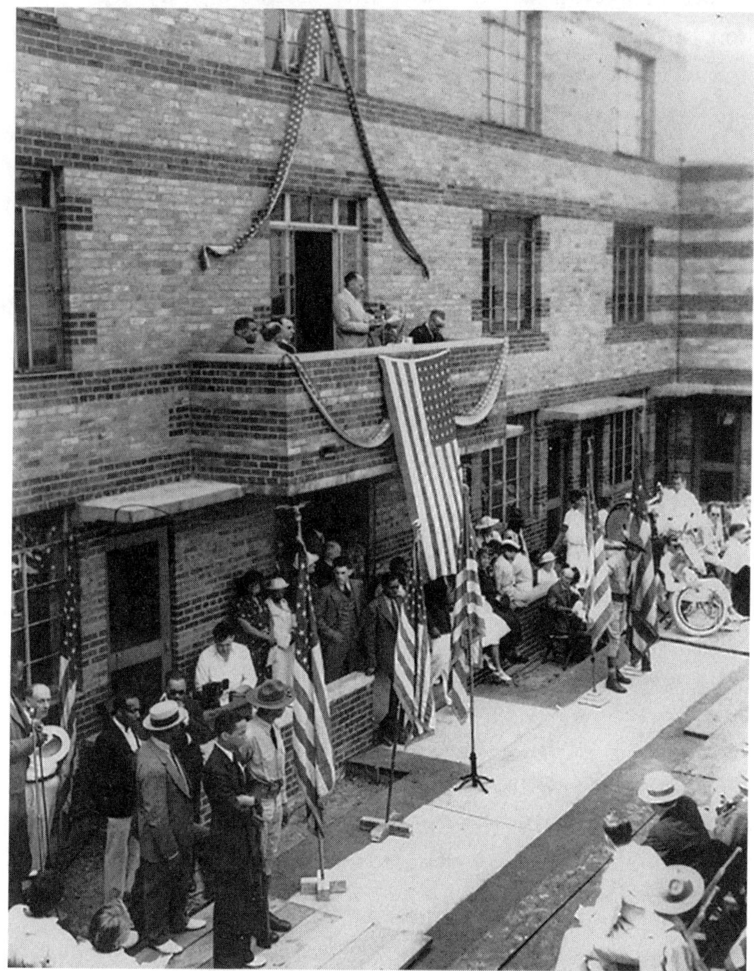

Outhwaite Homes dedication, 1945. Groundbreaking Cleveland Mayor Carl B. Stokes grew up in the Outhwaite projects, while Madison lived there with his family for a short time after he returned from the war.

al became the target of heavy negative media coverage. The media also slammed Locher for his handling of the Hough riots in July 1966.

So, as Locher's star began to fade, more people began to gravitate toward Stokes, including Dr. Kenneth Clement, who was quite a power himself. A prominent surgeon and a former president of the local NAACP, Clement, a brilliant strategist, became Stokes' campaign manager. Clement, the well-known politician Arnold Pinkney, and I were particularly close to Stokes—a kind of kitchen cabinet.

We began to campaign hard. We went out to raise money, mainly among blacks, though a lot of whites came along for the ride, too. They said Stokes seemed like a pretty good guy.

After he beat Locher in the Democratic primary, Stokes faced Seth Taft, a well-known Republican and an establishment politician. Taft was a member of the Union Club and the grandson of President William Howard Taft. Stokes, in stark contrast, was the grandson of a slave, and his mother was a cleaning woman at the Union Club. Stokes couldn't even enter the Union Club—except, maybe, as kitchen help. I wasn't welcome there either.

Anyhow, Stokes came along at the right time, and we began to get behind him. We started a movement, and people began to believe it could really happen. We worked hard.

I stopped practicing architecture to be with Stokes at all committee meetings, strategizing with Pinkney and Clement. For the first time, African-American professionals—an architect, a doctor, a politician, lawyers, all these important people who lived in the city—were getting behind Carl Stokes.

Stokes began campaigning on the West Side, because he needed the west-side vote to win. Since he was a very handsome guy, well-dressed, and a charmer, when he got across the river, many people who were prepared to hate him fell in love with him instead. Stokes is our kind of guy, they thought.

In Cleveland, people who supported him were mostly blacks, along with some whites. Of course, you had to have that in a city where at that time blacks made up a third of the voting population. There were not a lot of white people donating money to Stokes, or to the organization supporting him. It was Carl Stokes and a core group of us going to the West Side, wondering whether we'd come back alive after talking with white folks over there. We got people out to vote who had never voted before.

Then the debates began, and it was clear that Taft knew all about government. Stokes had been in the legislature in Columbus and was politically savvy, too. But Taft had been a county commissioner and seemed a natural to become the next mayor since he had local administration experience. It was shaping up to be quite a race.

I will never forget the last debate at the City Club of Cleveland. Both sides did very well. Taft was on the attack for at least half of his 20 minutes; Stokes was less personal. Taft called Stokes an "absentee legislator" and "absentee Democrat."

Taft administered the coup de grace, or so we thought at first, when he said, "Carl, you have missed so many sessions in the legislature, you don't deserve to be the mayor." How would Stokes come back from that?

Time was running out on the radio broadcast, so they let the debate run long, and Stokes countered with a letter from Taft saying, "Congratulations, Mr. Stokes. You have a wonderful legislative record." That quotation shot down Taft's "absentee legislator" claim. Once Stokes read all of the letter, it was wonderful. Taft had forgotten he'd written it, and Stokes turned everything around.

So that November 7, Stokes was elected. He took 50.5 percent of the vote that year, and did that again in 1969, when he beat Republican Ralph Perk to win a second term. The whole town—black and white—went crazy, mostly in a good way. At that time, there were no black judges, no black legislators in Congress representing Ohio.

Actually, in 1966, Edward W. Brooke, a Massachusetts Republican, became the first black senator since Reconstruction. I knew Brooke very well, from Howard. We both served in the Italian campaign, and I learned that, after the war, he was courting an Italian woman, Regina Ferrari-Scacco, whom he would eventually marry.

Bob Madison and Carl Stokes shake on success in 1967.

But Stokes' election, as far as we were concerned, began a slow, snowball effect that had folks saying, "We can be elected. We can win." We always had the hope and faith that blacks could be elected to positions of power. Now we had an example. We had proof.

Faith stood me in good stead then; it has never failed me. My mother was always saying, you got to pray, the Lord knows what's happening, and He'll take care of you. Our concern was always about keeping on doing what we could. My faith and determination kept us going.

Determination also got Stokes elected as the first African-American mayor of a major city. On the day he won his first two-year term, I remember thinking we were over the top now. It wasn't that he was omnipotent or omniscient, but his election meant that, at last, we had power, and people of color could actually win. He also had a white constituency that backed him, of course. To me, his victory felt like the beginning of the realization that this was America, a country in which the races understood each other and could cooperate and even coordinate. I think that was the essence of that year and of several to come.

The Stokes legacy

When Carl Stokes became mayor, he turned everything around, and momentum began to build. In a way, Barack Obama was a recipient of Stokes' great big snowball forty years later, when he won the first of two terms as the nation's first African-American president.

Like Jackson in Atlanta and Hatcher in Gary, Stokes was in touch with his constituency. For example, the city of Cleveland needed a new police station, which meant it needed an architect, which meant it needed contractors. When people asked if there were any African-American architects and the response was no, Stokes said, look for one.

That's when I got involved in city work. Mayor after mayor across the country also began to find African-American architects and engineers who could do that work—because they looked for them. You can't find what you don't seek. And you can't get hired if you're not given a chance.

The momentum didn't flag, even though Stokes lost political power after the Glenville shootout. His unraveling started when reports showed that some money from Cleveland Now!, an ambitious, federally funded program designed to foster black entrepreneurship, had actually been spent on guns used by Black Power advocates involved in the shootout.

While Stokes wasn't blamed for the shooting, he was held accountable for giving Cleveland Now! money to the wrong people. His decline began.

Still, Stokes had been able to shake up the establishment and make it more inclusive, resulting in more African-Americans in government leadership roles. What he did was change the orientation of city government to one for all of the people rather than for some of the people. And not in Cleveland alone.

Power is power. We felt strongly that at last we in Cleveland had achieved something never done before. Those achievements began to have an effect on the national scene. In 1968, Shirley Chisholm from Texas became the first African-American woman elected to the U.S. House of Representatives. Joining her in the 92nd Congress was Ohio's own, Carl's brother, Louis. Building from the path blazed by these and other African-American pioneers was the election in 2008 of Barack Obama as our 44th president.

Cleveland Mayor Carl Stokes lends his presence at the groundbreaking of a Madison Madison Madison project in 1968.

But Carl Stokes gets the credit for the breakthrough, for crossing that 50-yard line for the first time. After the first 50 yards, it gets easier.

Make me want to holler ...

All this political change in America played out against the backdrop of the Vietnam War, and I began to ask why we were there. When I went to war in the 1940s, I didn't ask why, I just went. I was not a supporter of the Vietnam War. I didn't have my heart in it; I didn't feel it was the right thing.

In World War II, I began as a student and ROTC cadet at Howard. We went to fight that war of our own free will because we believed that if we won, we would come home to America and demand to be treated with the same respect we received in Italy.

When we marched through Lucca, people came out and cheered. Italians invited us into their homes. They took us to operas. But when we rode a train through Alabama, people spat on us.

By the time Vietnam came around, my attitude had changed and war had changed. Over the years, demonstrations against the war escalated, cresting with the National Guard killings of four protesters at Kent State University on May 4, 1970.

I was on the board of trustees at Case Western Reserve University when students were protesting and the kids at Kent State got shot. That Monday, I left work to go up to Case to support Bob Morse, the president of the university. I knew Bob as a neighbor from the North Park area.

Bob, along with me and Herman Stein, the provost, were sitting on the steps of Severance Hall when all of a sudden the students rushed out; it was students wall to wall. Everybody marched up Adelbert Road in Cleveland's University Circle, and students clogged Euclid Avenue. Understandably, that demonstration made the university's old guard uncomfortable.

Members of the board of trustees at Case Western were leaders of industry, masters of the local universe. Most of them didn't concern themselves much with what was happening on the campus. But Bob Morse did, and so did a few others, so when students rallied and protested, we made a point of engaging directly with them.

Our plan was to show up to show we understood student's concerns. We marched not as a way of protesting but to show we cared. This was how we diffused tension and avoided violence on campus. Even though this approach worked, Morse came under pressure from other trustees for his handling of student protests.

Kent State was the turning point on that Vietnam issue. It was so senseless, just like the war we're in now is so senseless. We had to find another way. Even before Vietnam, I would have said war is not a way to solve problems. As for me joining in that protest after the Kent shootings, yes, I was out there in it. I just did it, because that was all we could do.

Dressed in native garb and reclining in his Cleveland Heights courtyard, Bob Madison presides as Prince of the Ibo Tribe.

CHAPTER TWENTY
HOTEL ROOM DIPLOMACY

With home remodeling, home design, doctors' offices and medical buildings under our belt, it was time to branch out. The civil rights movement was on the march, black churches started flexing their political muscle, and President Lyndon Johnson's plans for a Great Society were on the horizon.

At the beginning of the 1960s, our work on churches accelerated, thanks to connections in the A.M.E. system. Some friends, including the Reverend Nicholas Hood, had heard of my practice. Hood was then the minister of Plymouth United Church of Christ in Detroit, and he knew Robert P. Madison, Architect was involved in an urban renewal venture in that city, the first public housing project of its kind in America. After we did that, we got to build Plymouth Congregational Church, so the Reverend Hood and I became close.

▲

Cleveland State University Science Research Center, Cleveland, Ohio, 1978 | Designed by Madison Madison International

This was the first project of this scale for both me and a few of the key contractors we counted on to deliver on our design. Cleveland State was just beginning to emerge in earnest as a major state university, and I'd like to believe this building made a powerful visual statement to support that.

We began to get more commissions for churches, doing designs and preparing drawings and specifications. That pretty much sums up the early years of the Madison architectural venture, but there was far more to come.

The firm had already come a long way; after all, when it began, it was Robert P. Madison, Architect. Then, my brother Julian joined me in the late '50s, and we became Madison Madison, an architectural and engineering company. We really hit full stride when Bernard came on board full-time as an architect in 1967, making us Madison Madison Madison.

At the time, the idea of an architect and engineer working together was frowned upon because the architectural profession thought of itself as pure and superior. Architects didn't want their design vision sullied by the gritty details that engineers need to consider in executing that vision. But to the three Madison brothers, "pure" mattered less than success, and success required us to get the project, make it work—and make money. So we teamed up, at a time of great opportunity. The success of our firm relied on Julian sourcing and securing projects and me being able to design and produce those projects.

My mother had envisioned this great firm of ours: my dad, me, Julian and Bernard. Stanley was the exception. Mom thought Stanley should be a preacher, but he became a pharmacist instead, working at Shorter Drugstore, a black store on East 105th Street. He worked hard at that pharmacy, but he had higher ambitions, and decided to become a doctor. So he earned a medical degree from Western Reserve and became a general practitioner in Baltimore. Nobody ever faulted a Madison brother for lack of ambition or drive.

In 1954, when we started our architecture practice, 105th Street in Glenville was jumping. You could walk along 105 every single day and see success, one black business after another. We had black pharmacists, and there were companies owned by blacks who hired other blacks. You know, once upon a time black people had actual status, community, even material goods. But in achieving desegregation, we seem to have lagged behind in achieving meaningful integration.

There were growing pains, of course, and at Madison Madison Madison it became a kind of power thing. I was appointed chairman because I went to Harvard and had advanced study abroad, and nobody else had. I found out later that Julian's wife, Mildred, was never satisfied with Julian's standing in the firm.

The ideal arrangement was for Julian to get the work, I would manage the work, and Bernard would execute it. Unbeatable, I thought. But Bernard did not want to always be third man; he wanted his own firm, so he left in 1970 to launch just that in Baltimore. Bernard actually did pretty well—so well, in fact, that he started designing a building in Cleveland, a church, one of many he would design.

All of us kept in touch over the miles and the years, something that took much more commitment in an era of expensive, long-distance phone calls and challenging travel options. Through it all, the four Madison brothers tasted success in professional careers.

But one awful year forced me to view professional successes with a different, truer perspective; family and national tragedies have a way of doing that. In the summer of 2001, my brother Stanley died after a long illness. The baby of our family, gone. Of course, in September the entire country went through the horrors of 9/11, which changed our perspective then and still to this day. It turns out that shortly after that day, I travelled to D.C. to visit Bernard. That was a tough trip.

Logistically, it was tough because the National Guard swarmed all over the airports and everywhere. Emotionally, it was tough because at that time Bernard was getting treatment for cancer. After a successful operation, though, his doctors gave us reasons to be very optimistic. Just a month later, I received a call from his family; Bernard had died quite suddenly.

A time to grieve mightily. And then a time to recover, and roll with life's changes, and a time to keep going.

Hotel room diplomacy

Our firm really took off in the 1960s, a decade of tremendous change, especially for blacks. Black power was gaining traction.

After the election of black mayors in various major cities—with Carl Stokes in the vanguard in Cleveland—the late '60s signaled the first time in history that black people had some control over what was happening in America. And to better represent the cities' large black populations and produce the many infrastructure and urban renewal projects in the pipeline, the new leaders said they wanted to hire black architects. The stock answer at that moment was there were few to none—which made it just the right time to raise my profile. It helped that I had friends in high places. It also helped that Julian knew Kenneth Gibson, the new mayor of Newark. "Let's call him and go see him," Julian said. "He's a mayor now." Julian would hop in his car or on a plane, make a proposal, and often come back with a project. Julian was brilliant as a developer, the guy who got the work. He got the job, and I produced the job.

It wouldn't be far-fetched to say I led the charge for black architects in several major cities newly empowered by their first black administrations. That started with Maynard Jackson in Atlanta. We knew each other from Cleveland, and both of us were members of Alpha Phi Alpha. Jackson told me there were black architects in Atlanta who needed to be organized. Could I help?

I never turn down work. So I went to Atlanta and convened all the black architects there—there were about five firms of three or four men each—and said, "Look, Maynard wants you to succeed, but you've got to combine your forces. One or two men, they're not going to do it, so come together."

But they wouldn't. They scrapped and wrangled instead of collaborating. But I had a solution: I locked them in a hotel room and said, "You're going to stay in this room until you all come out with an agreement about working together." About two hours later they emerged, and we started getting black architects successfully involved in projects.

Same scenario in Newark—and in Gary, where my brother Julian flew to cultivate the Madison interests. Our reputation was on the rise. Mayor Richard Hatcher said we were welcome there, so we started working for the city of Gary. We also started working for the city of Newark.

Minority empowerment became even more of a cause when President Richard M. Nixon established the Office of Minority Business Enterprise in 1969, expanding it into the Minority Business Development agency two years later. For a while, it felt like even the federal government was on our side, and on the side of the cities—even cities that didn't yet exist.

Carolina dreaming

One venture we committed to wholeheartedly was designing and building a brand new city in North Carolina near the Virginia border. It was named Soul City, and it was to be built largely on land reclaimed from an abandoned tobacco plantation. Soul City was designed to fully engage and empower black people, and it was the brainchild of Floyd McKissick, an educated, ambitious and connected guy. At the age of 12, McKissick joined the NAACP. After returning from service in World War II, McKissick became the first black student admitted to the University of North Carolina Law School. His admittance didn't come without a fight, however. His case was successfully prosecuted by his lawyer, future Supreme Court Justice Thurgood Marshall.

McKissick was named the leader of the Congress of Racial Equality in 1966, but in the late 1960s, he switched political alliances in order to support Nixon, a Republican. McKissick believed that an innovative form of capitalism, rather than violence or protest, would serve as the ticket to black success, and he felt Nixon would be most receptive. Soul City was his grand vision. The idea was that it would connect workforce training to entrepreneurial acumen and capital investment. In the process, Soul City would transform a few thousand acres in a poor, rural area into a purpose-built powerhouse, with 24,000 new jobs for 44,000 Soul City residents projected by 2004.

Soul City was an ambitious, largely stillborn planned community project in North Carolina to which Bob and Julian Madison contributed.

To pull off this ambitious project, McKissick secured $14 million in U.S. Department of Housing and Urban Development money along with another $6 million from other federal and state agencies.

The project began with great expectations. Julian was on site the most. In Soul City, I designed houses, a fire station, the power plant, and other essentials for a brand-new community. Roads were built and ground was broken on such basic infrastructure as a wastewater treatment plant. We began work on an "industrial incubator facility"—today, economic development professionals would call it a "co-working" space—full of software engineers. Back then, McKissick envisioned the incubator turning out newly minted entrepreneurs who would fuel the growth of Soul City and make it a model for others. Despite its shaky political scaffolding, Soul City was at least 40 years ahead of its time.

But the project never got a grip. As I look back, many factors were stacked against it. Ironically, the Civil Rights Act of 1964 prevented Soul City from being exclusively black, removing one of the development's defining elements. The new law required Soul City to welcome all races. That confused the market, so too few new residents committed to the new city. Cities can overcome many obstacles, but they don't exist without residents.

Also, the Watergate scandal forced Nixon to resign in 1974, and about six years later, financial support for the project essentially shut down. In 1981, President Ronald Reagan wanted to dissociate the Republican Party from as many initiatives as possible of the disgraced Nixon, a fervent (if unlikely) Soul City backer.

After three years, Madison Madison pulled out, and McKissick faded from the scene.

I was deeply disappointed that Soul City failed—how could I not be? We had invested money in designers, in addition to a lot of time, talent and travel. We recouped some revenue from Soul City in architectural fees and Julian's engineering work on roads and sewers. The fire station we designed was built, but an entire community of homes we designed never made it out of the blueprint stage.

To draw, model and create something that never gets built may be the most crushing aspect of an architect's life. Part of your soul and your imagination is rolled up in plans destined to remain in drawers or tubes.

CHAPTER TWENTY-ONE
DAKAR

I have designed hundreds of buildings, from iconic institutions to modest residences. Each has mattered to me, for a variety of reasons. But the commission that continues to affect me the most is the first U.S. Embassy in Dakar, Senegal. That project connected me to my roots with unexpected depth. It also made me feel all my hard work had finally paid off.

For one, I got to design the building following a request for proposals (RFP). Anybody in the country could submit a design proposal for this project, but the prize in this competition was not a commission to draw the details of a home in D.C., a medical office in Cleveland or a public housing project in Detroit. The architect who won this contest would design the very first U.S. embassy to be built in an African republic. For an architect hoping to win a project when the client is the United States of

▲

U.S. Embassy, Dakar, Senegal, Africa, 1974 |
Designed by Madison Madison International

In the early 2000s this and other embassies around the world needed to be replaced due to serious security concerns. That was sad, sort of like an artist's work being painted over. Still, society's needs change, and buildings are repurposed. I haven't made it back to Dakar to see how it's being used—I hope I can get there.

America, that alone was significant. It also was crucial to me—and to Africa, a country with a special hold on me.

The selection committee consisted of the deans of architecture at three universities: Harvard, Yale, and Princeton. That's pretty good company. When those three get together and decide you're the winner, you have to believe you're pretty good. For me, the joy of being selected meant we—Madison Madison— had arrived.

As we prepared our proposal, I thought we had a good shot at this project. The call for entries featured a few major stipulations that worked in our favor. Because Senegal was a former French colony, it was a French-speaking country that employed the metric system. Because I was fluent in both French and the metric system, I felt we had an advantage. And, of course, we needed to submit proof of the professional credentials to get the job done right. So, on a professional level, securing the embassy job was validating and very satisfying.

Our victory also resonated in a far more profound, far more emotional way. For the first time in almost 30 years, since Julian and I visited Millry, Alabama, the home of our great-grandmother, I was in touch with a very distant past. That's because I realized that Grandma Land's grandparents might have been slaves who came to America from Dakar.

I had no idea how deeply Dakar would touch me but I began to sense it not long after I arrived and learned of its significance as a port of departure and trade. The major business in Dakar in the 1600s and 1700s was slave trading. I knew then that I had to know more.

My first step was a brief, solitary trip to Goree Island off the coast, about two miles east of Senegal harbor, to experience the encampment where slaves were confined. As I sat in that House of Slaves, I saw the very wall where slaves were shackled until gangs of men rounded them up, paraded them for auction, then marched or dragged them onto ships. These people were not passengers—they were cargo. And they were no longer men or women; they were slaves, property doomed to a life of bondage, most likely in the Americas. Confronted with this reality, I began to unravel inside.

I sat near that shameful wall for about two hours, weeping. There I was, three centuries on, thinking—no, knowing—that at least one of my forebears had been here before me. They left here in chains in a rotten cargo hold. About 10 percent of those who began the journey of approximately 4,000 miles died of disease, starvation, or suicide. Those who survived led a life of brutal labor and degradation in a strange land. And then, far down the line, there was me, with multiple degrees of higher education, earning a commission to sit in an air-conditioned office, sip coffee, engage in pleasant meetings, now in Dakar to design an embassy to represent my country. An architect's labor requires education, talent, and experience—and I was to be paid a fair wage for practicing a profession I loved. Quite a contrast to my forebears' situation.

Winning the embassy job felt like a kind of justice, providing a sense of vindication, validation, all of that. There I was, this little guy, coming along centuries after all the whippings and the deaths of people about whom I had no factual knowledge. Still, I felt it in my bones that some ancestor of mine—maybe more than one—had been on one of those slave ships.

So, yes, I cried.

Those are fundamental reasons that winning the embassy competition and getting the job, no matter how protracted its completion turned out to be, mattered so much to me. It had nothing to do with the money or the size of the building. It was all about who my people are and who I am.

I was an African-American architect, one who continually heard this comment, "Who ever heard of a black architect?" With the realization of the Dakar embassy, many more, certainly, would come to hear of at least one. This guy in Cleveland is going to design the American embassy? They're supposed to get architects from New York or Cambridge or New Haven to design something like this. But no, I earned this project; they didn't just give it to me. Those people from the selection committee weren't convened to make choices based only on sentiment. I worked for that job. I feel that when you earn it and you do it, you deserve it. And we did all that.

The road to Dakar

The embassy project was complicated. It started in 1964, at the beginning of Lyndon Johnson's presidency. It ended 13 years and three administrations later. What took it so long was the Vietnam War, which drained over $1 trillion in current value from the U.S. economy and incalculable pints of blood from nearly 60,000 dead and 300,000 wounded GIs.

Even as Vietnam churned in the background, the '60s and '70s marked an era of significant progress in civil rights in the U.S. It was also a period in which many African nations burst free of their colonial shackles, opting for independence, no matter how tumultuous the outcome.

We went to design the embassy at just about the time the French were leaving the country. Around 1960, when several former colonies established their independence, American diplomats decided to establish formal relations with these evolving countries. In Senegal, the U.S. had no embassy, so the call went out for a designer. I submitted my credentials and Madison Madison was called to D.C. to be interviewed by that highly credentialed committee. I got us past the first test. Then I had to submit some drawings, wait and wait some more.

Finally, we received word that we were awarded the job. Even though we were very confident in our abilities and knew our fluency in French and the metric system was critical, an architect—at least this architect—learns that celebration only comes once you receive the commissioning letter and sign the contract. The Dakar project officially kicked off when the building operations division of the State Department couriered the official commission documents to design the building. We cheered our achievement, but not for long. Tremendous amounts of work needed to be tackled, including many tasks we had never attempted before. Madison Madison would be spending a lot of time in Senegal.

As I visited and worked in Dakar, the city really surprised me. With a footprint similar to that of Akron, Ohio, Dakar is Senegal's largest city and its capital. Today, the city proper of Dakar has a population of well over a million, its metropolitan area over three million. Located squarely on the Tropic of Cancer, Dakar was simultaneously very African and very

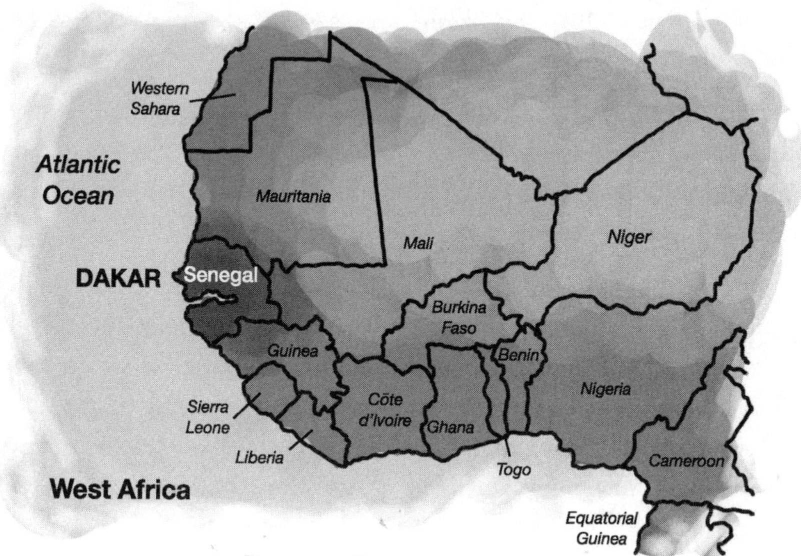

Being awarded the commission to design the United States Embassy in Dakar, Senegal, where Bob's ancestors boarded ships as slaves three generations earlier, marked a proud and profound moment for him.

French. Architects from Paris had a long heritage of traveling to Dakar to practice. Dakar was like a French city, with street names that sounded French and looked beautiful.

Compared to my native Cleveland, the central city of Dakar was much more dense and urban. Its high-rise offices, apartments and grand boulevards made Dakar comfortable and familiar for the French who lived there. Travel just a few kilometers to the outskirts, however, and you'd encounter mud roads and thatched-roof huts. In Dakar, it was easy to simultaneously be in two cities, two cultures, almost two eras, depending on how you chose to see it. For me, Dakar was the rare place where I could not be seen, either.

Invisible man

Early on in Senegal, I noticed that when I walked down the street, no body looked at me. When I sat in a restaurant, no one looked at me. Check into a hotel and it was like I wasn't there, I was just another man. It took a while, but I finally figured out why I felt such unease and at the same time felt totally anonymous. It was because I was black—as was virtually everybody else in Dakar.

When I was in that Norwegian train station in 1953, everyone followed me, but in Dakar, no one did. It made me feel good, but it was oddly uncomfortable, too, because I had never had this experience before in public, at restaurants, museums, and hotels.

I soon thought, maybe I fit in so easily because I spoke the language and I was assumed to be French. I was thought to be from Côte d'Ivoire, a country just a few hundred kilometers to the south. If I said or wrote on documents that I was born in the Ivory Coast, a layer of bureaucracy just melted away. It was easier (and far cheaper) to secure a driver's license, easier to ask for assistance or hire workers, and in general, just easier to live. I wasn't used to fitting in—but that was very welcoming once I adjusted.

In designing the U.S. Embassy for service in this majority Muslim country, I met with contractors, consultants, and government workers responsible for building permits. They were all, of course, Senegalese, and they spoke French, as I did. During our workday meetings and conversations, we all wore standard business attire: suit, necktie, shirt, and dress shoes. One Friday, we didn't have any work to do because it was a Muslim day of prayer. I decided to drink in the culture of Dakar from the balcony of my hotel.

In gazing down on the street, I couldn't help noticing one of the fellows I'd been in a meeting with the day before. Then, he wore a Western business suit. Today, while it was hard to recognize him, it was impossible not to notice him. He wore a boubou, a colorful, traditional African gown. On his head was a fez, and on his feet were wild, pointed shoes of different colors.

Just as jarring was the company he kept. Walking behind him were eight women, beautifully dressed but heavily veiled. His family? His wives? I tried to process all this to figure out what was going on and what I was feeling. Then it hit me: they were Muslims, with vast cultural differences I couldn't even begin to understand. All of a sudden I felt excluded—again. I was sad too, because I once thought all of these were my people and that in Dakar, for one of the few times in my life, I felt totally comfortable. Now I felt left out because Muslim culture was so very foreign to me—and likely always would be.

I realized that even though I'm black, I'm not comfortable with all the expressions of black culture, at least not what I witnessed that day.

Project in waiting

That first visit to Dakar in 1964 lasted a week and a half. My goal was to simply, and literally, get the lay of the land and walk the future site of the embassy. Then I returned home, designed the building, and went back to present it to the people on the ground in Dakar. That took up most of 1966. All was progressing nicely until foreign affairs intervened. The war in Vietnam was heating up and spreading to more of Indochina, so many of the U.S. government's resources were being funneled into that conflict. Plans were put on hold when I received a communiqué from the U.S. State Department: "We're placing a moratorium on this project. We'll let you know if it ever gets started back again."

The U.S. Embassy in Senegal glows in the Dakar night.

Orison Rudolph Aggrey, the United States Ambassador to Senegal (far left), an unidentified man in the middle, and Bob and Leatrice at Dakar embassy grand opening on July 4, 1974.

Years passed, and the Vietnam war escalated further, but the Dakar embassy never quite died. A project lull of several months is uncomfortable but not uncommon. But it's very rare for an architect's design to be shelved for several years, and rarer still for such a project to actually be built. But that's what happened in 1972 when I received another communication: The state department was ready to restart the project. Did I want to be involved? Of course I said yes, so I went back in '73 and completed the drawings. The following year construction began. That took an additional three years.

So from the beginning of the process to the ribbon-cutting ceremony, 13 years elapsed. In some ways, it was like a blink of an eye, but in many others it was as if a generation had passed. When we were awarded the commission, my daughter Julliette was a cute seven-year-old girl. When the project was completed, my baby was a beautiful 20-year-old woman. During that time, presidents and secretaries of state came and went. By the time the embassy opened, the only original professional or civic figures still standing were me and Leopold Senghor, the first president of Senegal. When we met, I joked to him, "we're still here." Senghor, considered the George Washington of West Africa, was a brilliant man. He lived in Paris for most of his life and married a French woman. He returned to Senegal in 1960 when it gained its independence from France and would serve as Senegal's president for two decades.

The building finally opened in 1977—fittingly, on the Fourth of July. There was quite a celebration, a combination of African and All-American. There were fireworks, marching band music, and hot dogs. Leatrice and I were treated like royalty. A chauffeured car met us at the airport, a long red carpet was rolled out, musical groups announced our arrival, and servants bowed as we walked past. We weren't watching the sort of ceremony you associate with royalty and movie stars—we had starring roles in it. I was some kind of celebrity in Dakar because I was a black man and I was the designer of that building. Because that had never happened before, I was hailed as somebody special.

A special place

The embassy I designed had a sense of dignity, of solidity. The design I came up with was very open and welcoming, with a lot of glass— the sort of building an embassy was supposed to be.

I was concerned about not having the configuration look exclusively African—that approach would risk making the embassy an inauthentic caricature. We needed to integrate African motifs into an authentic portrait. This was a balancing act, and we worked hard to pull it off. I also wanted it to reflect the evolving relationship between the American government and the Senegalese government. The symbolism of Africa was shown in murals and in details. You entered the building to find yourself in a two-story atrium. The ground floor was pretty open, so people could move around freely. Offices were on the upper floors. As you ascended, though, the structure became more and more secure, until we got to the top floor, the fourth, which I wasn't allowed to design. The United States Federal Building Operations at the State Department designed it, because its configuration and the technology needed to be held closely. I just gave them a shell, essentially four walls, to work with. It was strange to create such a substantial building that at the same time was substantially incomplete. But that's what I had to design.

The exterior of the embassy, however, was anything but incomplete. It was a beautiful, beautiful sight with gardens all around. It fit right into this striking city, which in many ways rivaled Paris. Even though it was not the tallest building in the city or even in that neighborhood, when lit up at night it was a gorgeous beacon. As an embassy, it worked well, but as in many other countries, people started attacking such buildings in incidents that were largely nuisances. But after the suicide bombing of the U.S. Marine Corps barracks in Beirut in 1983, the U.S. State Department started shutting down embassies, including that one in downtown Dakar. That building was something, and it still stands, though they've moved the embassy to another location. After all that political unrest, the Senegalese government was forced to abandon it and move operations to another, more fortress-like structure.

Despite these changes, the building continues to stand tall in my mind. I have designed many important structures of my own and have contributed to yet more, but the U.S. Embassy in Dakar was a dream come true, a dream that lingers.

CHAPTER TWENTY-TWO
CHINA

When I'm in the United States, whether at home or on the road, I'm acutely conscious of my color. When I leave the country, my sense of my color changes. In Dakar, blackness was the norm, so I was hidden in the blend and at times felt disoriented; the white people stood out. That was largely true, too, when I and Julian did business in the Caribbean.

In countries where whites control the culture, it's different for me. It's almost as if I have to prove myself all over again, asserting my professional value as if in spite of my complexion. That wasn't the case in Dakar, however. Or China. It counted ever less as my reputation grew and I came to be accepted for what I did no matter my color.

▲

Gate of Heavenly Peace, Tiananmen Square, Beijing, China, 1420

How can you not be humbled when you set foot in a building that involved one million workers laboring for 14 years? One of the nearly 1,000 buildings in the Forbidden City, millions flock to this site every year to be inspired and awed. I was one of those visitors. Fifty years later, I'm still in awe.

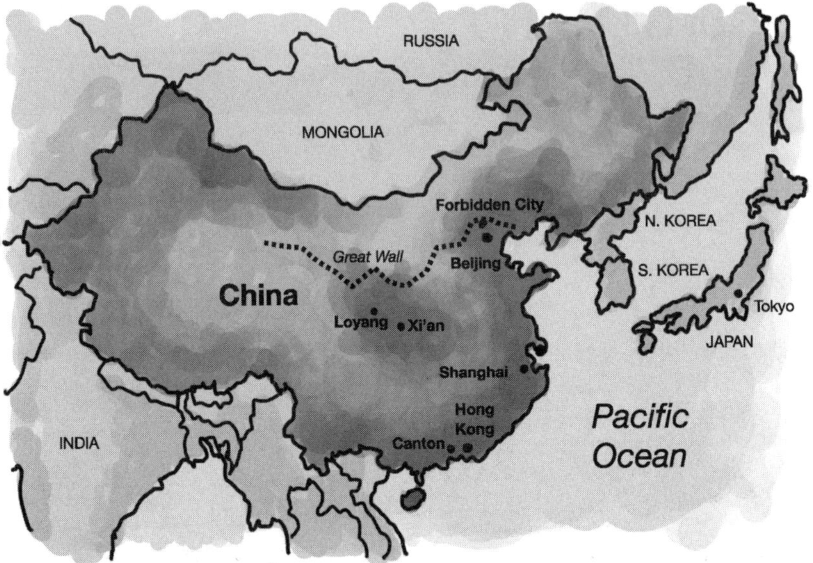

Cities on the map mark a few of the highlights of learning and teaching for the delegation of 15 U.S. architects in their 1974 visit.

It wasn't just the change in color context and color judgment that impressed me when I traveled. It was what the country tried to be and what my mission there was.

I would say China and Senegal were the countries that impressed me the most, and as of my first visit to Dakar, China was yet to come. Once I got there, I discovered a world I'd never imagined, not to mention architecture unlike anywhere else.

A new old world

It's hard to imagine what China was like when I went there in the spring of 1974 at the tail end of what was known as the Cultural Revolution. That was quite a year: President Richard M. Nixon, who had opened up China just two years earlier, was on his way out thanks to Watergate, and I had just been elected a Fellow of the American Institute of Architects. Nothing I have ever done exceeds that honor. It affirmed not only that I had arrived; it affirmed my value as an architect.

That spring, I was invited to join 13 other distinguished members of the AIA for a tour of China. To be accepted as one of the elite architects from the U.S.A. was such an honor.

Besides major cities, our tour covered farms, the countryside, the Imperial Palace, the Forbidden City, the Temple of Heavenly Peace, the Avenue of Lions, the burial tombs of the emperors, and ordinary homes of average citizens. We also visited the palatial home of I.M. Pei, the already-established architect who organized the trip. Pei, whom I would work with decades later on the Rock and Roll Hall of Fame, had not seen his Soochow home in 37 years.

After a stop in Tokyo, we got off the airplane in Hong Kong, and then took a train to Canton. Mao Zedong was still living, as was Chou En Lai. This was little more than two years after President Nixon, Chairman Mao and Secretary of State Henry Kissinger opened up mainland China; remember ping pong diplomacy?

We were the third group to visit Communist China after Nixon, who was followed by a group from the political arena. All 14 of us were archi-

Bob was among the most distinctive in a distinguished group of American architects visiting China in 1974. Here they are in Tiananmen Square in what is now known as Beijing.

tects; I was the only black. We were in China for three weeks that April, and we visited 11 cities all told. I was very upbeat about China. I still am. My positive views have not changed.

The governments had made an agreement with the architects of China to create an exchange program, so we took a bunch of books used by American architects to give them. We found out they could use the help, because the then-contemporary architecture of China was mostly modeled on architecture from the Soviet Union, and it was brutal, really awful stuff, nothing creative.

Where drab buildings ruled in the cities, farmers working in rice paddies represented the countryside. What bound the two together were trains and bicycles, conspicuous players in China's landscape.

Trains, like bicycles, were ubiquitous, as were trains that ran on time. It was fascinating to see the contrast between old and new, among airplanes, trains, and bicycles, all in a landscape that looked like it came from an earlier century. Imagine taxiing down the runway of a modern airport on board a Boeing 707 and looking out the window to see a peasant in an ancient-style hat plowing a rice paddy behind his buffalo.

During that leg of the trip, we didn't see a single internal combustion engine. In mainland China in 1974, everyone traveled by bus—and bicycle—from place to place. There were millions of bicycles but hardly any cars. There was no way to be prepared for the scale of the place. This was China under Mao, and everybody was dressed alike: Men and women wore the same kind of outfits.

The Chinese people, who moved en masse, were very generous with us, very gracious. They were classier than the accommodations. At one point, we stayed in what felt like a fifth-rate hotel in Quanzhou in the far west. It was clean, but it hadn't been updated since it was built; things were very, very primitive back in those days. At the same time, you can understand that when we saw Beijing, all of us could see the majesty of the architecture from the 15th century. We had a dynasty chart so we knew which one created which building.

Bob atop the Great Wall of China.

They let us into the Forbidden City in central Beijing (it was called Peking then). We also saw parts of the Imperial City, like the Gates of Paradise and the Palace of Heavenly Peace. It impressed me that once upon a time the Imperial City—with the Forbidden City at its center—was really magnificent, really majestic.

One Sunday, we visited Shanghai, more than 800 miles southeast of Peking but only a few hours' flight on an airplane dedicated to our group.

There, too, we saw wall-to-wall people. I mean, wall-to-wall people. They were out there just parading around and were all dressed alike, with the Mao Zedong jacket—I still have mine—the cap and all that.

At the same time, there was occasional individuality. I'll never forget seeing someone fixing transformers on an electricity pole. The person wore a belt for equipment, and when she got down, we realized this was a lady. It was the first time we'd seen a waistline since we got there.

After Shanghai, we traveled to Luoyang, one of the four great ancient capitals of China. It was also the site where they famously buried statues of soldiers. We got there just as they were excavating the mounds that became known as home to the Terra Cotta Army. There, we also saw caves where Buddhist monks lived and inscribed history on the walls. I have a rubbing from one of those caves dating back to the last dynasty, at the start of the 20th century.

It wasn't just the vast numbers of people or the scale of the place; at that time, the population was 900 million. Today, it's almost 1.4 billion. The other thing that really impressed me was how subservient to Mao the people were. Mao was the father, the Grand Leader, generally considered the man who led the advance of modern China. He also created the Long March.

The Chinese were a wonderful group, and very courteous to us. I was very famous because in my delegation, I was the only black. Max Irvine was the leader of the group; he was a white guy and he had white hair. I had black hair, so the two of us stood out. We had fun with that.

On an academic note, each architect was asked to give a lecture on one or more aspects of the manmade environment. My topic was large-scale housing developments, an obvious concern in a country of nearly a billion people.

I had to give my lecture—on the housing of poor people—at the University of Shanghai. After my presentation, I invited the audience to ask questions, and I'll never forget this one, posed to me through an interpreter: "Mr. Madison how do you house your peasants?"

American architects touring China in 1974 made an excursion to Luoyang where they witnessed an extensive cave system featuring carved artwork, statuary, and cultural inscriptions. A print of a rubbing taken from one cave dominates a wall of Madison's dining room.

"We don't call them peasants, we call them 'low-income families,' " I said.

To the Chinese, at least at that time, aesthetics didn't matter that much. All that mattered was functionality. Housing was a tool for achieving the ends of the state, and there it was functional in the extreme.

Solid landing

Upon my return to Cleveland, the local chapter of the AIA and the Ohio Architects Board invited me to present a lecture about my trip. I accepted the invitation and prepared my slideshow and lecture material. And now came the most glorious triumph.

The screen was in place, the lights were ready, and I was poised to begin the lecture. The secretary announced my name. As I walked slowly on stage, I surveyed the audience and had a moment of sheer ecstasy: sitting in the front row were all the heads of architectural firms waiting with great anticipation. Years earlier, I remembered them all telling me, "We don't hire colored people."

I stared at each one of them, a wry smile on my face.

That lecture and the China trip as a whole weren't the only reasons 1974 was a good year for me. That same year, being elected to the College of Fellows of the AIA put me in mind of another African-American, the singer Marian Anderson. As I walked across the stage to receive my medal in the Daughters of the American Revolution (DAR) Constitution Hall in Washington, D.C., I remembered how the DAR had refused to allow Anderson to perform an Easter concert in their hall because of the color of her skin. Eleanor Roosevelt, wife of the president, resigned from the DAR because of that snub.

Anderson didn't take this lying down. Just a few days later, she gave a historic concert from the steps of the Lincoln Memorial. Instead of the 3,500 people she would have sung to in the DAR auditorium, Anderson performed for more than 75,000. She had turned what must have felt like defeat into a wonderful victory. And there I was, 35 years later, a black man, walking across the very stage Anderson was denied.

When I returned to Cleveland, I dashed to see my mother, who was in hospice care. I told her where I had been, explained the significance of the

FAIA distinction as an honor bestowed by my peers, one that only three percent of architects ever achieve. Then, I opened a small box to show her my FAIA medal. A great big smile flashed over her face. She reminded me of her prediction, first proclaimed when I was only six years old, that I would one day be an architect. Two days later, she passed on to join my father. A transformative month, indeed.

Becoming FAIA is the second-highest honor an architect can attain. Ten years later, I would achieve the highest honor possible for an AIA member when I was elected as the Chairman of the Jury of Fellows. The Jury is the group of AIA Fellows who evaluate and select those deemed worthy of FAIA designation. During the investiture ceremony at the AIA Conference, after much pomp and ceremony and swearing an oath, I again walked across the stage to accept the accolades of my peers.

This time, I didn't see any of the heads of architectural firms who wouldn't even consider me for a job 30 years earlier. Perhaps they were hiding from my view. Or maybe I was too focused on moving forward.

CHAPTER TWENTY-THREE
STRAINING THE FAMILY FABRIC

The 1960s and '70s were a time of growth for my young business, and we began to take on all sorts of new projects, including prisons and public works. My expertise in architectural drawing and planning, combined with Julian's engineering skill and salesmanship, made for a winning team.

A lot of jail work arose after the Attica Prison riot in western New York on September 9, 1971, to this day the largest jail rebellion in U.S. history. We read books about building prisons; we were ready.

At nearly the same time, we became involved in a sewage treatment plant in Milwaukee, a job Julian brought to the firm. We also had the Plymouth A.M.E. Church and that 221(d)(3), 220-unit housing project in Detroit, along with all of the interior concessions for the $400 million Hartsfield-Jackson

▲

Justice Center, Wooster, Ohio, 1978 | Designed by Madison Madison International
The Center, located in the city's central business district, was designed with varying volumes in order to reduce the impact of a very large building in relation to the size of existing, surrounding structures. Mass and volume were carefully organized to relate to the scale of street elevations, stepping up to the largest volume in the center.

Atlanta International Airport. We were not the lead architect for the airport project—we didn't have the capacity to take on something that big. But we could interpret it and make it work. That's what we did: We made it work, benefiting several of Atlanta's African-American architectural firms.

Building on such successes, we expanded mightily. At our peak, we had about 150 employees in six offices. Besides headquarters in Cleveland, we had outposts in Atlanta, Philadelphia, Detroit, Milwaukee and Chicago. These were actual operating offices, with mostly engineering work. We also designed transit stations for the Metropolitan Atlanta Rapid Transit Authority, or MARTA, after Mayor Jackson invited us there. Public transportation also was a focus of mine in a bedeviled project in Houston in the early 1980s, and years later, in Cleveland—where it was a great success—with the Healthline. The '70s and much of the '80s were good years.

We also had a portion of the Chicago Deep Tunnel Project, a complicated storm-water-abatement effort to reduce flooding and the deleterious effects of flushing raw sewage into Lake Michigan. The idea was to dig a tunnel far below the earth to form a reservoir, with a valve system that could control release of treated water into the lake. We also had that sewer system work in Milwaukee. We not only had a large number of projects; we had different design and engineering responsibilities on projects in various industries, with new partners, in new regions.

Heady times.

Our growth was so rapid that I didn't know all my employees and vice versa. When I walked into a branch office, the receptionist might not know who I was. On the one hand, it felt exhilarating; we were a large and growing company. On the other, it made me realize we had lost that family feeling at Madison International. It felt like we were spreading ourselves too thin, and not only in the United States. We even did some work in the Caribbean. Friends of Julian in the Bahamas called him up, so we went down to do a job there.

Flying high

I'll never forget sharing a hotel room in the Bahamas with Julian and changing into tennis gear. Before we stepped onto the court, I said, "Can you imagine this? Two black guys from the projects playing tennis on a court in the Bahamas?" We laughed as we realized how far we'd come.

Julian sure was an entrepreneur, but sometimes he'd swing too wide. He even became involved in trying to develop a company to sell clothes to people in the Bahamas, not exactly our field of expertise.

Still, the two of us were terrific together, just like when we were kids. Whether picking cotton in Alabama or shining shoes in Washington, Julian and I were in sync, getting stuff done. But eventually, that relationship frayed.

Julian was a great guy. We had differences, but, when we were together, we were a powerhouse. We'd play good cop, bad cop. We could even switch roles, telling which ones to play just by looking at each other's eyebrows.

Except in places where I wouldn't want to go, I closed the deal because I was the practical brother. In Soul City, for example, I was only interested in the buildings, not the bigger picture. When Julian was in South Carolina helping Floyd McKissick get that land together, he handled matters McKissick couldn't. Julian was terrific in that area; he had the gifts of vision and persuasion.

While Julian dreamed and schemed creatively, even brilliantly, he couldn't always deliver. Still, because he went to Howard, he knew a great number of black people and could deal with all of them, from the finest to the crudest. That was not my forte, but I could deal with white people, like the dean of the school of medicine in Rootstown, where we designed the gross anatomy laboratory at the Northeast Ohio School of Medicine (NEOMED).

We were invited to make a presentation to design the Gross Anatomy Lab there. I wasn't sure I even wanted to make a pitch, but I warmed to the prospect, and once I got there, took quite a bit of time explaining my presentation. Even though the chairman signaled his impatience, a board member intervened, saying, "Don't stop him. He's selling, and he's doing a good job."

Much to my surprise, we got the project. I guess I could sell after all.

I was there because I could talk to that dean eyeball to eyeball. I also was the one who went to Washington to secure a prestigious federal job because

I was comfortable dealing with professionals at all levels. I went to Wooster to win over the local powers so Madison Madison could land the job designing a jail and an administration building in Wayne County.

I'm particularly proud of the Wooster jail, a replacement for a facility dating to 1865. Even though we'd been invited to make a presentation, I was reluctant to make the trip because I thought our chances were next to zero. Wooster, Ohio? There weren't enough black families there for a church meeting. No NAACP, no Urban League. These were farmers. This was country.

About 10 firms—from Akron, Cleveland and Kent—vied for that job. I put on my best show and, to my delight, found that the commissioners were simpatico. Once we got the job to design the Wayne County Justice Center, we worked well with the county sheriff and with Ralph Insalata, the project manager. We ultimately designed that city's Community Center and the County Administration Building.

Danger zone

I had the long view, and Julian was the master of the pitch, but there were times we nearly lost it. One time, I almost went to jail.

One summer day in the late 1960s, I got a notice to come down to FBI headquarters. The Madison brothers found ourselves in a room there. An employee checked us all out. What is going on here? We didn't know. And then someone said to me, "Mr. Madison, you have not paid your withholding taxes for your corporation for three months, and you owe $250,000." I said, "What?" I was stunned. I felt like the FBI was ready to put the handcuffs on me. "I don't know what you're talking about," I told them. "You run the company, Mr. Madison," the FBI told me.

"I'll pay it all right, I'll pay it," I said. I felt like they were ready to run me into jail right then, but then they huddled together and I overheard them saying, "Maybe this guy is telling the truth." They told me I needed to return to my office and investigate what was going on, and then report back to them.

So I returned to the office, marched to the office of the comptroller—she wrote checks every day, and I just signed them—and demanded to know what was all this about unpaid withholding taxes? She explained that when we didn't have the funds in our account, she simply didn't pay them. When I reported what I had learned to the FBI, they gave me a month to secure financing and write a check to Uncle Sam. A great big check, in fact. By that time, with interest, penalties and taxes, my company owed $500,000. If we were to survive and keep my mother's dream alive, it was time for action. And money.

I was able to secure a business loan from First Bank, a minority-owned bank. After five long years and 60 monthly payments—the first couple of checks were especially hard to write—we eventually came to consider those payments as just another bill we had to pay. And pay we did, every penny of that loan. Going back to the time of Julius Caesar, experience is said to be the best teacher. But it's also an expensive teacher, one I never wanted to learn from on these matters again.

After the worst of this was behind us, I reflected on this scary and unsettling event. I realized that I never was in a position to understand tax laws and salary distribution practices for an architectural practice. I was never offered a course of studies related to professional management,

The Madison brothers team—Bernard, Julian and Bob—developed a presentation model of the Dakar embassy.

probably based on the belief that a black architecture graduate would never actually ever run his own practice. And during my brief tenure at Robert A. Little as a junior designer, I did project and assignment work, so I learned nothing there about how financial matters worked.

In order to ensure financial and tax compliance moving forward, we hired an outside firm, Dingus & Daga, as our certified public accountants to manage our finances and audit our processes. Our practice and our business—we now came to fully appreciate we had to view it as both—was continuing an upward trend of strong growth. We couldn't afford another incident like this.

I could draw and design, but the practice needed to be tightly managed. But it turns out I couldn't design an approach broad enough to manage Julian's imagination, initiative, and sometimes overly active ambition.

Dubious dreaming

The boldest venture Julian ever dreamed up would come to be known as Madison Madison of Tobago. Here's how it began.

Julian called a classmate who lived in Tobago and told him he was looking for work. After about a year of discussion and travel, Julian told me his plan. "We're going to develop a cement plant on the island of Tobago," he said. Imagine two brothers from Cleveland, an architect and an engineer, investing in a rough-and-tumble industrial process we knew little about on a small island country 2,500 miles south of home. But that was Julian.

He saw himself as a project developer who could convince people we could pull all these different forces together and successfully execute on a project of this scope. He also convinced people in Tobago they needed a concrete mixing plant.

But first, he needed funding, and he decided the best way to raise that was to sell shares in the endeavor. Before we could become cement plant operators, we had to become venture capitalists. Much to my surprise, it worked—people started buying stock in the company.

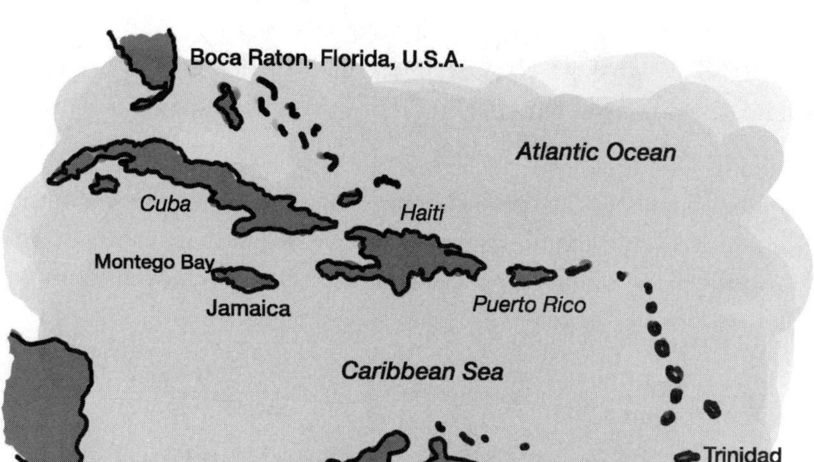

An overview of several Caribbean project sites that mark perhaps the most far-flung of Madison endeavors.

The next thing I knew, Julian bought a used cement mixer from England, which he arranged to have shipped to Tobago. I went down for the mixer's island debut. There was a great big celebration, and, all of a sudden, we were going to "do cement."

And we did, but only for a short while. More than 40 years later, the idea of running a cement plant in Tobago seems even more exotic than it did at the time. Still, I admired Julian for his initiative and limitless imagination. I just wish I'd put greater limits on it.

The project could have worked and even made money, but as fast as we put money in, shady locals siphoned it out. The locals bilked former classmates of Julian's, taking their investments and spending much of the money before dispersing what was left back to Cleveland.

I went down to Tobago to find out what happened. The people who had absconded with the money had vanished. I felt terrible. All kinds of people had put their money out there, and it didn't work, but the idea was just brilliant.

The cement plant in Tobago wasn't our only venture into the Caribbean. We also explored projects in Trinidad and Jamaica, and even designed buildings, but none of our efforts bore fruit. We had nothing to show for our investment in time and money.

All our far-flung work meant we needed offices for manpower on site. When you're doing engineering work like a sewer system, you need people. But we hired too many, bloating our payroll, and we lost money.

We could design all this stuff, but we weren't nearly as good at financial management, so at best, we broke even—or we lost money. We had a payroll of around $4 million a year in the '70s. We had lots of people and lots of work, but I couldn't even balance the budget. It didn't help that at the same time as I was trying to tighten up and reduced fixed costs, Julian was trying to loosen the purse strings even more.

We had some tough times, and we had some great times, but money became more and more of an issue between us. Finally, I told him, "Look, Julian, we don't have the money to hire another person." Even then, Julian would hire that person anyway. I stepped on the brakes, but it didn't work.

That ongoing argument is why we broke up in late 1983, when Julian left Cleveland to oversee branch offices in Detroit, Milwaukee and Chicago. Another reason we broke up was that botched Houston project, which eventually cost me a lot of money.

The rift deepens

The '80s were remarkably productive for the Madison interests—except in Houston. Designing a subway system in that sprawling Texas city ultimately didn't happen, and that was a deal breaker; its failure was the beginning of the end for me and Julian. We had a contract to design and engineer subway stations along the Buffalo Bayou, a river that goes through Houston, as part of a $2.1 billion project set for referendum late that spring.

Before the vote that would decide the fate of the project, we went to Union Commerce Bank, which is now Huntington, and borrowed $300,000. Our contract was our collateral. The bank loaned us the money, we were doing great, and we finished the preliminary designs. But on

June 11, 1983, the project was voted down and our contract was canceled, leaving me holding the bag on that $300,000 loan.

So we had to pull out of Houston; we had an office there, two cars and three staff people, and I had been flying back and forth. It was like Exodus. I said, "Julian, we owe $300,000, based upon this contract. We've got to pay this back, so we've got to cut back on everything."

Two days after I told him this, I discovered that Julian had hired three more people. "Wait a minute, Julian," I said, "we've been doing too much spending—and we don't have the money." This was the fourth time we had had this conversation.

The Houston crisis broke this camel's back.

CHAPTER TWENTY-FOUR

IT'S A THIN LINE

Cutting the cord with Julian was painful, largely because we'd been such dynamic and successful partners for most of our lives. Up until then, we'd been able to leverage our different personalities and reconcile issues. But disagreements over money and differences in style finally caught up with us, making the split inevitable. I was chairman, he was vice president, and we were clashing. Severing business ties with Julian was one of the most significant personal disappointments in my life.

Because he was my brother, and because we'd been a hell of a team, no way would I fire him outright. But I had to cut the cord. "Let's quit, it's time," I told him one day in the fall of 1983. The following year, we officially dissolved Madison Madison International.

▲

Frank Lausche State Office Building, Cleveland, Ohio, 1979 | Designed by Toguchi/Madison/Ireland

I've heard it said that when a group of skilled people get together to get a job done, it's amazing what can be accomplished when nobody gets caught up in who takes credit. That, in a ziggurat nutshell, sums up this great project.

Our partnership had worked until we got down to the nitty-gritty and needed to make difficult financial decisions; Julian wouldn't cut back. Together, we crafted a breakup strategy. Julian would assume control of the Chicago, Detroit and Milwaukee offices, where all the engineering work was booked. As for me, I would have ownership of the offices in Cleveland, Atlanta and Washington, where the architectural projects were. Seemed like a sensible decision. But I had reasons to be worried.

After nearly 30 years of building a business together with Julian and other family members, all of a sudden I would be on my own. Ending my business with Julian was like a divorce, and, no matter what they say, few divorces are ever truly amicable, and none of them are painless.

Still, our split was positive in that it addressed our conflict and cleared the air. But from a professional standpoint, it also left me with little architectural work, so I had to scuffle like the dickens. Eventually, I would do okay.

Fortunately, I had the St. Martin de Porres project, involving a building on St. Clair Avenue near Superior that the Catholic Church bought for use as a recreation center. I got the job to redesign and restore it, but that was the only job I had in 1984. Between that year and 1989, I was hustling like mad. I've never minded hard work, but scrambling like this was different, and very pressured. And it wasn't as if I was starting a business with no major liabilities. Because I was responsible to pay off that $300,000 bank loan we took out for the failed Houston job, I remained on the hook for that. Heading a corporation means you have power. It also means you're liable when things go south.

Going it alone

The split with Julian was really painful, even nasty. It strained the family. In some ways, it still does. By the time Julian left, we'd been disagreeing and reconciling and disagreeing and reconciling for 30 years. We were caught in this cycle for so long, I think that jealousy was at the root of our conflict. I was getting all the glory since I joined the AIA in 1956, became a Fellow in 1974, and was elected chairman of its Jury of Fellows in 1984.

Julian, meanwhile, was trained and certified as an engineer; in fact, he earned Professional Engineer (PE) status. Engineering is a technical

Whether in a meeting or traveling to faraway sites to close a deal, Julian was a force.

discipline and all about foundations, structures, HVAC, fire suppression systems, power supplies, telecommunications—everything that allows a building to stand and function efficiently. So, of course engineering is critically important.

Architecture, on the other hand, is all about silhouettes, color, form, and what's new and cool and dazzling. An architect's work is done in the studio but then becomes visible both from the street as well as on the inside. I guess an architect is more like the star performer, and the engineers are the backstage crew. It might not be fair, but unless the sound system goes down or the heating in the performance hall doesn't work, the audience or critics don't pay much attention to engineering. So perhaps it's natural that engineers can feel overshadowed by the work of architects.

Our split may have involved class, too. I think Julian's wife was very upset because she came from the top black family in Milwaukee while her husband was in second place at Madison International. The former Mildred Thomas was the child of one of the most prominent black doctors in Milwaukee. Her parents owned a pharmacy and a daycare center. The Thomases were very high society.

When I first met Mildred, I'd just returned from the Army and went to meet Julian at Howard, where he introduced me to her. I thought she was cute, and I could tell she was in love with my brother. But I didn't quite understand her aloof attitude toward our family; perhaps she thought we were less than her own. I tried my best to get along with her, and to her credit, Mildred did hang in, becoming Julian's right-hand person. I bet she figured that because there was all this engineering work out of the offices in Chicago, Milwaukee and Detroit, who needed Bob Madison? Mildred and Julian probably thought they could do all this engineering work on their own, so when it came time to separate, they were happy.

My wife, Leatrice, didn't mesh with Mildred, either. In part, I think this was due to the fact that Leatrice's parents were uneducated, and Leatrice's own education didn't register with Mildred. I guess it was a matter of social class distinction. My wife got along with Bernard's wife and Stanley's wife, but not Mildred.

At the time of the split, we had a project in the pipeline involving a proposed U.S. Customs station between Detroit and Canada. Julian and Mildred said they didn't need me as an architect—and they even hired our brother, Bernard. They probably figured I would fade away. But that didn't happen.

Running Robert P. Madison International on my own meant I needed to reorganize and streamline in a major way. When Julian was with the firm, we had structural, mechanical, environmental and electrical engineers. When I cut back to strictly architecture, we hired consultants to do the engineering; we outsourced. Now I could hire people when I needed them and not have to pay them every day. I could design structures on spec, then flesh them out by hiring engineers once I got contracts. It was a bit scary at first, but the approach really paid off.

As the 1980s transformed into the 1990s, Robert P. Madison International was on solid financial and organizational footing. A large part of that improvement was due the fact that from 1989 to 1999, the firm doubled in size from a revenue standpoint. But just as important as revenue growth was our need to manage that growth. And that's where my daughter Jeanne came through.

Jeanne became comptroller and operations officer at the Madison firm, and good things happened. There was the Rock Hall, the stadium, the arena, and another sizable commission—the state of Ohio computer center in Columbus. All those projects came together at almost the same time.

With Jeanne managing the finances and enacting better processes and procedures, we began to recoup expenses that often slipped through. With a structured receivables cycle in place, we received progress payments on large projects so we had a more predictable revenue stream.

For a time, things seemed to be looking good for Julian, too. When we split, he had all the confirmed projects. He had a $1 million contract to staff a Milwaukee office with four men, and a half-million-dollar contract in Chicago for engineering work.

Julian did great for a while, but people kept calling me, complaining that he wasn't performing, especially on that Milwaukee sewage-treatment-plant project. They wanted me to take it over, but I said no, I wouldn't do anything to hurt my brother, I'd starve first. I'm an honorable person.

Things began to fall in place for me, like that jail job in Wooster, and then the administration building there. And then came work for Cuyahoga Community College in my hometown.

The college is known in the region simply as Tri-C, and it opened on September 23, 1963. Tri-C was Ohio's first community college, and it hit the ground running. More than 3,000 students enrolled in Tri-C's first semester, the largest enrollment in any community college's first academic term in the United States. By the late 1990s, more than 55,000 students enrolled at Tri-C, Ohio's largest community college. Not only did we have the original campus construction, we earned commissions to design for expanded campus sites.

At Tri-C East, I designed the master plan for the athletic fields and later, the athletic facilities, the performing arts center, and the classrooms. This occupied me for the better part of the early '90s. The Tri-C work involved $30 million in '90s dollars in construction costs.

Evolving regulations played a favorable role, too. In the late '80s, when laws began mandating minority participation in construction projects, everybody looked to hire a minority-owned firm, and we were qualified. We were ready when they said, "You want some work? Come by." That's when Cleveland started a big building program and its modern transit system.

Specific projects included the Willard Park Garage at the rear of Cleveland City Hall, providing about 3,000 spaces for cars in five stories; Cuyahoga County's Jail II, next to the existing city and county jails and the county court system offices at St. Clair Avenue and Ontario Street; the Rock & Roll Hall of Fame, and the Great Lake Science Center. We did the county jail as lead architect, while we were associate architects on the Rock Hall and Science Center.

There was virtually no competition, and I started getting significant work, because laws and administrations had changed, affirmative action was getting a grip in the workplace, and we were prepared. There were issues, however, particularly in labor.

The school of Madison

When I started my practice in 1954, I had trouble finding qualified contractors who would work on my jobs. At that time, members of the building trades were virtually all white and not interested in working on a black architect's project. Had I wanted to hire African-American labor, I couldn't, because black workers didn't belong to unions. I took it upon myself to go to the headquarters of the United Association—shorthand for the plumbers union. "Why can't I get some of these black guys to work on my projects?" I asked.

"They can't read blueprints."

So I put on the educator hat I last wore at Howard after the war and started holding classes Saturdays at my office to teach blueprint reading to qualify people for union jobs. All I was trying to do was help guys coming out of high school find work.

At that time, people were scared to death of the unions, and the unions were powerful, sometimes dangerous. Not to me, though; union officials must have thought I was some dumb jerk, so nothing happened to me. Guys I taught how to read blueprints had work five or 10 years later. Anybody black could come out of high school and learn at my shop, and over my career I must have taught 200 people, all of whom got good-paying jobs.

This involved mentoring. I would give people who came to work in my office a T-square and a triangle and teach them how to draw. They couldn't design—understanding space and volume comes with further education and experience—but at least they could do meaningful work.

And they succeeded. A number of these people went on to start their own firms. Nearly every African-American architect in town worked for me during my company's first 50 years, including William and James Whitley, who went to Kent State University and began working at my company for college credits.

When the Whitley brothers went looking for work experience, nobody would hire them except Bob Madison. Everybody came to work for me to get that college co-op credit. The Whitley brothers eventually founded their own firm, Whitley and Whitley.

Education has always been part of the plan: to build a company with a diverse workforce, a raft of skills and the ability to tackle virtually any project that might come along. It wasn't easy, but by the 1990s, Robert P. Madison International was on very solid ground, with me solidly in command. It was about time; it was my time.

Still, the split with Julian marked a painful turning point. His departure, no matter our differences, was very sad, dashing my hopes for a family business, a family legacy. My vision for the Madison company was that it would be like the Fords, Henry Ford's family. I had three brothers, and two of them were in the field. My father died all too soon, but at least he was in the field. Had he lived, the potential certainly was there for us to all work together. But it fell to me to maximize my mother's vision, even if I had to do it virtually all by myself.

After all, I was the one to build the Madison architectural enterprise into the power it is today, and I was the one to lead it from crisis to triumph. That meant keeping its Cleveland foundation steady and growing, and those satellite offices Julian now ruled began to fade for me.

Actually, despite that profound split with Julian, my firm has survived to another generation. Kevin is my nephew, Bernard's son, and president

All hands on deck collaboration is the Madison International way.

of Robert P. Madison International. His wife, Sandra, is CEO and chairperson of the firm, and both are good architects. I'm their champion. People need champions.

The story faded to black for my brother, however. For a time, Julian thrived and made Detroit the base of a firm he put together with his daughter, Sharon. He even bought a downtown building, years before the city turned chic again. But he also fell—hard. Julian was killed on March 1, 1989. At his funeral services at Plymouth Congregational Church, the Detroit church I designed years earlier, Mayor Coleman Young eulogized Julian as a key force in the city's renaissance. There was a separate service for Julian in Cleveland.

I was left desolate. My oldest brother and longtime friend was gone.

Keep going

In Cleveland, we evolved into a well-managed and tight-knit firm. We would have staff picnics in the Metroparks, along with Christmas parties. These were wonderful occasions. I felt proud that we were doing our job and that all these people were working together and liking each other. Nobody had ever done that before.

At the same time, companies are vulnerable, and personnel problems would occasionally arise. One guy came to my firm from jail on a work-release program. He could draw like you wouldn't believe, he worked diligently, and I was ready to take him on full-time. I paid him after two weeks but never saw him again. He could have had a career with me.

I tried to help other hard-luck cases, but most didn't work out. Still, I felt an obligation to give people a shot at success. Through all this, I never lost sight of the client and always sought excellence and improvement in whatever we did. Architecture is a delicate business, and when a client says, "I want you to design a house for me, and I've only got $250,000, and that's it," you have to know what you're doing. If you don't, you'll let that client down, and your reputation will take a hit.

When someone entrusts you with their money, you must be demanding in terms of excellence and execution. You must be just as exacting with yourself and your partners. I didn't demand that others do everything my way, but in this profession you have to know how to add and subtract—for starters. I could prepare a sketch, and our staff could translate it, as long as the dimensions in the sketch were correct. Get the basics right.

I assembled a great company, with a staff of many colors and faiths. I wanted a fully integrated workforce, which differentiated us from our competitors and still does. But any workforce needs to get the job done, and it has to be reliable. And I personally required steadiness, a quality my wife embodied.

Over the years, Leatrice influenced me personally and, at least at the start, kept the firm going in a very fundamental way. She provided the financial backstop and support with her teaching career. And while she was not on our board or a member of our architectural firm, she was my emotional and professional bedrock.

I couldn't have done all this without her. I wouldn't even be here without her. Leatrice was the one who always said, "Go, we're going to go, we'll do it." She was a promoter of all things Madison. Even at her funeral, people came up to me to reminisce about all the times she had told them about "Monk this" and "Monk that."

I felt I could walk with the mighty because I've done it, I've proved it. My hope is that out of this can come a belief. Ruth Bader Ginsburg, the Supreme Court justice, has done that. She's just like me: If you really give it all you got, you've got to make some sacrifices and take some lumps. Be aggressive and be prepared for the worst. If you have the right stuff, you can do it.

I remember when we got our first school, the Captain Arthur Roth School, and people said I didn't have the experience to design a school. But a lady on the board of education stood up for me, even though others in the profession were pretty hostile to me. There was the same kind of reception when I was chosen to design the Rapid Transit Authority Healthline stations: "Madison has no experience designing rapid transit stations in Cleveland," opined James Dixon, then president of the Cleveland chapter of the AIA. I earned the job anyway.

The minority architecture firms in town were Hisaka, Fred Toguchi—and Madison. I'm black, Toguchi was Japanese, and Hisaka was Chinese. I felt really driven to prove I was as good as anybody else and that I could do architecture, too.

I guess I proved that. When I.M. Pei, whom I had met decades earlier on that great trip to China in 1974, came to Cleveland to choose a local architect to partner with on the Rock and Roll Hall of Fame, he weighed the credentials of several major firms. When he said that Bob Madison was his choice, I was proud but not surprised. I knew I was the right guy.

CHAPTER TWENTY-FIVE
THE MADISON LANDMARKS

Advanced knowledge might be a professional's most valuable asset. As you build up a large storehouse of facts, information and skills, you give yourself the best chance to get the job, deliver excellence on the most challenging projects, and advance your career or practice. But while nobody can know everything—we all know people who claim they do—everybody has the ability to learn and improve. If you're ignorant about a topic, the remedy is to be schooled, and sometimes school yourself, in that topic. Whether it's how to safely contain nuclear radiation, how to comply with federal regulations or manage the idiosyncrasies of a building site, knowledge is golden. Nobody can take away from you what you learn.

▲

Rock and Roll Hall of Fame and Museum, Cleveland, Ohio, 1995 | I.M. Pei, principal architect; Robert P. Madison International, associate architect

I'm not sure any of us who worked on the Rock & Roll Hall of Fame could have imagined how that building would become an icon for Cleveland. Big ballgame or a big news item or feature that involves Cleveland? You can bet an image or video of the Rock Hall will be shown. Maybe one day when a statue of Superman, who was created in Cleveland, finds a home, that image will be used. But for now, the Rock Hall is Cleveland's signature landmark.

Any honest professional will admit that some knowledge you gain just through luck or circumstance. For example, I learned French and the metric system in large part because I attended great schools with great teachers. As I acquired that knowledge, I had no plan for how I would use it 15 years later when I studied in Paris.

Domestically, I proactively learned about radiation control strategies before I designed the Tuskegee Institute's nuclear and engineering facility. That Alabama project was tough but rewarding.

The 1960s was a very busy period, and, in particular, 1965 stands out for me. In addition to more routine projects, three major commissions swamped my firm: the new U.S. Embassy in Dakar, Senegal; the Tuskegee facility, and the nation's first moderate-income housing project in Detroit.

It was wonderful to be a pioneer on such projects. This was the first time we had this kind of breakthrough work, which we were going to do even if we had to put in 24 hours a day. I didn't know what to expect when I opened my practice; mind you, this is only about 10 years after stepping out on my own. The embassy? Of course we were going to do it. You don't turn down work. We always found a way to do these kinds of jobs, unless it meant working for people who were dishonest. That's when a different type of knowledge and ability comes into play—including when to say no to a project, prospective client, or partner. I wish I could offer a formula for deciding when to walk away. No one can, though.

When we learned of a legitimate project, we would do our best to secure the work. From the very beginning, I didn't know day to day whether we would survive, so we did not turn down anything. If it was genuine and good, we would find a way to get it done, and do it well.

I sure had a lot of things going at once. At the very same time I was working on that embassy in Dakar, my firm responded to a request to submit architectural plans for the Tuskegee project. During the interview period, they posed the kinds of questions I had become accustomed to as a trailblazer like my deceased comrade-in-arms, architect Robert Taylor.

Like me, Taylor was a pioneer. He was the country's first accredited African-American architect, and the first African-American architect to enroll in and graduate from the Massachusetts Institute of Technology.

At Tuskegee Institute, a historically black university, Taylor designed the Science Hall. Even more remarkably, Taylor supervised its construction, entirely by students using bricks made by students under Taylor's direction. This project, completed in 1893, was inspired by Booker T. Washington, Taylor's idol. The goal was to motivate descendants of former enslaved Africans and embody the dignity of physical labor while showing the world the capabilities of African-Americans in the building trades. Taylor went on to design the entire campus of Tuskegee. Ever heard of Robert Taylor Homes, that huge public housing project on the south side of Chicago? It's named after him.

Taylor's personal life and professional achievements spurred me to do whatever I needed to secure the Tuskegee job, including expanding my fields of knowledge. My motto: You can never know too much.

I have to admit that I really wanted the job because a new administration at Tuskegee felt the need to open up campus projects to white architects. One of those was Paul Rudolph, chair of Yale University's Department of Architecture, who collaborated with graduates of Tuskegee's architecture school to design the institute's chapel. Once the administration decided it didn't want to limit the work to white architects, it invited me down.

The key question at my initial interview sounded familiar; I'd encountered many versions of it before. "Well, Mr. Madison, have you ever designed a nuclear facility before?" Tough question.

I went through the whole ritual of the interview, answering all the questions, and admitted I had no experience designing a nuclear facility. "But give me two weeks," I said. "I'll get the information I need."

After a few weeks, Tuskegee called me back for a second interview, based on my acquiring the appropriate information about a field that really only began in the 1940s. So, before I returned to Alabama, I went to Case Institute of Technology, connected with a nuclear physicist there and consulted with him for three days. I guess today you'd say I immersed myself in the topic. To me, it was simple: Find out what you need to learn to get the job, then learn it—and get the job.

Most of my learning stems from that kind of technique because I had many gaps in my formal education, especially in completing my architectural degree at Western Reserve University.

For me, the lasting lesson from Tuskegee is I didn't need to return to class to find out about nuclear science. Instead, I sought the advice of a consultant in the field of nuclear engineering. Among other technical details, I learned I would have to design in four feet of concrete and four feet of bermed earth to surround the building and contain nuclear radiation. So, when I returned to Tuskegee, I was ready and eager to present to the committee.

"Here's what we're going to do," I began, detailing how the facility would be designed and built to operate safely while complementing Taylor's original campus plan. "This guy knows what he's doing," the leader of the selection committee said. I was proud when my firm was named lead architect, with no partners involved. I designed the Engineering and Nuclear Facility at Tuskegee Institute, a landmark achievement.

I took a similar approach—deliberately moving from lead to inquiry, to practical education and application—to a project in Detroit. I designed the Medical Center Courts Housing Development, a $2.5 million, 221-unit complex that unfolded in four phases over five years. I got the work largely thanks to Nicholas Hood, a minister at Plymouth Congregational Church.

"They've got this program here," Hood told me. "Let's go after it." So I discovered at the housing authority of the city of Detroit a proposal to build a Section 221(d)(3) multifamily, moderate-income housing program administered through the Department of Housing and Urban Development, or HUD.

I did what I needed to learn the building requirements—occupancy levels, square-footage restrictions, accessibility, material and structural details—as well as the economic development aspects such as required occupant income levels. My team assembled all the data necessary to qualify for the program and the perfect design to match the desires of middle-income occupants with the constraints of the program. We also had perfect timing on our side: HUD was clearing cities for urban renewal and needed to fill vacant land with quality projects that addressed real needs. That 221(d)(3) project was very dynamic and full of complications that needed to be solved, just like the embassy in Dakar and the Tuskegee nuclear facility. But then, any project worth completing is challenging.

Unusual footprints

Sometimes the biggest challenge of a project is right beneath your feet: the site itself. Take the Frank J. Lausche State Office Building at West Superior and Prospect avenues in downtown Cleveland. The project came about in the mid-70s when James Rhodes, then Ohio's governor, decided a state office building was needed in Cleveland and of course would feature the work of architects from Cleveland. So he decided to put together a team: Robert P. Madison of Madison Madison International, Fred Toguchi and W. Byron Ireland, from Columbus. Ireland was Rhodes' favorite. He would come north to work with us on this tricky project.

Teams and partnerships come together in all kinds of ways and for all kinds of reasons—financial, political, industry expertise. All came into play in forming the architectural partnership that would bring the Lausche building to fruition.

The Tuskegee nuclear facility was solely my project, the embassy in Dakar strictly me. But the Lausche building was a team effort, largely politically motivated. Different people promoted each of us, but I was the only qualified Ohio architect who was black. So we became this team of Toguchi, Madison and Ireland—Japanese, black, white, Cleveland, Columbus, all different backgrounds.

Toguchi would be the managing partner and design the skin. My job was to design the shape. We all agreed the building would be glass, but we had to work hard to determine the kind of glass and who would detail it so it wouldn't leak. Ireland worked on the details of the mechanical systems.

Teamwork pays

When you think of a typical building site, you visualize a rectangular shape. Instead, the Lausche building would have to be placed on an irregularly shaped plot of land with seven sides. Complicating the project was the fact that the site is kind of an island, bordered by streets with heavy car, truck and pedestrian traffic.

So we needed a unique shape for the building, which I call a ziggurat. I got the idea for the building's irregular form from the pyramid-like temples of the Assyrian, Babylonian, and other ancient cultures. Ziggurats also were basically flat-topped, which this was, and on a floating platform that was believed to connect people with the divine. I came up with the shape. It was unique, it was the right solution, but shape alone doesn't make a building.

To make a building stand solid, you start at the bottom, digging a deep, sturdy foundation. Not on this project, though. The "land" we had to work with was mostly air. Major rail lines travel below street level, so this building had to be 15 stories and more than 200 feet high, providing space for more than 1,300 workers, all while essentially floating midair.

We pulled that off with a creative structural solution. Large iron piers were driven deep through street level to the rail lines about 75 feet below, and then perhaps another 50 feet below grade. We engineered an ironwork scaffolding to serve as the foundation itself. Amazing: 1,300 workers on-site, almost 500,000 square feet, all there 45 years later.

Whether the Lausche Building and its ziggurat shape symbolizes an inspired connection between its government occupants and the citizenry below, I'll leave to others to decide. Still, pulling off such a complex job as this could only have been achieved with a multi-firm team effort. We pulled that together right there.

Such teams are the norm for most large projects today. Take FirstEnergy Stadium, which was built from May 1997 until its opening in September 1999. The prime architect was HOK Sports Facilities Group, a St. Louis firm that designs most major-league sports venues. Despite its size and market dominance, HOK needed a local architect registered in Ohio. Its people were not experts on the laws of the city of Cleveland, so HOK selected Robert P. Madison International. Companies like HOK need a local firm unless they register in all jurisdictions, which is not practical.

I can design a house or a small building myself, but something as big and complex as the Cleveland Browns stadium engaged 15 people on our staff.

The main design scheme was prepared at HOK headquarters, but the details had to be fleshed out locally. I did the working drawings. There are 72,000 seats, and it was our job to draw in every one of them. "Bob, this is Section E," HOK's people said. "Put the seats in." That was my job, that kind of thing.

When it came to unearthing the whole underground—the locker room, the visiting locker room, as prescribed by the National Football League—HOK knew what to do. We didn't have to go back to school to find out how many lockers they needed. But we did the construction documents for the lower level of the stadium and all the tasks that an associate architect needs to tackle to make a project like this ready for massive crowds.

The very first crowd that gathered for a large event at that stadium that wasn't related to athletics was for an arts benefit. What a wonderful convergence of profession and passion.

Leatrice and I had a particularly delightful evening in late November 1999 when the Cleveland Opera honored us at a black-tie benefit at what was then known simply as Cleveland Stadium. That night, the opera board honored our "transforming vision" that "made Cleveland a finer place for us and for generations to come."

The fact that the opera gala was held in a stadium for which I was associate architect was especially sweet. Talk about bridging two worlds.

Cleveland rocks

A lot of projects I've completed originated from outside leads, like the stadium and the Rock and Roll Hall of Fame. For the latter, I.M. Pei was the lead architect, but he's not registered in Ohio. I am.

The Rock Hall was Pei's job. I was his Cleveland associate, the guy who prepared the local documents after he gave his plans to me. I frequently went to New York for design and review meetings. During one of these, after he had designed a dance hall on a cantilever over Lake Erie, I asked him about sympathetic vibrations.

You know what sympathetic vibrations are? They're what happens when a column of soldiers walks across a bridge in lockstep. As they

I.M. Pei (center) with Jim Lim and Bob Madison.

march, each boot hits the pavement at the same moment, creating a "boom, boom, boom." The harmonic resonance that march creates can crack the bridge. Think of it as tension failure. Architects learned the sympathetic vibrations lesson the hard way when two walkways at the Hyatt Regency Kansas City hotel collapsed in July 1981. The structural failure resulted in more than 100 deaths and 200 injured.

The way to prevent this is to take the soldiers out of their parade routine and instead have them walk normally, with natural variety in their stride. Simple action, catastrophe prevented. At the Rock Hall, Pei and I may have prevented a calamity similar to the one in Kansas City, not by changing the structure but by changing the function of the space. Instead of a hall where dancers might move to the beat in dangerous unison, that cantilevered space became an exhibition room.

The Rock Hall was Pei's building and very much his design, but I felt like a partner. He was very good about our relationship. Why did he want me? Pei is an aristocrat and an aesthete of the highest order. He appreciates Beethoven, Brahms, Braque, and Kandinsky. He told me that when he learned of the opportunity to design a rock 'n' roll building, he was concerned. I don't know anything about rock 'n' roll music, he said to me. Perhaps Pei saw me as both a cultural and architectural sounding board.

Pei decided to go to rock concerts in New York. After he went to three different shows, he said, "Bob, now I realize that rock 'n' roll music is unpredictable. It's erratic." If you look at the Rock Hall and notice that column sticking out to the west, perhaps it's as a result of experiencing those concerts. Rock is unpredictable; you never know what's going to happen.

We prepared preliminary drawings for his proposal and the documents and drawings required for construction. We were on site in a supervisory capacity as the building rose from Cleveland's harbor.

Bookish but bold

Two years after the Rock Hall opened, we were named local architect for the 10-story Stokes wing of the Cleveland Public Library.

Named after Louis Stokes, the longtime U.S. congressman and brother of former Mayor Carl Stokes, the wing was built in 1997. The architects on that project were my company and Malcolm Holzman, a New York company that worked on numerous libraries.

I headed the local design team, which included one engineer from Columbus and one from Cleveland. The ground next to the existing library, where the footings were, was potentially unstable, prompting an argument between the engineers over how best to address the issue. They were at each other's throats, and Holzman was up in New York.

Time for some hotel room diplomacy, using the same approach I had taken during the Atlanta airport job decades earlier. I said, "Look, guys, come on. We're going to go into this hotel and into a room, and you guys are going to stay there until you all decide which one is right. Either the building is going to fall down or it's not. One says it is, one says it isn't. Here's the hotel room. Go in there and don't come out until you agree."

They eventually came out with a solution—together. I was tough; I had to be. The building's still standing.

My office also did all of the restoration of the old library. The main library was designed by the Cleveland firm of Walker & Weeks, which

The architect with Ohio Rep. Louis Stokes, namesake of the major Cleveland Public Library project Bob completed in 1997.

also designed Severance Hall and other classic buildings of that era. When the library opened in 1916, it was one of the largest open-stack libraries of its time. My group took great pride in getting the nuts-and-bolts details right. The original library building had no air conditioning and we brought air-conditioning ducts to the stacks, where it is distributed all the way down under the floor.

Being bookish also means doing your research. We studied hard to get the 45-unit Amasa B. Ford Lodge at Eliza Bryant Village in Cleveland right. We designed those units to maximize the quality of life while keeping initial and continuing costs as low as possible.

The two goals don't have to be mutually exclusive. Of course, trade-offs always come into play, especially with materials and accessories. But with some planning, including talking to residents to learn their hopes for the space, you can achieve great outcomes. At Eliza Bryant, residents wanted a space of their own—so we built units that shared some but not all walls.

Security and a sense of community mattered, too—so we oriented the units so every door to a unit was visible to the doors and windows of at least four other units. This way, people were more likely to interact during everyday life, whether in conversation, sharing outdoor chores, or maybe just being watchful. Sometimes a "nosy neighbor" is the best neighbor.

Barring none

Designing scientific institutions, public housing, government buildings and educational facilities is one thing. Designing prisons is another.

First, I got a job designing a prison in Grafton. I told Julian, "J, we're going to do something with this. We're going to make it so that the prisoners can grow there and come out better citizens." That was our mission.

Then I was invited to make a presentation to officials who wanted to build the Wayne County Justice Center in Wooster. As I considered the offer, I thought to myself, "We're going down here for what? These people don't know black people, and they'll never hire me."

About 10 other firms were competing, and I'd been up against them before—and lost. Still, I love a challenge, and, much to my surprise, I was selected.

After about six months on that job, I was awarded the commission to design the county administration building, which made me wonder why. This could be the reason.

The selection committee was made up of farmers; Wooster is an agricultural town. To me, it looked like those other architects were arrogant and looked down on the locals. I think my presentation was respectful, and I'm pretty sure that's what got me the job.

I completed three major buildings in Wooster, Ohio. The justice center was kind of special. Of course, there were cellblocks, but there also were libraries with meeting rooms. The dining hall was really wonderful, and the garden was terrific.

Later, I was told that in the wintertime, people would actually break the law so they could go to jail and live in this wonderful building, with good food and a recreation center. That jail earned an award from AIA as one of the best-designed buildings in the state of Ohio corrections system. I saw the one they had before, and it was just a cold dungeon.

Then I got a job to design a prison in Ashtabula. When I visited the old one, I met this kid, about 18 years old, and asked him, "Why are you here?"

"I killed somebody."

"What's your term?" I asked. "Life."

After that, I stopped building jails. We've got to find the roots of the problems that send people to jail. I couldn't see a kid of 18 spending the rest of his life in jail. It just wasn't right.

CHAPTER TWENTY-SIX

GRACEFUL EXITS

One Friday in late July 1988, I arrived at the office as usual, only to observe a different look on the faces of the 45 employees at our Cleveland headquarters. My secretary seemed a bit off, as if she was expecting something to happen. I couldn't trace anything specific that was different, but when you reach a certain age and you've been close with a group of people for a long time, you develop a sixth sense. Something seemed to be going on.

The day proceeded normally until lunchtime, when we all gathered in the dining room. It was then that I understood: My 65th birthday was July 23, a Saturday, and all of Robert P. Madison International wanted to celebrate that milestone with me during the workweek.

▲

Regional Transit Authority light rail station, Cleveland, Ohio, 2002 |
Robert P. Madison International, architect

From the surface level of Ninth Street, this station seems small. But descend the stairs to the tracks or view it from near FirstEnergy Stadium to the west and you can begin to appreciate its complexity. Servicing multiple train lines, elevators, staircases, pedestrians, vehicles—all on three levels—was a chore. But it was fun to figure out, fun to bring in all that light, and fun to complement the look of the nearby Rock Hall.

A beautiful cake, a heartfelt "Happy Birthday to You" serenade from about 25 people along with the typical jokes related to so many candles ("Do you think he has it in him?" and, "I think we better alert the fire department"). Making a wish, blowing out the candles, applause and cheers, followed by my brief, embarrassed but genuine thanks. It wasn't until the staff presented me with a set of beautiful golf clubs that I appreciated the symbolism of the moment.

"What am I supposed to do with these?" I asked.

"Well, Mr. Madison, aren't you retiring? Have you thought about what you're going to do tomorrow?"

"Thank you very much," I said. "I'm really gratified, but I'll be right back here on Monday, just like I have been for the past 35 years." That was my way of ending any discussion about my retiring.

After all, there was work to do; there always is. It has been noted that architects live notably long lives. Take just three of my colleagues and contemporaries: I.M. Pei turned 100 in 2018, Philip Johnson reached 98, Oscar Niemeyer lived to be 104 years old, and they made tremendous contributions late in life. Of course, I'm no spring chicken now, but back in 1988, I was ready for more work—and the work was ready for us. No way was I going to stop at that point, and so began the most productive, most lucrative, highest profile and most satisfying 15 years of my career.

The work came thick and fast in the 1990s, when Mike White became mayor of Cleveland. White was Cleveland's 55th mayor, and just its second black mayor after Carl Stokes. Members of the Union Club and other pillars of the establishment came to the conclusion that the city of Cleveland needed a rebirth, with all kinds of new government buildings on city-owned land. The mayor agreed, the money materialized, and the search for architects, engineers and bankers who could execute these plans became critical.

As the search began, White said each building must have a team that included a qualified, minority-owned architectural firm. Robert P. Madison International had been around for nearly four decades and was the most qualified minority firm in the state—and more qualified than many firms with white ownership, too.

Designer's rendering for a key station in the Waterfront Line, part of Cleveland's light rail rapid transit system.

We began to be included in major city projects like; the Rock and Roll Hall of Fame; what is now known as First Energy Stadium; what is now known as Quicken Loans Arena; the main Cleveland Public Library; and the Healthline, the city's innovative rapid transit line, which features large buses traveling on dedicated lanes throughout the heart of Cleveland. We had earned the right to do this work.

"All my life, I have been hoping for true recognition as a professional architect and for what we can do," I told my staff. "After all these years, we have proven our capability—at last."

With all this work coming on line, we needed staff to really step up, become fully engaged and become leaders. And they were eager and up to the challenge. How wonderful. How exciting. How great.

As an increasing number of these projects came to completion in the 1990s and early 2000s, older staff members were reaching 65 years—like me—but unlike me, they chose to retire. They included: Art Pimm, who was five years older than me; Khai Lim, who had risen to president and been with me for 40 years; Chester Henderson, who joined me right out of college and rose to serve as a vice president; Chinnaya Paramasivam, aka Siva, a vice president who returned to India; Vjekoslav "Slavko" Zlataric, who retired; and Doris Jackson, my longtime treasurer.

As these veterans left, young people advanced slowly, but quite properly. My nephew Kevin became vice president, his wife Sandra became CEO, and Robert Klann took over finance.

Slowly but deliberately, I delegated more responsibility, even as the jobs kept coming—and getting better. I began to slow down toward the end of the '90s after the opening of the Rock Hall. In the first decade of the new millennium, it seemed to me that winding down took up more of my time than work did. I kept busy, but family preoccupied me more than my business.

After all, Robert P. Madison International was well-established, Leatrice and I had made our mark on Cleveland society, our daughters were well on their professional ways, and—face it—we were getting older.

My company was in good hands, good younger hands. I had vice presidents galore, and I had been promoting people since my brother left in the early '80s. I had Khai Lim, who became president when I stepped aside to become chairman of the board.

Promoting Khai was a big deal, but 2004 also turned out to be a big year in another way: It was the year doctors at University Hospitals told me I had prostate cancer. I didn't do anything at first; physically and psychologically, it was easier to do nothing. The doctors monitored my condition for quite a while, but not only didn't the cancer go away, its progress began a new phase. In 2006, they told me, "You better do something; you'll die from this."

"You have advanced, aggressive cancer," they said. "If you do nothing at all, you will die in three years."

So I began radiation treatments at University Hospitals that fall. From October to December, at noon, five days a week for six weeks, my body was the target, and a powerful beam of radiation was the weapon. They said, "You got it." That felt like such a victory.

Leatrice and Bob in the Smith Lobby of Severance Hall, home of the Cleveland Orchestra.

Leatrice with her daughters Juliette and Jeanne. The two generations of Madison women speak to the dignity and power of the family.

At the same time, I was taking care of my wife, so getting rid of that cancer felt like two steps forward, one big step back. I was cured, but the very next year, I learned some bad news. Leatrice was suffering from dementia. That devastating diagnosis explained many things.

When she was a young girl, Juliette would come home from school to find her mother in the same spot, reading one newspaper after another: *The Plain Dealer*, *The New York Times*, *The Call & Post*, *The Cleveland Press*. Leatrice's attention and intellectual curiosity were powerful. Years later, however, long after our daughters had left home, her lack of focus and drive disturbed me. She might read most of one newspaper, then return and read it again. Some days, she'd stare out the window for an hour. I began to wonder what was happening to my Leatrice.

For months, I had noticed gradual changes in my wife's behavior, but I figured that was just part of getting older. People used to dismiss symptoms like hers as a memory lapse, something normal and benign. Actually, what she was going through was consistent with a defined, progressive disease—and, unfortunately, an incurable one. I never really understood her dementia until it was too late, and ultimately, no medical professional in the world could prevent or treat her condition. So sad, so frustrating to have your life partner in the room with you, but without her intellect and spirit. We were together, but alone.

I kept thinking it was my fault Leatrice was so slow getting up in the morning, that it was my fault she would have a habit of standing in the kitchen not moving, as if she were lost. I couldn't understand why she'd get stuck on a sentence in the newspaper where she used to zip through it front to back. "The president says he's going somewhere," she'd say slowly over and over. Very painful to watch.

So, after my illness was successfully treated, I could turn my attention to take care of sweet Leatrice. In sickness and health. I also traveled to work in the office every day, and even though some help came to our home every day to care for Leatrice, my attention to my practice began to decrease. I was trying to keep myself, my practice, and my wife alive.

That was how we spent Leatrice's last six years, caught in a battle on three fronts. Those were very tough years.

Team picture of Madison International staff at its peak, perhaps the best illustration of Bob's commitment to creating and maintaining a diverse, high-performance workforce.

During that period, we had plenty of architectural work. I made the decision not to retreat but to at least pull back a bit, observing and more or less supervising. I wasn't really doing the designing, account management, or business development. Life itself, Leatrice's and mine, became more important than my practice; my wife died in 2012.

By that time, the office had been effectively reorganized. We had people of all races, religions, and countries of origin, and they all worked together. As the months and years passed and the list of successful projects grew, the differences dropped away. They stopped asking about each other or talking behind each other's back. They genuinely liked and appreciated each other for who they were.

In most of our lives, we can only plan so much; circumstance and accident play a large part in what we become and what we accomplish. But the composition of that firm, a United Nations of architectural professional? That was by design. I planned that to prove it could be done.

Our success was a victory. I didn't beat them at their own game. We created a new, better game, and we won, over and over. I don't think any architectural firm has tried that since.

Still, no matter how great the victory or how enjoyable the environment, the time comes when you have to let go. To do that well, it's important to know when and how. An architect friend of mine—an older man—is having a hard time because he won't let go. It's very difficult to take your hands off the wheel when you designed the car.

These young people wanted to move up, and I wanted to give them a chance to do that. Like Sandra Madison, my nephew Kevin's wife. She's good. We were doing the performing arts building on the eastern campus of Tri-C and I laid it out and she started drawing it. I would come back and check and say no, I want to do it this way. She said no, we do it my way, and she just grabbed it and ran with it. Same with Lim. Same with Henderson. I'm a headstrong guy, but I know when to back off and let someone else run the project. It's not easy, but it's necessary.

It didn't disappoint me that my daughters didn't join my firm as full time designers. I was fine with our relationship as it was. I also don't think Jeanne felt I discounted her because she was a woman, and I did everything with her that I would have had she been my son.

As for Juliette, the inside joke all of us have enjoyed is that maybe she should have been an architect, given her interest and abilities in art, design and recently, construction and development. She never asked whether I wanted a son, but if she had, I would have told her I was happy with her and Jeanne. How could I not be? As the old saying ends, ". . . but a daughter is a daughter for the rest of her life." So fortunate for Leatrice and me that this saying applies to us.

Besides, even if Juliette had considered joining Robert P. Madison International after college, she couldn't have looked forward to being the new Madison, the one to carry that water there. As much as anyone, I'm sensitive to the struggles of carrying on a family legacy.

In any case, family still matters strongly to me, with Kevin and Sandra in charge of my company.

Pulling back from the business I founded and built became a combination of laying on of hands and letting go. I'd done that before on specific projects. Take the time we were associate architect on the Great Lakes Science Center, with E. Verner Johnson, a lead architect from Boston, and we had to get him to comply with Cleveland codes—which we knew.

It finally felt right to stop those daily office visits, relax, and live a different kind of life. That cancer was a pain, and those last years with Leatrice were difficult. But the demands of home life weren't the only reason I let go.

Another reason was things were changing technologically—the way an architect produces designs and specifications. While my favorite tool has always been a pencil, young architects need to be computer-oriented and tech-savvy. They may not know how to draw on a piece of paper, but they know the right buttons to push.

Architects of my era could draw lines on paper. I could draw from when I was a little boy. Most of today's designers can't draw; they have a machine, they have a keyboard, but no pencils, no T-squares.

I like pieces of paper more than keyboards. I knew I couldn't design with computers, and I didn't want to. I didn't feel I had to learn that. I'd been out there all day for years, for parts of eight decades.

I officially retired when I was 93 years old. The last major project I personally designed was the Gill and Tommy LiPuma Center for the Creative Arts on 30th Street at Woodland Avenue at Tri-C in Cleveland. It's home to the Rock Hall archives. That was an exciting thing to do. We were on a tight budget of around $35 million.

Like that nuclear engineering facility at Tuskegee Institute I designed a lifetime earlier, the LiPuma building involved a learning curve. The site is within shouting distance of a very busy freeway, so acoustic controls and dampeners had to be built in. It also required special glass to blunt ultraviolet rays, as well as saddle cantilevers to help block the sun and protect valuable archives from fading. Designing it meant I had to go to a whole new school—again.

Some people said the 75,000-square-foot LiPuma building didn't have flair to it, but the whole campus is red brick and white, and we thought it was vital to stay within that vocabulary. I was proud at the ribbon cutting. I stopped by for a visit in the fall of 2018, and I'm still proud.

But after the LiPuma building opened in 2009, it was time to step back, because these young people have bright ideas, and they have to have a chance. As much as I could, as hard as I could, I said, I've done my thing.

I ran my race; I did my part in life's relay, so here's where you take it from here. Grab the baton and hold it tightly. Run steady through the curves. Swing your arms. Breathe, breathe. And know that you'll pass it on to someone worthy and ready.

I still visit the office. It has my name on it, and my name has currency. It's a brand, too, and the people want it there. I ask how they're doing, and I get reports on projects, but really all I do is listen; I don't work on them. I come home at night and shed a tear. But it's not a tear of pain or sadness. It's a tear of acceptance and, I guess, satisfaction.

Everything is still there. And it's theirs, all theirs.

CHAPTER TWENTY-SEVEN

THE ARCHITECT AS ARTIST

To me, architecture has always been a mission. It is also, of course, a trade and a skill. But above all, architecture is a statement of purpose: to create a space in service to people. I've always tried to build what my client wants, whether the client is a city, a country, an agency, a private homeowner, a group of doctors, or a church congregation. But sometimes it's an architect's job to give clients not just what they want, but what they need, now and in the future. When you're just starting out, scrambling for commissions, it's difficult to walk away from the income even if you know the client is making shortsighted choices.

But when you're a professional, you sometimes need to model your behavior on that of an air traffic controller. An air traffic controller respects the professionalism, training, and instincts of the pilot in the air. But that

▲

Quicken Loans Arena, Cleveland, Ohio, 1994 | Ellerbe Becket, principal architect, Robert P. Madison International, associate architect

This wasn't the house that LeBron James built—after all, the building opened as Gund Arena a few months before LeBron was born. But for many around the world, it will be noted as the place he worked his basketball magic for so long and for so many.

controller has specialized training, instrumentation, and perspective. If a pilot is heading for the side of a mountain, the air traffic controller had better do everything to avoid that collision. After all, everyone has a stake in keeping the plane aloft. An architect needs to adopt a similar mindset, to inform and do what's best for the client and the public.

Social stakes

My favorite buildings are ones in which I have a personal stake, buildings that also contribute to the social good. My deepest hope is that the structures I design—from the U.S. Embassy in Dakar to low-income housing in Detroit to any number of A.M.E. churches—better the human lot.

I may be as far away as possible stylistically from Frank Lloyd Wright, but I wholeheartedly agree with his view of architecture: "All fine architectural values are human values, else not valuable." At the same time, I subscribe to Louis Sullivan's famous architectural guideline, "Form follows function." I'm a generalist, and I've always wanted my buildings to work well.

I never thought that much about specific types of buildings, however; I did not specialize in museums or hospitals or anything like that. I like to work, I bucked history to stake my architectural claim, and I was happy to design any kind of building that came along. In a way, each one was very special to me. Special because my buildings contributed to social progress.

With the perspective of so many decades, however, I now think that some types of projects stand out for me—medical clinics and churches, in particular. Those clinics were where I really began, shortly after I opened my office in 1954.

I started out by remodeling houses to accommodate clinics and doctors' offices. I designed these for African-American doctors who at that time were not able to rent space for their practices in existing buildings because the owners wouldn't rent to African-Americans. These were basically repurposings, remodeling existing homes to clinical specifications. They were modifications and adaptations.

I soon got to design my first true, purpose-built structure, the Mount Pleasant Medical Center, a four-suite commercial structure, with a pharmacy, on Kinsman Avenue. That really put me on the map.

Not only did it win a design award from the American Institute of Architects, it surprised the whole city. All of a sudden, people were saying, here's a black architect who can not only design buildings, he designs prize-winning buildings.

Another project of mine that drew notice was the Medical Associates Building on East 105th Street. In the summer of 2018, that building played host to FRONT International, a months-long, regional arts program; nice to see it repurposed. Nice that the reason it was built doesn't exist any more—at least not in the law books. Nice also that it's no longer called the Medical Associates Building. It's simply called The Madison.

Medical buildings were always very compelling because designing them meant creating spaces where doctors could practice, saving people's lives. That became exciting and personally rewarding.

The next type of building that was really important for my company was a church. That's largely due to the fact that, in 1959, the African Methodist Episcopal Church designated my firm as its official architect. The A.M.E. Church was the first African-American religious organization established after slavery in this country; Wilberforce University and several other historically black colleges originated from it. So, when I was designated the church's official architect, we did buildings in Niagara Falls, New York, Pittsburgh, Little Rock, Arkansas, Washington, D.C., Detroit, and, of course, Cleveland—really all over.

The A.M.E. Church is my keystone in more ways than one. It became important to my family not only because of the work it generated but also because we were doing the work for African-Americans, we were very religious people, and it was my personal church.

The very first church I designed marked a very special milestone for me. How I got the job is quite a story.

Stepping up

I'd been practicing for about three years and advertising a lot in the *Call & Post,* Cleveland's powerful black newspaper, when one day I got a call from the Reverend Robert L. Fuller. "I am the pastor of Mount Hermon Baptist Church, and Mr. Madison, we would like you to be our architect," the reverend said.

I was stunned; nobody had ever called me out of the blue with such an offer. Naturally, I said I was interested, so the Reverend Fuller invited me to a meeting a few days later at a storefront in the Central area. That unforgettable gathering marked a turning point in my career.

Here was this pastor talking about how Mount Hermon was a black church and he said, "Now, Mr. Madison, we want you to be our architect for this church. This is the most important thing you will ever do."

Most important thing I'd ever do? I was shocked—especially when the pastor said the church planned to spend $250,000. Where would it get that kind of money? I wondered. The establishment banks wouldn't even loan me $300 to establish my practice, and here's this little storefront church with about 75 people talking about a quarter-of-a-million-dollar building.

As these thoughts were running through my head, the church and congregation were already way ahead of me, ready to act. Very soon, the pastor said, "All right, we're ready to call the roll now. Please get in line and come on up." Twenty-five ladies stood up. These ladies worked at basic service jobs, in laundries, in hotel housekeeping, as caretakers of children. If they were middle-class, they were only on the very lowest rung. But that didn't matter to them or me. They were resolute.

They stood up, as the reverend demanded. After he called each one by name, they went up to him one after another, each with a brown paper bag in hand. The pastor took something out of the bag and put it aside. When all of them had made it to the front, he shouted out: "We have achieved our goal."

What is he talking about? What goal did they achieve? I wondered.

Turns out each of those bags contained a bank savings book, and each book showed at least $10,000 in the bank. Twenty-five of those meant $250,000—cash. I was so moved I couldn't believe it. These people in a storefront church had been selling chicken dinners, barbecues, that kind of thing, for I don't know how many years.

What particularly touched me is when they came up to me and said, "Mr. Madison, you're our architect now." They couldn't spell architect, and some of these people were old enough to be my grandmother. I will never forget one lady who said, "Mr. Madison, I pray to the Lord I will live to see our church completed."

I was so moved that they picked me that I vowed to do perfect work and not make a single mistake. My wife and I went home after that storefront meeting and we prayed. Then I worked seven days a week with the little staff I had, we drew every line, and we watched that building come up piece by piece. It took about eight months to do the drawings, then another year and a half to build the church. Our fee was about 10 percent of the cost; $25,000 was a lot of money at that time. And even though I didn't put a brick in place myself, I rode herd on the contractors; after all, those people came up with 25 bank books of $10,000 each or, in today's figures, about $100,000. And when it was over, they came up to me and said, "Mr. Madison, thank you."

It was then that I realized I wasn't designing this building for me. I wasn't really designing it for the pastor. With this budget, these specifications, this would not be one that would win any design awards for me or my firm. But that was not the point. These people looked me in the eye and shook my hand. They literally put their faith—and their life savings—in me to build this church. I could not forget that. Still can't.

A personal mission

When I speak about the meaning of architecture, it centers on somebody entrusting that kind of faith and confidence in you, so you have to deliver. For the rest of my career, architecture became a matter of providing a satisfactory structure for people who had come up with the funds and who had a vision, an image and great desire to make this thing come to pass. I could name at least 10 other A.M.E. churches where people simply put their faith in me. I was 34 when I got the Mount Hermon job; those people definitely put their faith in me.

What's fundamental for me is that an architect has a responsibility to provide for the client the very best—that he or she puts together a design and a structure that reflect the client's wishes and desires and becomes a benefit to the environment in which the building finds itself. That's particularly true for private institutions like churches and private homes.

Bob and co-author Carlo Wolff outside Cleveland's FirstEnergy Stadium.

Public institutions, like stadiums, jails, or the Rock Hall, are different. There, you don't know who the users are. People come and go in a stadium, but a stadium doesn't have that connection to a particular person with a stake in it.

At the same time, all forms of architecture, even institutional architecture, can be a persuasive force. That was the case with LeBron James, the basketball superstar who joined the rebuilding Los Angeles Lakers in 2018, two years after leading his hometown team, the Cleveland Cavaliers, to its first world championship.

A key weapon in the arsenal Lakers president and CEO Jeanie Buss deployed to woo James in his free agency period was the new Lakers facility. The UCLA Health and Training Center in the Los Angeles suburb of El Segundo is awash in natural light. The building is all about transparency and community. It aims to integrate basketball operations and business operations by creating an environment that feels domestic rather than corporate. That $80 million facility was designed by the Detroit architectural firm Rosetti, working with Los Angeles firm Perkins + Will.

"The architects that we ended up choosing talked about how architecture can change culture in an organization," Buss says, recalling a conversation she had in 2012 with then-Laker Dwight Howard. "He came up to my office, and he said, can I ask you something? I said, sure, and he goes, where are all the people that work here? And it was then I realized it was important for them to know how we operate behind the scenes, so this building is a walkable building. There are no barriers, and you can make a full circle without having to divert through anything or be stopped and backtrack." When you hear a ball in play in one of the three basketball courts at the center of the building, "it's like the heartbeat of the building."

Corporate though she may be, Buss clearly has an emotional stake in her team's innovative, new facility. When you design for people you know and you're emotionally invested, it becomes more than a mission, it becomes a life—and a commitment beyond anything I've ever had to do before.

Churches are much more personal than any other building. Medical clinics are next, but a church, and a home—I find a commitment and impassioned feeling for those kinds of buildings because of the owners and the users I get to know.

Into the great unknown

When you start designing, you have no idea what the project will cost until you've completed it. A square joint could cost one amount, but a round joint could cost far more or less. It then becomes a measure of how the building comes together that really drives the final cost. A lot of schemes that we came up with would drive the project over budget so we cut back and cut back and cut back, and sometimes cutbacks are bad, and we don't like that. But generally, we knew—eventually—how much we could do, how much it would cost per square foot, and how to stay within those parameters. Yet the square footage for a school is different from the square footage for a detached, single-family home.

Architecture books provide standards, but standards can't provide all the learning. Even the most professional learn by trial and error. Grasping the fundamentals is a critical first step.

When we talk about design, we talk about space, volumes and materials. Space can be defined by a collection of lines. But ultimately materials are what make a structure what it is.

For example, back in the Dark Ages, when those great churches in Europe were built, laborers could handle a piece of glass that was about three feet by four feet, so stained glass was a matter of small pieces of glass joined together. Structural steel was not around at that time, so they had to put one brick on top of another brick on top of another. But as materials became more applicable, structural possibilities opened up. That's why, in my view, design has become a function—maybe reflection is more accurate—of the kinds of materials that permit you to do things.

Where in the Dark Ages you could only work with smaller volumes of glass, now pieces of glass as big as a wall can be formed. Therefore, the ability to create and enclose space—which is what buildings do—is dependent upon the kinds and flexibility of materials. The creation of prestressed concrete in the last century meant thinner floors, which meant higher buildings with taller floor-to-floor spaces; same thing with glass. So now, architecture, in my view, becomes a function of how you take materials and place them.

The architectural magazines I continue to read show pieces of glass that can span 10, 20 feet. When I was designing, we really only had prestressed concrete. Glass didn't offer similar design flexibility.

Expanding opportunities

Since I began my practice, architects have gained the ability to use materials much more creatively because there's much more flexibility in the materials. It's the ability of the materials to conform to whatever you want that gives an architect the opportunity to create any kind of space.

A long time ago, we were much more conservative in how we placed walls, columns, and other architectural features because we had to be very concerned about the structural system of support. Now architects and builders have much more flexibility because the materials can be specified to accommodate nearly any design we can dream up.

While building materials have become much more sophisticated and malleable, the skill set hasn't kept up.

Today, you don't have contractors with the kind of skill and affection they used to have. Take those elaborate structures in Lake View Cemetery in Cleveland; most of those artisans came from Italy. They lived up there

Bob with Ugochukwu-Smooth Nzewi, the Cleveland Museum of Art's Curator of African Art, at the First Annual Distinguished Lecture in African and African American Art. The lecture was made possible by the Robert P. Madison Family in Memory of Leatrice B. Madison Endowment, in November of 2018. Bob and Smooth both trace their heritage back to the same tribe in Western Africa. Bob continues to proudly serve and consult with the CMA.

and knew how to put those together; they learned over centuries how the Italians did that. It's difficult to find legacies like that in the trades.

In the 1960s, finances increasingly became a determining factor in what was built. Developers were building skyscrapers in New York with a life expectancy of 20 years because someone could tear them down and get some money to refinance. Built-in obsolescence started to replace built-to-last.

In the old, old days, when the Cathedral of Florence was built, it was meant to last; it's still there. It took 100 years to build it, though, because they put one brick on top of another. Filippo Brunelleschi did not know how to build that cathedral dome. It took him and other people years of trial and error, materials were limited, and everything had to be done by hand. So the fundamental issue is workmanship, not materials.

Ego is another sticking point. Take the race to create the tallest building, which has created all kinds of weird configurations. The engineers are the ones who can do that. But you've got to make sure to guard against the stresses of wind—if you're on a top floor, top floors sway, and you have to make sure the materials don't snap. They used to; that's what Brunelleschi was up against in Florence in 1400.

The environment is another consideration that has grown prominent, even crucial, since I began my practice. Even 50 years ago, energy conservation didn't matter that much. Warm up your house? Install a few more radiators. Now windows are double- and triple-paned. Again, it's the materials. Their increased flexibility gives architects more opportunity to be both creative and responsible.

As an architect, my favorite tool is the pencil. You can mark things with the lead, grade 4B. Bold, soft. By the pressure of the lead, you get different shades and creations, and you can overlay designs with vellum or tissue paper. That's what a pencil can do.

With a pencil and a piece of paper, you can do so much, two-dimensional, three-dimensional. My colleague Le Corbusier said it best when he proclaimed, "I prefer drawing to talking. Drawing is faster, and leaves less room for lies."

For me, the pencil came before the computer, AutoCad and Photoshop as a tool for drawing.

I don't know how to use a computer. Oh, I know how to push buttons, and I send text messages and receive photos of my family on my smartphone. But these students now, and my staff, can do so much more. They can take a computer and draw virtually any shape from any perspective and with any texture or transparency. Add a filter and change the season from summer to winter in a rendering illustration. Pull off the building skin and look at the skeleton of structure and mechanicals; they can do it all.

What many of them can't do, however, is articulate what they're doing. I remember one time a couple of guys came by with beautiful work. Let's talk about this, I said. Why did you create it like this? How will it help society? They couldn't answer. It was just one picture after another picture after another picture. Why? They didn't know why.

I don't want to be critical, because I understand that computer technology is what every architectural firm needs to master to be competitive today. But to me, someone who at least has some background with artfully pushing a pencil can add an important dimension better than someone who can only push buttons.

With a pencil, the canvas is unlimited. While you can't build a building with one, you design with a pencil—at least that's what I did— and any building starts with a design. With the right design—and programming, purpose, structure, sustainability—those buildings should last, too. The best buildings have long careers, like the greatest athletes.

I lived through the careers of Jackie Robinson, Jim Brown, Larry Doby, Jesse Owens. I'm still in the LeBron James era, and what an era it's been. I'm a major LeBron fan, no matter where he's playing. What he does on the court is amazing. What he's done for Northeast Ohio, the game of basketball, and the advancement of African-Americans has been remarkable as well. What he's done as a philanthropist and as a family man is inspiring.

Still, even a talent as great as LeBron needs a place to play. How many people watching a game think about the building it's played in? Somebody designed that building. I designed the Quicken Loans Arena, the building LeBron James played in. Even though LeBron is gone from Cleveland, the Q is likely to still stand tall after its ongoing upgrades. And after LeBron retires and passes the baton to the next basketball wonders, they will need arenas to demonstrate their talent. And a team of architects will have to design them.

That's what makes sense to me, and that's what I tell people about my profession. They often look at me with absolute disbelief that a black man could design such important buildings. Of course, black men and women can—with training, talent, opportunity, and a little bit of luck. And a lot of hard work.

That work pays off. Whether it's crossing a stream under enemy fire, constructing a building over a river, breaking through academically and professionally in a way that no African-American had done before, building a home on a hardscrabble lot in an inhospitable city, or designing bulwarks of faith like Mount Hermon Church and monuments to progress like the U.S. Embassy in Dakar, my life has been a triumph. While the color of my skin stacked the odds against me, I often needed to find a workaround. Perhaps it was a unique alternative approach, or finding a way to beat them at their own game. No matter what, I always played the long game.

In the end, the long game is the only one worth playing.

Bob surveys examples of his architectural handiwork in downtown Cleveland. From a single vantage point on the East Ninth Street pier on the shore of Lake Erie, it's possible to spot nine major projects designed by Robert J. Madison International.

AFTERWORD

I have spent more than a year writing for and about Robert P. Madison, Ohio's first African-American architect. As a result of our many discussions, I have learned a great deal about prejudice, racism, determination, intelligence, common sense, endurance and dignity. As the only child of parents who fled Hitler's Germany and later fled Mussolini's Italy for America in 1939, and one of very few Jews in my early school years in Columbus, Ohio, I know that fear of the other that motivates people who live in the seamier outposts of the American psyche. As the oldest of four brothers growing up in both the South and the North, Bob knew all about racism from the time he was a kid. My "otherhood" pales next to his. At the same time, the way we two deal with such unwanted distinctions bonds us.

Helping Bob write this memoir has been fascinating, rewarding, and a great honor. Best of all, it has deepened a friendship that began more than 20 years ago when I wrote an article about Bob for the Case West-

▲ **Gill and Tommy LiPuma Center for Creative Arts, Cleveland, Ohio,** 2009 | Designed by Robert P. Madison International ern Reserve University alumni magazine. I got to know Bob a little then. I also became acquainted with his wife, Leatrice, and visited the home Bob built for his family in Cleveland Heights. Over the years, we would run into each other at cultural events. It was always good to see Mr. and Mrs. Madison. I always find Bob engaging, opinionated, proud, funny, and sartorially advanced. The equally stylish Leatrice was unerringly gracious and polite.

Where my CWRU article focused on the Madison firm's architectural projects, this book goes deeper, tracing Bob's remarkable and fully lived life.

The work has involved channeling Bob's thoughts; transcribing and editing two dozen interviews; curating and editing hundreds of pages of his notes and manuscripts; and sourcing and selecting supporting material. It's been enlightening, occasionally jaw-dropping, and routinely surprising. One could call his story a personalization of the story of civil rights. It also is the account of a singularly talented family and the chronicle of a self-made professional who overcame great odds—even history itself—to not only prevail but also make quite a mark.

What Bob overcame in his journey to prominence and influence is inspiring and instructive. His saga—that is what this is—also attests to his modesty. Although he has enjoyed more than his fair share of honor and acclaim over the years, Bob isn't one to trumpet his achievements. In fact, ever since we started working on this book in late fall 2017, he has questioned whether anybody would be interested in reading about him.

I have never had any doubts.

Small wonder that the Bob Madison story is called *Designing Victory*. It tells of a mover and shaker who expresses himself through the buildings he has designed in a way that connected to the politics and the faith by which he lives. Bob has put a major stamp on his native Cleveland, Ohio, designing its "look" in various university buildings, the state office building, the Cleveland Public Library's Stokes addition, and the Rock & Roll Hall of Fame.

Look around downtown Cleveland and your eyes will land on a Madison structure. How Bob developed such a high professional profile attests to a singularly focused intelligence, his curiosity, his willingness to learn and adapt, his appetite for work and for beating the odds.

One of the key hurdles in crafting this memoir was memory itself. Memories lose definition and accuracy, no matter how immediate they feel. One can only imagine that at 95 years, Bob's memory bank is incredibly rich in quantity and detail. Along with his archives, it is those memories that make his story come alive. One memory from my own, younger life connects me with Bob beyond being his co-author. It's a painful but important path of re-discovery I travelled.

As a teenager, I joined a picket line protesting Woolworth's on Brattle Street in Harvard Square. The store had infamously refused to serve blacks at its lunch counter. I picture the picket line vividly. It was circular, with people holding signs and chanting. My mother had brought me to my first such march.

Walking that walk cemented my intolerance of intolerance and my aspirations for a colorblind society. What put it all together was a little old white lady spitting on me as I walked that sidewalk in Cambridge, Massachusetts, home to Harvard University, home to the best and the brightest—and at least back then, home to many of the most bigoted.

Helping Bob craft his story forced me to think more deeply about the larger picture of civil rights, and even though what I've had to deal with in no way measures up to what Bob had to overcome, there's a kinship there, as well as a sharing of warmth, respect, and a drive toward social justice.

The way I vote and pontificate about social issues are expressions of my beliefs, but I can't say I've dedicated my whole life to a more just society. Bob Madison, through his buildings and his example, has. May his inspiration live on.

Carlo Wolff

For editing, observations and insights well beyond the call of duty, I wholeheartedly thank James O'Hare of Act3, the executive producer of this book. I also thank the other principals of Act3: Ron Hill, whose drawings brought so many Madison projects to life; Jaime Lombardo, the digital wizard who contributed so much to the book's look and tone; and Kyra Wells, whose fresh eyes enhanced the book's visuals and marketing. A special thanks goes to Nina Gibans.

C.W.

EPILOGUE

Just days before this first edition was slated to go to print, Case Western Reserve University came full circle for me, catching me by surprise on campus at a board of trustees meeting on February 22, 2019. After the meeting was called to order, the board chairperson asked CWRU President Barbara R. Snyder for opening remarks.

In a loud voice, President Snyder asked, "Will Robert Madison please stand?" She then directed everyone's attention to a wall in the Toepfer Room in Adelbert Hall. What I saw startled me: portraits of six honorees including: former Congressional Representatives Louis Stokes and Stephanie Tubbs Jones; Fred Gray, famed civil rights attorney; Sara Harper, the first African-American to graduate from CWRU Law School; David Satcher, former Surgeon General of the U.S.; and Robert P. Madison, architect. Snyder explained to the crowd that these likenesses were an important way for the university to recognize exemplary CWRU alumni who have honored their professions and served the community.

More than a very impressive gesture, this was an authentic statement from the leadership of CWRU. I am honored to be in such great company, and honored by a great way to cap my long, often troubled, but finally harmonious relationship with my old school. The recognition was part of "The Trailblazer Project," an initiative that includes recognition for African-Americans, Asian-Americans, Latino-Americans, American Indians and other typically under-recognized groups. Almost sounds like the multi-cultural group that charged with me across the Arno River in Italy, or my colleagues at my architectural firm.

I guess I always viewed myself as someone who is willing to go before others to lead. So now I'm honored to be officially named a "Trailblazer." Heartfelt thanks go to President Snyder and Vice President Marilyn Mobley for their graciousness and consideration in mitigating the treatment I received as a student over 70 years earlier. About 20 years after my graduation from Western Reserve, as I was developing a business and designing buildings, I began to capture details and stories of my life and career that might be helpful to others.

First, during vacations, I spent time writing about people, events, and emotions that I encountered. Time passed as more stories were written and filed away for some future time. Then came retirement, and the flood of memories only increased: places I lived and visited, schools attended, buildings I designed, obstacles, awards and honors, people—the hundreds of people who have influenced my life.

Wow, I said to myself, what a life. I realized that all these people, places, and projects have formed the fabric of my life. In some future time, I thought, I really should format these stories in a way to inspire others—maybe they, too, will decide to dare mighty things, win glorious victories, give all they have in order to achieve them.

Then I realized that that future time is right now. Time to publish words and stories to not simply tell my story, but also to honor my mother and my wife. After all, what kind of mother coaches and supports her young sons to be an architect, engineer, minister, preacher, or other professional? My mother, Nettie Brown Madison, that's who. And what kind of wife sacrifices her professional ambitions and personal needs for the sake of her husband, her family, and society? My wife, Leatrice Branch Madison, that's who.

So, I sought advice, first from two other important women in my life—my articulate, professional, and artistic daughters. Jeanne is a business consultant, strategic planner, and actress, while Juliette is an artist, designer, and developer. They both enthusiastically said, "Go do it, Dad!" They wrote their memories to spur me along; I thank them for their encouragement and honesty.

Next step—get a professional to help. I immediately thought of Carlo Wolff, whom I've known for many years. I knew nothing about writing a story and nothing about publishing a book. Carlo eventually agreed to write with me, and not only that, he introduced me to a partner organization.

Act 3—Jim O'Hare, Ron Hill, Jaime Lombardo and Kyra Wells—specializes in publishing, media strategy, and production. This team became completely involved with all aspects of this book—editing, researching, illustrating, designing, printing, promoting, and distributing. They made all this come alive and for that, I am grateful. So I thank Carlo for being my friend, confidant, and muse, and I thank him for connecting me to the resources to get this moving and keep it going.

Many friends were enthusiastic supporters of this adventure, including Steve Bullock, Ted Long, David Whitehead and Elaine Pinderhughes. Thanks to those who provided technical assistance, proofing and critical reading of drafts; a partial list includes Dave Lange, Dorothy McMahon, Barbara Green, and Andrew Jarrett. For assistance with photos, thanks to Tim Diamond and AnnMarie Wieland of the Cleveland Public Library, Dr. Bill Barrow of the Special Collections Library at Cleveland State University, Jennifer Trivelli of the Cleveland Foundation, Clemency Christopherson of Adjaye Associates, and Patty Lampert of the Cleveland AIA.

Also, I can never forget or thank enough each of the 300-plus members who worked for me over the past 60 years. I especially acknowledge four members of my staff for a combined 120 years of service until their own retirements: Jim Lim, Chinnaya Parmamasivam, Chester Henderson, and Vernada Davis. Enough said, because I could never say enough.

And finally, Kevin and Sandra Madison, my nephew and his wife; and Robert and Sarah Klann, longtime employees and now the owners of Robert P. Madison International. Thanks for carrying on with enthusiasm and excellence.

So here we are at the end of this book, but certainly not the end of the story. Anytime some poor square perseveres to overcome long odds, I see a new page turning. When a new business or design is created to inspire or serve, there it is, the beginning of a new chapter. And when someone does his job with dignity and respect for all, a new character carries the story forward.

But for me, the best way for the narrative to continue will be for someone now reading this to take a moment to write down his or her own story. It doesn't have to overwhelm you. Begin like you begin any other journey, with a single step. Jot down notes on one brief account of your life; memorialize someone who inspired you, an obstacle you were determined to overcome. Then write another, and another. Gather them up and then pass them along to others who might benefit from your unique experiences, perspectives, stumbles. . . and victories.

R.P.M.

ABOUT THE AUTHORS

Robert P. Madison, FAIA, is an architect, entrepreneur, and civic leader. Born in Cleveland, Ohio in 1923, he studied architecture at Howard University before serving in Italy in World War II. Madison earned a B.A. in architecture from Western Reserve University, an M.A. in architecture from Harvard University, and completed additional studies as a Fulbright Scholar at L'Ecole des Beaux Arts in Paris. In 1954, Madison opened the first African-American architectural firm in Ohio. Major projects include the U.S. Embassy in Senegal, the Engineering & Nuclear Facility at Tuskegee Institute, the Stokes wing and Main Library renovation in Cleveland, and the Rock & Roll Hall of Fame and Museum. Madison lives in Shaker Heights, Ohio.

Carlo Wolff writes about popular culture, music, books, hospitality and travel. A contributor to the jazz magazine, DownBeat, he is the author of "Cleveland Rock & Roll Memories," lead author of "Mike Belkin: Socks, Sports, Rock and Art," and co-writer of "The Encyclopedia of Record Producers." Wolff also reports and edits for newspapers and magazines. A native of Dallas, Wolff grew up in Columbus, Ohio and attended schools in the Boston area. He moved to Cleveland in 1986. Wolff lives in suburban Cleveland with his wife, Karen Sandstrom, two dogs and a cat.

PHOTO CREDITS

Architectural illustrations are property of Robert P. Madison, Robert P. Madison International or its affiliates.

Photos from the personal collection of Robert P. Madison used with his permission.

Special thanks to:

Rodney L. Brown Photography, www.rlbphoto.net

Cleveland Public Library, Main Branch, Photo Archives

Cleveland State University, Special Collections.

The Cleveland Foundation

Karen Sandstrom

And watch for...

To dare mighty things...

Robert P. Madison, ARCHITECT

Robert P. Madison's inspiring life story designed for young readers.

Available from

act3creative.com